Group Portrait
South Africa

Group Portrait

Nine family histories

South Africa

Compiled by: **Paul Faber**

Edited by: **Annari van der Merwe** and **Paul Faber**

Kwela Books - KIT Publishers

Foreword

Can we learn from history?

If we are able to learn, then we must be able to learn from history in particular, because by definition learning is based on knowledge collected over time. Even intuition, they tell us, is made up of genetically stored insights from the past! None of us can remain unaffected by what happens around us. We are shaped by events that came before us and processes that unfold in our own lifetime. In a way, history is rooted in our hearts and our minds, but it is also ever-present in our environment – and not only in obviously man-made things, such as buildings and objects of art. Even in nature do we see its effects.

This is also true of South Africa. Our country has been formed by the events of history, of which we have been the masters to a greater or lesser extent. We find evidence in the ancient metal foundries near Rustenburg, the Big Hole at Kimberley, the Johannesburg mine dumps, the sugarcane fields of KwaZulu-Natal, the wheat fields of the Free State and the vineyards of the Western Cape – all are imprints of history. Ours is a history of nomads, smallholders, slaves, labourers, traders and fortune hunters, foreign powers and local resistance; of rulers and the oppressed, of landowners and the landless. Tangible proof exists in the rock paintings in the Drakensberg; the Fort at Cape Town, with Sheik Yusuf's tomb not too far away; the Voortrekker Monument in Pretoria; the prison on Robben Island, and the shanty towns on the outskirts of all our cities. There are other remains too, transient but no less poignant: our various traditions and customs; mieliepap, bobotie and braaivleis; colourful beadwork and the wearing of school uniforms; rugby, soccer and cricket; the click and nasal sounds in some of our languages;

folk songs and praise poetry; our different places and ways of worship; the way we dance.

The traces of history do not disappear. Yet despite ever-present reminders, nothing is as elusive as history. We cannot hold onto the present, and the past can only be reconstructed – from memory, which is at best unreliable, and from documents: diaries and photographs, if we are fortunate. But even these records were created by individuals, often very self-centred, with only limited knowledge and understanding. No two people will ever record a shared or witnessed experience in exactly the same way. Their different versions will be coloured by individual emotions, convictions and beliefs, interests, physical limitations and earlier experiences. Nevertheless, personal records and memory are crucial when it comes to reconstructing the past.

This has become abundantly clear in recent times: the world over, official versions of history have proved to be as subjective as those of individuals. In authoritarian states, history is written by those in power, so what survive are the stories of kings and generals, chiefs, power-mongers and tyrants. The stories of ordinary people – the farmers, workers, sailors, housewives and children – are lost. For years, historians distorted South Africa's history, some deliberately, others perhaps unknowingly. The story of the powerful and wealthy was told in great detail, while the story of the majority remained largely unheard. Much of the history of ordinary persons has been lost and is still in danger of disappearing. For this reason this particular publication is so welcome. Like *The Story of my Life* (and the Afrikaans version *Ek en my Mense*), in which twelve South African children portray their own

Photograph: George Hallett.

reality through photographs and short written pieces, *Group Portrait South Africa* presents us with a composite picture of our "rainbow" nation – in this case, by looking at the weal and woe of nine different South African families over a century and beyond. It is interesting that both these projects were initiated in Holland, but executed mainly by South Africans.

No book can compensate for a lost past; that would be an impossible task. But *Group Portrait South Africa* goes a long way towards 'writing" a different kind of history.

It presents us with a handful of stories, not an ultimate, definitive history of our country. But can such a history ever be written? I leave that question to those better qualified than I to answer. It does seem very valuable, though, to sample as many as possible of the countless stories of ordinary folk, their reconstructions of their own past and their memories, in order to arrive at a more intimate understanding of what lies behind the official versions of history. This history of ordinary people and families has indisputable value. It reveals the impact of major historical events, such as colonialism, the growth of African nasionalism and apartheid, on individuals and their small circles. It takes us from the national stage and places us in a local setting. We encounter, not nameless representatives of a group, but unique, real persons. What in the end emerges is not their cultural or religious background, their colour, language or position in society; but their humanity, how they related to others and coped with prosperity and adversity.

I trust that this lovely book will remind us that recognition and knowledge of the past is a first, crucial step towards true understanding of the present; that despite all the outward differences, personal experience of loss and loneliness, happiness and success, is universal.

Nelson Mandela

Robert Papini & Sibongiseni Mkhize   The **Mthethwa** family

Elsabé Brink   The **Nunn** family

Dumisane Ntshangase & Derrick Thema   The **Rathebe** family

Steve Lebelo   The **Plaatje** family

Sonja Loots   The **Steyn** family

Henry Bredekamp   The **Le Fleur** family

Rayda Jacobs   The **Manuel** family

Bongani Mgijima & Carohn Cornell   The **Galada** family

Shamim Meer   The **Juggernath** fam

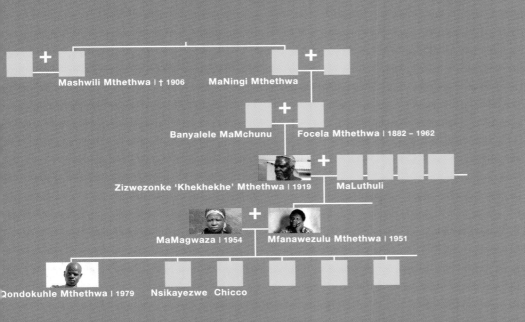

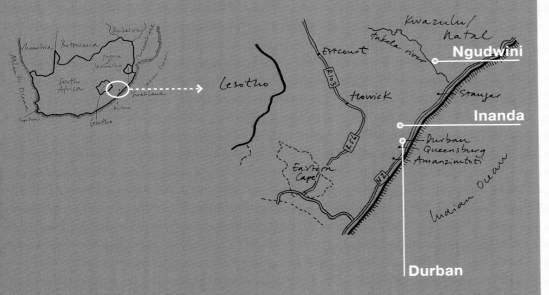

It is just before 10 a.m. on a Saturday. Ten vehicles are already queued at Gilubuhle in southern Zululand, the divination training centre, consulting practice and dispensary of octogenarian Zizwezonke "Khekhekhe" Mthethwa – KwaZulu-Natal's pre-eminent traditional healer, who combines attributes of both *inyanga* (doctor) and *isangoma* (diviner). Gilubuhle is also Khekhekhe's "new" family seat, dating from 1947 when he broke away from his Lutheran father's homestead and established his own.

The healer is dressed casually in an old white vest and khaki cut-offs, with a narrow band of smooth hide high on his forehead, and consults very unassumingly from the passenger seat of his red Venture 2200 parked in the courtyard. One of the bumper stickers proclaims in Zulu: *"The world over, goodness begins with you. So said God of our forefathers."* It is a typical day in the life of the master herbalist.

To the south of Gilubuhle (which means "Attempt the good"), a deep blue-green haze softens the contours of the forest-decked lower reaches of the Thukela River as it meanders the last few kilometres to the sea past sheer rock formations soaring out of the valley floor. With an expansive wave, Khekhekhe reminds the visitor that it was in this majestic green Mthethwa patrimony that the founder of the Zulu kingdom, Shaka, grew to manhood.

CELEBRATING THE ANCESTORS

Around 1794, Shaka's mother Nandi was banished from the court and domain of his father Senzangakhona, hereditary ruler of the amaZulu, at the time a modest chiefdom numbering perhaps half the Mthethwa with whom the adolescent Shaka and his mother eventually found sanctuary in about 1803. Not long after this, around 1805, a Mthethwa prince named Godongwana, facing certain execution for conspiracy against his royal father, fled south to the British outpost of Grahamstown on the northern border of the Cape Colony. After some years, he received news of his father's death and returned home to claim his birthright. Godongwana became known as Dingiswayo – "The Exile". Keenly aware of how Xhosa resistance to the British advance had failed in the eastern Cape, he took stock of his own domain – the coastal region of what is now KwaZulu-Natal. Since about 1750, the area had been on the brink of drastic change as various European maritime companies with trade links and possessions in the East were operating along the coast – the VOC, which already had a foothold at the Cape of Good Hope and a vast trading empire in East India; the Portuguese who were firmly established in Mozambique as well as in Goa on the Indian subcontinent, where the British, too, had established various outposts, among others at Bombay. By the early nineteenth century, the British had become the major foreign power to contend with in east and southern Africa.

During his sojourn behind the colonial frontier, Dingiswayo had grasped the relentlessness of the colonial threat and the fate that awaited indigenous people who failed to unite before it. So in order to prepare his own more effectively for what he knew was inevitable, he pioneered a military alliance that was much more than that. Within just a few years, he had created a confederacy of chiefdoms, which required a complete reorganisation of the various groups living along the seaboard. In so doing, this cattle-raising region that for many centuries had had only tenuous links with the outside world, was put on a war footing and braced for any eventuality.

For some Africanists today Dingiswayo rather than Shaka is the real originator of resistance to colonisation, a visionary political organiser they also regard as the true architect of the unified forces, which Shaka Zulu would later lead. Khekhekhe subscribes to this interpretation. He considers Shaka the protégé of the Mthethwa and believes that the Zulu dynasty owes its modern status and designation as a nation to their great forebear Dingiswayo. He states this claim in a polite way: *"We Mthethwa still regard Shaka as one of us, because it was we who raised him to be a strong man. He grew up under Dingiswayo's wife MaNhlapho, just like one of her sons, and used to train his regiment – all bachelors – on a precipice at the Izinsimba stream near here. I don't celebrate Shaka's Day,"* Khekhekhe declares, *"because it takes Shaka away from his Mthethwa upbringing and emphasises his Zulu birth."* Shaka's Day became an annual event in 1980, but already in the 1920s, moves toward celebrating the founder of the Zulu Kingdom had begun under Solomon Maphumuzana, grandson of Cetshwayo, the last king of independent Zululand. At that time urban Zulu intellectuals and rural chiefs founded the original Inkatha, a cultural movement. Khekhekhe spurns this "national" ceremony, holding instead an *isikhumbuzo* –

Members of the Mthethwa family, 2002. From left to right: MaMagwaza, Mandlenkosi, Mfanawezulu, Zizwezonke, Qondokuhle, MaNtuli, MaYengwayo, Nduduzo, MaBiyela and MaNtshangase. Photograph: David Goldblatt.

a remembrance of his ancestors – on 23 February every year. The celebrations feature dances by trainee diviners and teams of local youths, while the great Khekhekhe himself recites his forebears' praises and demonstrates his snake-handling powers.

Proceedings begin the previous day when a two-metre-high display of various "first fruits" – maize, sorghum, pumpkin, sugarcane – is set up at the edge of the forecourt and livestock are sacrificed; people attending the celebrations are fed and the divination trainees trance-dance for most of the night. The same routine is always followed. Around 2 p.m. the next day, after a crowd of about 200 people from surrounding homesteads would have gathered, the trainees and Khekhekhe's wives and sons – all in traditional garb – proceed to the "church", a small four-square structure (rather than a traditional dome-shaped rondavel) with kudu horns mounted over the entrance, to invoke the Mthethwa ancestors by burning incense herbs and singing the clan hymns. Everyone then files off to the dance ground, where, once Khekhekhe has recited the family praise poetry, the trainees dance and recent graduates thank their mentors (one or other of the Mthethwa sons) by pinning banknotes of R100 or more onto their fur headbands, and giving a short speech. Khekhekhe then thrills the onlookers by bringing his snakes out of their baskets, draping his green mamba on the visiting locals – and tourists, who these days swell the numbers of his followers. Camera crews are also increasingly in attendance in recent years. Khekhekhe withdraws at this point to talk to some visitors, while the entertainment continues in the form of local youth outfits performing *ingoma* (dance style developed by migrant workers) and *isicathamiya* (modern Zulu music style).

This *isikhumbuzo* is explained by Khekhekhe's eldest son Mfanawezulu as his father's *"way of entertaining the community and paying his respects to the ancestors"*. But there is an additional political significance that goes unmentioned: Khekhekhe holds the ceremony at about the same time as the ancient harvest Festival of First Fruits (*ukweshwama*), which used to be held independently by every chiefdom until Shaka's unification of the region from 1816 onwards. Hereafter the celebration became the prerogative of the Zulu overlord only – until it was banned by the British, to be revived by present Zulu king, Goodwill Zwelithini, as recently as 1980. Today it is once again an important national gathering. But Khekhekhe holds his ceremony independently,

and calls it not just *isikhumbuzo*, but explicitly *ukweshwama*.

Although celebrating the Festival of First Fruits has great historical and political significance, observing it is only a part of Khekhekhe's plans to reintroduce and restore precolonial African ritual, symbol and knowledge – an ideal that lies at the core of what he is all about.

NO ORDINARY SANGOMA

Born in 1919, Zizwezonke "Khekhekhe" Mthethwa is no ordinary *sangoma*. Not only is he the country's sole "snake diviner" (no equivalent Zulu term exists), but he is also the self-appointed upholder of "ancient pre-Zulu traditions". As such he is always the first stop for post-1994 visitors in pursuit of an older Africa. This practice began around 1950, but his special relation with snakes dates from much earlier: *"In my childhood, my parents would see snakes sleeping near me and club them, thinking it was the work of witches; they did not notice that the snakes never harmed me. I started handling snakes from age 17 or 18; they can't harm me because they are part of me. If you do things according to the laws of nature, you can eat poison and handle snakes and still survive. I always tell people that what gives me power to handle poisonous snakes and to heal sick people is the power of my god, Mvelinqangi ['First Cause']. It is even written in the Bible that when you believe in your God alone, you*

will be able to heal the sick and to touch deadly snakes."

As is often the plight of those with extraordinary powers, Khekhekhe had to live down much scepticism and outright suspicion before winning his bona fides. *"When I became a sangoma, many people thought I was a charlatan; I had to prove my powers to white*

Khekhekhe consults from his bright red Venture 2200, parked in the courtyard at Gilubuhle. The words on the door – *"He who rises under your feet (i.e. Khekhekhe himself). May there be complete faith in your heart, so that it doesn't breed maggots like flies"* – also appear on stickers on all his vehicles. Photograph: Paul Weinberg.

men first before black people realised I was not a demon, but a person with a special talent … The Chief Native Commissioner [head of the former Native Affairs Department] would invite me to Pietermaritzburg and Durban to demonstrate my snake-handling skills. The people from the Natal Parks Board and the scientists from Durban, like Dr FitzSimons [South Africa's leading herpetologist], also wanted to use my knowledge. They acknowledged my powers, and invited me to show them that I had the same powers as a magician. Even white magicians were curious to know my secret." One memorable highlight was when he was requested to demonstrate his snake-handling skills to the man who called himself "die groot induna" (the great counsellor), but whom Khekhekhe calls 'the king of apartheid' – Dutch-born Hendrik Verwoerd who was Minister of Native Affairs in 1950 and who later devised and implemented race-based "separate development", becoming South Africa's prime minister in 1958. Having to perform for Minister Verwoerd

and maize, beyond big rainwater storage tanks. *"My father's home was where my maize plot is today, so I built mine just above his."* At the centre of Gilubuhle, overlooking the reception forecourt, lies the ancestral graveyard. The five tombstones (*idlinza,* the term for a royal grave, is used, not *ithuna,* which indicates the grave if a commoner) differ

relationships with the Bushmen [San] who came from the south." Khekhekhe's grandfather Maningi, son of Mngoye, is commemorated with a more imposing edifice than Dingiswayo's. The polished marble headstone has a shield engraved on it and a genealogical list followed by the legend: *"Our ancestors used to sleep in anthills; they were Bushmen."* The grave rests on a cement plinth supported by six pillars, with three glazed ceramic cattle (one a Brahman) reclining on the quartz-chip grave bed. The size of the grave reflects Khekhekhe's increasing prosperity over the years rather than his grandfather Maningi's historical eminence. Khekhekhe's great-uncle Mashwili – Maningi's brother, and one of the leading lights of the Zulu Rebellion of 1906 – was a much more important figure, but his grave is missing from this family cemetery because his body was never recovered. The rebellion broke out when a cluster of Zulu chiefdoms refused to accept a British poll tax. Mashwili died in a surprise attack by the colonial forces and, like Bhambatha Zondi, the main leader, was decapitated. *"Mashwili's story is sad,"* Khekhekhe reflects, *" I've just gone to cleanse his family because he was buried without a head."* (In Nguni culture, cleansing rituals are performed for any ancestor who died a violent or unnatural death.)

The admiration he feels for his great-uncle – the traditional leader who took a patriotic stand against the coloniser – evaporates when Khekhekhe comes to speak of his own father, Focela (1882–1961). Focela became lineage heir after Maningi passed away soon after the Zulu Rebellion. Focela's grave is the smallest of the three, having only the terse epitaph: *"The one who surveys from afar [wanders in faraway places] like the hadeda ibis",* which can also be translated as: *"The one who does not mingle with the crowds".* In his youth Focela was converted to Christianity and as committed Christian became an evangelist. He helped to build and staff the Lutheran by-station at Ngudwini and flatly refused any "heathen" titles. *"The church had taken control of his life,"* Khekhekhe laments, *"and he refused to become chief of this area. That is how we lost the chieftain-ship."* (Mashwili re-established the Mthethwa leadership of the southernmost reaches of Dingiswayo's old domain after he was forced to flee Zululand for rousing the ire of Zulu king Mpande, who ruled from 1840 to 1872. He fled south into what was the Natal Colony and resettled in the old Mthethwa territories south of the Thukela.)

was nevertheless considered an honour. *"So while people were looking down on me, I rose up and became a prominent man. That is why I am known as 'Uvuka ezinyaweni zamadoda [He who rears up under men's feet]; I surprised them like a snake."* (It is interesting that when Dingiswayo returned from Grahamstown, he was given the praise-name "He who rose from the dead".) Today Khekhekhe, probably the country's most prominent practitioner of traditional medicine, operates from an imposing establishment. More than 20 rondavels and veranda-fronted four-squares, all matching – whitewashed, with earth-red corrugated iron roofs and neat guttering – form an imposing tableau. Aloes and other broad-leaf plants ornament the paved walkways. Nine rondavels, built on the steep, terraced hillside behind the complex, are reached by whitewashed cement steps commencing from an entrance arch. A tractor is parked under a green PVC awning. *"I was born here,"* Khekhekhe says, looking over the hillside's large fenced fields of banana

The landscape around Gilubuhle. Photograph: Paul Weinberg.

considerably in size and cost, indicating Khekhekhe's progress over the years in honouring his forebears. The earliest, a polished marble headstone with the inscription "Elephant of Delwase" on the front and an elephant engraved on the back, is marked as Dingiswayo's "grave". A text in Zulu explains how this can be the resting-place of one who died at the hands of his archenemies in far northern Zululand, almost two centuries ago: *"[Dingiswayo] passed away at the mountain of Isigwegwe, at Nongoma. He came to me [Khekhekhe] and said to make a home [proper grave] for him, and a spear, to be collected by Zizwezonke [Khekhekhe]."* Every year, at the *isikhumbuzo,* Khekhekhe carries a tall "ancestral spear" made according to the instructions received from the spirit of his great forebear. *"We don't know the spear's history,"* he allows, but *"it is part of the Mthethwa heritage – connected to our origin and*

n Zululand, the traditional order initially offered stiff resistance to Christianity, and most missions had only a limited hold. After the Zulu kingdom's defeat in the Anglo-Zulu War (1879), however, conversions increased – even in the face of persistent strong opposition from chiefs and family heads. When "white Zulu" John Dunn, until not long before allied to King Cetshwayo, was appointed to a chieftainship by the British in recognition of his assistance against his former Zulu master during the war, the Norwegian Lutheran Mission won exclusive rights to all of southern Zululand, which included Ngudwini. Conversions increased even more rapidly after the British occupation of Zululand in 1887, with Eshowe – the nearest Lutheran mission station to Ngudwini – counting over 1 000 converts by 1906.

"These Lutherans," fumes Khekhekhe, "were really causing turmoil around here, encouraging people to abandon their ways." And indeed the Norwegian missionaries did their best to undermine traditional social and political structures: in their testimony before a 1907 govern-ment commission on chiefs, they insisted that "chieftainship must be abolished, and the tribal system dissolved and replaced by direct white rule".

With the end of Zulu independence in 1880, itinerant preaching became possible, and permanent by-stations and so-called "preaching places" were established in outlying districts. Focela's younger brother, Funumuzi Genius, who "converted many Mthethwa", built one on the Ngudwini ridge. This is the church to which Focela devoted his life, until his death in 1961. For this, Khekhekhe, his voice harsh, calls his father "very irresponsible – not interested in

Zizwezonke Mthethwa during the annual *isikhumbuzo* (ritual to commemorate the ancestors), 2001. *"My ancestors come to me in dreams and tell me where the snakes are waiting for me. It is always different snakes, and they cooperate when I use them in ceremonies. I've been bitten many times, but my body is strong and the poison no longer affects me."* Photograph: Paul Weinberg.

history; he abandoned all Mthethwa traditions and customs, took only one wife, and worked as a servant for the whites". A note of satisfaction rings through when he says: "What I can tell you is that all those who turned to Christianity and joined the Lutherans did not live long."

The Lutherans were the strongest mission in

Mfanawezulu's niece Baficile whitewashing the inner walls of the *ihoho* (ancestral chapel) in the courtyard at Gilubuhle, 2001. Formal addresses to the Mthethwa forefathers, which precede all ceremonies, are held here.
Photograph: Paul Weinberg.

the Eshowe magisterial district (they counted twice as many as the Catholics, and were four times more than the Anglicans). Yet they were outnumbered, not only by non-Christians, but also by "the sects" – the so-called "Ethiopian" breakaways. Impatient with the endless delay in their long-promised appointment to leadership positions alongside the whites,

some African preachers had broken away from the formal Christian missions to form their own church movement. The Natal government, fearing that they would fall under the influence of the "Ethiopians" – perceived to be politically militant – prohibited African evangelists throughout the early 1900s from settling permanently at mission by-stations. Mfanawezulu, Khekhekhe's eldest son and heir, and not his father, says that Focela was in fact precisely the kind of convert who worried the British (and after 1910, the Union of South Africa) officialdom – a "syncretist", one who accommodated his new Christian faith within his African heritage. His grandfather, though a Christian, "had some knowledge of medicine: war medicine, medicine for stick-fighting, which made him invisible; also medicine to fortify homes, and love potions: many young men and women used to come to him. He was a kind man; there is nothing bad I know about him."

The story behind his son's name certainly attests that Focela, as young father, did show a ready acceptance of messages from the spirit world. Approached by *uthikoloshe* (a river troll), instructing him to name his heir "Zizwezonke" – because one day all peoples (*izizwe zonke*) would come to him for healing – Focela obeyed, even though it greatly upset his Lutheran brethren.

Perhaps this is one of the reasons why Khekhekhe seems to be softening his judgment of his father. "Recently," Mfanawezulu reveals, "[Khekhekhe] stitched a Zion church gown, and said he wants to keep it in his hut, because the spirit of our grandmother [Focela's late wife, Bunyalele MaMchunu] wants it. He instructed all of us to buy gowns; we all have them just hanging in our houses."

The "Zion church" arose in early 20th century, shortly after the emergence of the "Ethiopians". Unlike the "Ethiopians", it was however entirely grassroots in structure and character. Even though inspired by American faith healing, the movement was thoroughly African in nature in its response to the intense dislocation and suffering of black people. At one point, Mfanawezulu confides, Khekhekhe did join a Zionist church: "They say he used to wear a white gown, but he does not want to talk about that. It seems the ancestors took him out of the Zion church."

Khekhekhe does not refer to this, just as he

makes no mention of Focela having been a mission Christian with a difference. He relates only how the ancestors early on demanded that he withdraw from the domestic job, which his father had arranged for him in Durban. While working for a white family in the leafy suburb of Essenwood, he *"became very sick"* (possessed by ancestral spirits), and *"cried so loud my boss heard me. He tried to calm me down, but I told him that I see my God, and he wants me to go back home; I dreamt of my ancestors urging me to salvage what was left of the Mthethwa."*

Though he only began his healing practice when he was 30, Khekhekhe had grown up "sick": *"I began my strong communication with my ancestors at age 18. I respected them and followed what they were saying. I went through the training as* isangoma. *I never looked back after that, although my parents did not like seeing me return to the old ways; they hated me for abandoning Christianity and reverting to what they called a ' heathen lifestyle'. But I became sick every time I went to church. The Lutherans saw me as possessed by a demon."*

THE PEACEMAKER

Though most of his work today consists of treating every manner of condition, Khekhekhe also offers three months of divination training for those who come to be healed of the possession sickness, so in time they themselves become healers. When asked about his own spirit calling, he gives the classic diviners' answer: *"I went under the water and lived with a blue person there."* He would, however, refer a patient to another diviner in cases of sudden or violent death (which in Africa are generally considered "suspicious", likely to have a human cause), or if he can't determine the problem.

Patients arrive at Gilubuhle from all over southern Africa, from as far afield as Pondo-land in the north and the Eastern Cape in the south; even from Swaziland, Mozambique, Zimbabwe and Malawi ("Nyasa") do they come. Among them are the infirm, the insane, the infertile and loveless, small-business people in need of breaks and others needing protection for their households. The stream of clients include Indian business people and white farmers. Khekhekhe is known to specialise in *intelezi* (protective magic): should someone be out after you, R300 to R400 may secure you "invisibility" from that person. But, he gamely admits, while his spells can help, good luck, too, may be important. When Khekhekhe finally emerges from his consulting seat in the red Venture, it is clear where he ultimately puts his

Barbara Tyrrell: Drawing of Zizwezonke Mthethwa, early 1950s.
The artist visited Zizwezonke Methethwa in the company of
her husband. He was making a film, while she did drawings.
Ink and gouache on paper, 36 x 21 cm.
Collection of the Killy Campbell Museum, Durban.

rust: in a 9-mm automatic strapped to his hip. It is hardly surprising when R200 notes are coming through his window all morning, in a volatile, little-policed area where armed banditry is not unknown.

Yet Khekhekhe insists he has always refused

for many moons, learning all the different types of healing by discovering the uses of edible and medicinal plants and by watching the behaviour of animals, but *"today, the learning is only about war medicine"*. So Khekhekhe frequently invokes God, to whom

[Mangosuthu Buthelezi] and Mandela [Inkatha and the ANC] was not a gentlemen's war: people were being ambushed in the streets or asleep in their homes. During the days of Dingiswayo, people fought in the open; we did not kill people in the dark and then call ourselves heroes. You're no hero if you ambush people. This was not a real war: it gave birth to crime that would become uncontrollable, and haunt us for many years. The leaders were arming people with guns; children were being taught to be criminals. I can tell you the increase in crime started during the era of political violence. Drugs began to be distributed into our communities, and many vices began during that time, like the increase in rape – something, which was very rare in the past. That's how I see it as an old man. It was not an open war, and that is why we have all these problems today."*
(About the World Trade Center attacks, he says: *"The Americans were ambushed, and they retaliate using technology, rather than facing their enemies in the open. That's not real war; I regard it as criminal. In the olden days, armies used to fight in the open."*)
According to some written sources, the killing of King Dingiswayo was the result of treachery on the part of Shaka, an act that can be considered the first instance of dishonourable "non-open" war waging. In Dingiswayo's hour of greatest need during his struggle with his main challengers, the powerful trading chiefdom of Ndwandwe to his north, he was allegedly betrayed by the protégé whom he had only recently installed as leader of the Zulu. Shaka, it is said, deliberately failed to meet the Mthethwa forces according to an agreed plan, with the result that Dingiswayo was captured and put to death by the Ndwandwe after a few days in captivity.

For Khekhekhe this episode was the first of many perfidies committed against his forebears. For the Dingiswayo-Mthethwa lineage it meant total collapse, because Shaka then proceeded to thwart any possible challenge from Dingiswayo's descendants by appointing, not Dingiswayo's legitimate heir, his eldest living son Mngoye (Khekhekhe's great-grandfather), but Mbiya, a son of one of Dingiswayo's uncles, who, some say, had acted like a father to the outcast Shaka Zulu. Then, after Mbiya's death, his son Mlandela – supposedly Shaka's consort and confidante throughout his exile – inherited the Mthethwa chieftainship and lands. This infamy was compounded by the victorious British, when, after the Anglo-Zulu War of 1879, they proclaimed Zululand in June 1887.

Zizwezonke "Khekhekhe" Mthethwa demonstrating his power over snakes in front of the Municipal Native Administration Department in Durban (now the KwaMuhle Museum), 1950s. In the background, men are waiting in line to receive work permits. Photograph by S.B. Bourquin. Ethekwini Collection, Unicity Heritage Department, Local History Museums.

to have anything to do with war medicine: *'When there was a lot of fighting here, people used to come to ask me for* muthi *[medicine] called* intelezi *to strengthen themselves and their homes against attack. I never made* muthi *for people to go kill others, because as* inyanga *my main responsibility is to save lives."* Around Ngudwini Khekhekhe is indeed *"known as a peacemaker"*. *"I come and stand between the two fighting factions,"* he says. *"Everyone is fighting nowadays, and I don't know why."* He does know, however, that his own profession is deeply implicated: a true *inyanga*, for one thing, should train in the veld

he prays for luck in healing people: *"If God wants you, you'll feel it in your blood and dreams."*
Gilubuhle means "Attempt the good", but *ubuhle* is also the term for "beauty". Seeing himself in service of "goodness and beauty" may be the reason why Khekhekhe feels that part of his prophetic calling is to awaken people to the worrying signs of the age: *"There are many evil things happening: HIV/Aids, cholera, rabies, malaria fever. Why is Aids incurable? It is because it is a curse, not a disease? You cannot cure a curse. You see, at Gomorrah they were doing evil things, and did not listen to Abraham. In Egypt, they were also doing abortion, like you do here. So our Father in heaven is using the same way as he used before. If you go astray, you need to be shown the way. God is angry with us."*
Also to blame for the present horrors is the outbreak of black-on-black violence during the liberation struggle: *"I complained to many people that the fight between Gatsha*

An open-air school in Kwazulu-Natal, circa 1900-20. As a young boy, Khekhekhe attended a similar school. Ethekwini Collection, Unicity Heritage Department, Local History Museums.

Staff and converts at a Lutheran mission station, circa 1900-20, at the time when Khekhekhe's father, Focela, was converted to Christianity. Ethekwini Collection, Unicity Heritage Department, Local History Museums.

Thus, the chieftainship of coastal Zululand passed from Dingiswayo's house to a junior line, which holds it to this day. Though Khekhekhe does not directly say so, for him Shaka's treachery marks the beginning of all KwaZulu-Natal's recent and present straying from *ubuhle* – the good and the right. The marginalisation of Khekhekhe's family constitutes but a single example of a profound historical rift, or rupture, to which he traces all the world's present malaise.

Current rulers, he laments, lack the faculty of future sight; their leadership is no longer visionary: *"Among the Mthethwa,"* he insists, *"it was important that, in order to be king, you be* isangoma *– a prophet of the people."* Dingiswayo was the last diviner-king, an office now long forgotten, under which Khekhekhe includes Pharaoh, Jesus and *"many ancient lords"*. This crucial combination of leadership powers has, fortunately, come down in his bloodline (*"I am no ordinary* sangoma*"*), as well as in certain others, from pre-Shaka times. But those in office today are mainly usurpers: *"People without powers are called* amakhosi *[lords, chiefs]. They do not have the power of dreaming [prophesying]. They don't have enlightenment from God. What I have experienced is the love of God; He gives me powers ... On the day I was born, wild animals came to this home and raised a cacophony. My grandmother told the family it was standard occurrence when a leader was born."*

In dealing with his patients, Khekhekhe blends the imperious and common touch: his sonorous voice rises to an exasperated peal when chiding them, to the unfailing amusement in the queue waiting in front of him. When an old lady complains about adultery taking place in her (polygamous) household, he insists that, far better than buying any medicine, she should expose it right away, otherwise *"there will be poison in the family"*. So much of their sickness, he scolds his patients, has a psychological cause: *"It's not just about* imithi *[medicines]; they can't help unless you deal with home problems yourself!"*

(With a grizzled grin he will suddenly recommend *dagga* (hemp) as not toxic at all but a curative for any poison: *"Just grind and drink it."* Or if it must be smoked, *"the proper way is to put water into the smoking horn, as our ancestors did; you are killing yourself if you roll it with paper and mix it with tobacco."*) Khekhekhe is passionate about the virtue and integrity of ancestral ways. He keeps strictly to the old African diet and culinary techniques: his maize must be stone-ground; he never drinks water, and eats only indigenous beans (*izindlubu*). *"Urban people are weak,"* he insists, *"because they eat everything – salt, curry, rice, cabbage, oranges, beans. If you eat and drink everything, you kill yourself. Today you see people grow old quickly because of their diet and the kind of beer they drink. In the*

Two Zulu chiefs in captivity after the Bambatha uprising, July 1906. Along with Khekhekhe's grandfather Mashwili Mthethwa, chief Meseni of the Qwabe (left) and Ndlovu kaThimuni (right) resisted British colonial rule. Ethekwini Collection, Unicity Heritage Department, Local History Museums.

olden days, people drank sorghum beer. There was no sugar." Food was homegrown and people were healthy, but today's children receive a schooling from which they learn *"nothing but to be clerks in offices"*. *"My children are also attending schools, [but] I want them to learn to safeguard their future without depending too much on being employed. I want them to learn to use their*

hands and work in the fields. When I was growing up, the soil was our employer. The land was the key. It worries me to see children being sent to school, only to come back and no longer want to work with their hands, which have painted nails. They also paint their mouths red. That has killed our nation. That is my opinion."

Khekhekhe's progeny span a half-century, his youngest child being about five years old. When he last made a count of his children and grandchildren, *"many years ago"*, they totalled *"about 94"*. Whatever modernisers and modernists might say, for him polygamy works: of the 14 wives he has taken, half are now *"no longer here"*, but the remaining seven are happy and relations between them amicable, he insists. While this may be due to them all being distant blood relatives of varying degree, he also ensures that they routinely rub into skin incisions a preparation moistened with his blood. As a result, he says, not one has ever complained or run away, and all respect him by never quarrelling among themselves. (Another measure of his adroitness with love medicine is that not one of his brides was older than 20, and that he proposed only to the first girl, who then *"dreamed of the second and went looking for her till she found her"* – a process which repeated itself right to his fourteenth wife.)

In Khekhekhe's house of many mansions certain "complications" did however arise, which resulted in the lengthy banishment of the customary-law heir to his entire estate.

TRADITION, BUT NOT AT ANY PRICE –
MFANAWEZULU'S STORY

Mfanawezulu, the eldest, is Khekhekhe's only son not to have remained in the family business at Gilubuhle, which had *"just one traditional hut"* when he was born there in 1951. His name – "Son of Heaven" – is a reminder that his mother, after numerous fruitless consultations with diviners and other healers, conceived only after Khekhekhe had a vision of a baby boy brought from above and sat down before him.

Mfanawezulu chose to become a bus driver. Today his route takes him through Umhlanga Rocks, an upmarket oceanfront suburb of Durban, and just a few kilometres from the sprawling, relatively new but under-serviced township where he stays with his six older sons. Inanda Newtown began as a post-emergency housing scheme, constructed after an outbreak of cholera in the early 1980s, when, in spite of the apartheid policy of "influx control", massive migration to the Durban shacklands took place.

Mfanawezulu and his sons occupy a standard four-room "matchbox" house, still the ashen grey of unpainted zinc. They have no electrical appliances, neither stove nor fridge, television or audio, and their only furniture consists of a few iron-frame beds and wooden benches. The walls are bare except for the clothes hanging on pegs. Dry bundles and corked calabashes of umuthi are stashed in Mfanawezulu's room, for he does a little consulting on the weekends. These very basic quarters were acquired *"after a lot of hardship, during the time when black people had no rights to live in Durban"*. (This situation dated back to 1937, when all Africans other than servants and migrant labourers who were housed in hostels, were forced out of Durban's central and residential areas, into the emerging shack settlements. In accordance with the Group Areas Act, removals to the new townships for black people began in 1958. Influx control policy was finally abolished in 1986, and a Free Settlement Areas Act proclaimed in 1988.)

Humble though these premises might be, they are important to Mfanawezulu: *"I don't want my children to suffer the same way, so the Inanda*

Langa Magwa: Abakwe Mthethwa, 2001-02. Goat and python skin on a metal frame, 300 cm tall.

house will be kept; my children will do the extensions if they want to. I plan to go back to Ngudwini." Mfanawezulu now yearns for the land, but his trials began well before his move to Durban. A lack of schools at Ngudwini in his youth meant that he could not obtain a high-school education, so his father employed him as a driver. Like most people living around Ngudwini, Khekhekhe used to raise cash from selling wood from his wattle trees, and by 1974 he turned his profits to a transport business. It was the days of six-seater sedan taxis –

Six of Zizwezonke Mthethwa's seven wives, 2001. From left to right, in front: MaYengwayo, the eldest, MaNtuli, MaYengwayo, the youngest. At the back: MaBiyela and MaNtshangase, who are sisters, and MaYengwayo.
Photograph: Paul Weinberg.

Chevrolets, Valiants, and Fairmonts – and there was no public transport in the area. Khekhekhe paid his son's *lobola* when he married in 1970, and then for his driver's licence.

This happy relationship lasted until Mfanawezulu made a girl pregnant some years later, before any *lobola* for a new wife had been discussed. Because he was the first-born, this meant not only defiling customary law, but also disgracing all at Gilubuhle. So Mfanawezulu found himself and his young family – now numbering two wives and "many"

children – cast out by his out-raged father. He set them up at Ndulinde near Zululand's second city Eshowe, about 60 kilometres from Ngudwini, and got work in Durban with the KwaZulu Transport Company. After many futile attempts at reconciliation with his father, it dawned on Mfanawezulu that, as future heir, he had become a casualty of the efforts of Khekhekhe's other wives to advance their own sons. His own mother, the "great wife", had passed away and there was no one to intercede for him. *"I then decided to burn impepho [incense] at my home in Ndulinde, and tell them [the ancestors] I had tried everything."* But it was a full 13 years before

his father summoned him home, in 1992. Then the real trouble started. Khekhekhe insisted that his first-born stop working in the city and return to be a full-time driver for him. By now, Khekhekhe owned some minibus taxis, and two buses doing the Eshowe and Mandeni routes. Mfanawezulu complied, but of the seven days he was expected to work, he was allowed as wages only Friday and Saturday's takings. With business slow on his allotted days, Mfanawezulu's children were soon going hungry. Besides, he lived in fear of reprisal, because he had shot and killed one hijacker and wounded another when his bus was hijacked on the Eshowe route and the passengers robbed. As a safety precaution, he had switched to driving the Mandeni route. Then he fell ill and had to stop working alto-gether. When he returned after a long convalescence, he discovered his brothers had

Mfanawezulu Mthethwa behind the wheel of the bus he drives on the Umhlanga Rocks route, 2001. Photograph: Paul Weinberg.

Mfanawezulu Mthethwa with his sons in Inanda Newtown, 2001. From left to right: Qondokuhle, Nsikayezwe, Mandlenkosi, Nkululeko, Sibusiso and Mzwandile. Photograph: Paul Weinberg.

deposed him as driver. Only after he reproached his father for having made him leave secure employment in Durban was he promised a vehicle of his own – a new Toyota minibus. Instead, he received a second-hand Volkswagen, entirely unfit for the harsh gravel roads. *"It never made any profit. On the contrary, I ran deep into debt, having to fix it almost every day. It's still at the garage at my workplace; the parts to repair it are too expensive."*

All this misfortune Mfanawezulu puts down to conspiracy against him by his father's other wives. *"They wanted to isolate me because they thought that, as the first-born, I was going to start taking over my father's business. I had no plans to take over anything; I just wanted to carry on working to feed my family."* Khekhekhe had stopped listening to his first-born's side of the story and, with his family going hungry at Gilubuhle, Mfanawezulu was forced back to Durban.

The mid-1990s was a bad time to be looking for a job, with thousands of workers retrenched as the new government adopted privatisation as part of their new economic policy. Luckily he got a job with the recently privatised municipal bus service, and he has stuck with it, while back home his surviving wife MaMagwaza safeguards their interests against the envy of Gilubuhle's other six.

Not surprisingly, Mfanawezulu's view of polygamy is far removed from that of his father: *"What I can say is that a lot of bad things have happened to me because I was born into that system of marriage. To be honest, I can say that it brings a lot of complications."*

Mfanawezulu wants his sons to be what his father would deride as "monogamists". This doesn't mean he underrates the temptation that polygamy holds for men: *"I also fell into the trap ... But I always advise my kids to learn from what happened to me; I don't want them to experience the same hardship. I tell them about how my father changed before my eyes."*

The opinion of Mfanawezulu's third son, Qondokuhle – or Qondo – suggests that this advice has not gone unheeded.

WE NEED TO KNOW HISTORY – QONDOKUHLE'S STORY

Qondo was born at Ngudwini on 8 March 1979, the fourth of his father's 15 children – 14 with

MaMagwaza, the *nkosikazi* (senior wife) and one with his late second wife. Qondo attended school up to Grade 4 at Ndulinde near Eshowe during his father's "banishment", but finished

Mfanawezulu Mthethwa at Inanda Newtown, 2001. Photograph: Paul Weinberg.

his primary education back at Ngudwini. Since 2000, he has been living at Inanda Newtown. Mfanawezulu's tribulations with his father's other wives following his own mother's death have left Qondokuhle with few doubts:

"Personally, I can say I don't like polygamy. I grew up under that system, I know the bad things about it."

The name Qondokuhle means, "Aim for the good". Qondo says his grandfather is a good man, and that he enjoys going home to see him. Although he regards him as a healer, in the first place, he is also enthusiastic about Khekhekhe's project to restore family name and traditions: *"I love what my grandfather is doing; we should follow on his footsteps. I love history."*

Qondo is at Gilubuhle and sitting next to Chicco, a 17-year-old half-brother nicknamed after the popular South African composer and arranger Chicco Twala. The last word on things historical has always come from his History teacher, Chicco says. Yes, his grandfather can recite the family's praise-poetry, but he has never directly imparted its history; there are no special occasions for doing this.

Chicco echoes their father Mfanawezulu, who complains that Khekhekhe has *"only passed down to me knowledge of* umuthi, *not historical knowledge. But it is important for him to pass the information down; I wish there was a way we could acquire the knowledge he has about our history and tradition."* Qondokuhle concurs: *"We need to know history, and it's not good that he's the only one who knows; he's getting very old now. We're lucky he's still alive. It'll be very difficult when he passes away. He's the only one who has that wealth of knowledge, and I really want him to pass it down to us. The problem is there's no time – he's always busy with people coming for consultation. In the evenings, he's usually tired, and just wants to sleep."*

Qondokuhle thinks for a moment and continues: *"The problem is that my grandfather is not someone you can approach lightly. It's okay if you're not a member of the family, but we find it very difficult to go straight to him and start asking questions. We usually listen when he narrates historical events to other people."* It is also not easy to approach Khekhekhe with requests. *"He raised me up with a strong hand. I still remember his beatings. I'm still uneasy around him,"* Mfanawezulu says. *"I only talk with him when he calls me to come to him, and then I get an opportunity to ask him questions about history."*

Then the formidable old man brings the conversation to an abrupt end by breaking into the Mthethwa *izibongo* (historical praise-poems) and one wonders if there really is need for formal lessons: Khekhekhe's five-year-old son, till now larking about in the van, suddenly listens, rapt, and you witness how "family history", stretching back many generations, is handed on to the little one without him even being aware of it. Change is nevertheless undeniable, even in the senior house of the Dingiswayo-Mthethwa: Mfanawezulu's experience of paternal remoteness and rectitude has resulted in a vow that he will not be following his father's example as far the upbringing of his own children is concerned. *"I experienced that condition of not being close to my father, and I didn't like it. I don't believe*

in fathers distancing themselves from their children. I want to be a friendly father, so they can talk to me when they have problems. I don't want my children to run away the moment they see me." When at Gilubuhle, visiting his wife and younger children, Mfanawezulu spends as much time as possible with them, passing on the traditions he considers worth keeping. With the youngest, this happens through music. After his guitar broke a few years ago, he took up the *igenkle*, the

Footwear for town and countryside. Qondokuhle and his father Mfanawezulu, who sports neo-traditional sandals – *imbadada* – made from rubber car tyres, 2001. Photograph: Paul Weinberg.

herdboy's single-stringed musical bow, to accompany the songs he was teaching them. With his older sons, he shares what he learnt, as Khekhekhe's errand boy, about the uses of *umuthi*. Qondokuhle is appreciative: *"He has already taught us some basic herbs. He's done a good job in that. I regard traditional medicine as a good thing, and I want to know more. I'm sure he'll teach us more later."*

Yet Qondokuhle recently moved to join his father in Inanda, primarily to be able to get a better formal school education. At Gilubuhle, the long distance to school and unreliable transport often made him late for class; but more serious were the frequent disruptions of schooling by faction fights in the area. *"We always felt unsafe – you don't know who your enemies are. The school is surrounded by forests, and getting there was unsafe. We couldn't concentrate on lessons because we were never sure whether people might be waiting for us outside the school gates."*

Consequently, Qondokuhle joined the steady rural exodus that is fast emptying South Africa's countryside: young people leaving for better opportunities in the city. Mfanawezulu supported his son in this: *"I wanted them to get something better. They are now attending multiracial schools. I want them to be exposed to different things, broaden their horizons."* So Qondokuhle now goes to school in the former Indian "Group Area" housing estate of Phoenix near Inanda Newtown. He wanted to study auto mechanics, but apart from languages, only commercial subjects are offered: Accounting, Economics, and Maths.

He is repeating a year because adjusting to the new environment was not easy. Communication, for example, is exclusively in English and, as he magnanimously puts it, *"the quality of teaching at Ngudwini didn't prepare me well enough"*. Qondokuhle is nonetheless resolved to succeed. *"My plan is to finish high school and see if my parents can send me on to tertiary. If not, I plan to look for work, and use that money to further my studies."* Over weekends, he stays in, doing homework when not helping round the house. No girls feature in his life yet – he doesn't want the focus on schoolwork to be "disturbed". Could this single-mindedness have anything to do with his rejection of the whole ethos of polygamy, which he writes off as *"no good at all"*? *"There's always competition and unnecessary rivalry between your wives and your children. It is very bad. Sometimes your wives use love potions to make you love them. The husband just becomes a ball to play with. I prefer one wife, no matter what other people think, even if they call me a dog – as people usually call men with one wife."* Qondokuhle certainly knows about the bind of tradition: *"You know, in some areas you can't have a say in a discussion if you're a man with one wife."* He shrugs, glowers briefly. This would certainly be the case in the house of grandfather Khekhekhe, who contemptuously dismisses his own, converted father, Focela, as *ulindifindo*, (derogatory term, meaning "one who waits for the knot or marriage tie").

Qondokuhle, 2001. Photograph: Paul Weinberg.

Girls in gala dress waiting in line to dance during a girl's coming-of-age ceremony (*umemulo*), Gilubuhle, 2001. From left to right: Khekhekhe's daughters Ganile, Khangelephi and Ne, and Mfanawezulu's niece Bonile. Potograph: Paul Weinberg.

MaMagwaza preparing traditional sorghum beer (*utshwala besiZulu*) for the December holidays, 2001. Photograph: Paul Weinberg.

was the duty of Baphendlile ("They've opened the way" or "They've laid the foundation"), as MaMagwaza was called as a teenager, to look after her baby brother when he was born. She often accompanied her mother on further visits to Khekhekhe, who in time began chaffing the young girl about becoming his eldest son's first bride. This happened only after Khekhekhe himself had married two of Baphendlile's paternal aunts, and she accompanied them when they moved to Gilubuhle. With that,

"I started to become a member of this family. As a grown-up girl, I gradually developed love for Mfanawezulu. But it was Khekhekhe who brought us together by his constant hints and intimations."

So she became *nkosikazi* (chief wife) to the *nkosana* (heir) of Gilubuhle. Her co-wife died soon after marrying Mfanawezulu, so when voicing an opinion on polygamy, she candidly admits: *"I can't say I've experienced it directly."* But her family did, however, live in the main Gilubuhle complex from 1992 – after Mfanawezulu's father rescinded his banishment – until 1994, when space became limited for their growing household, and they relocated to the nearby hilltop overlooking the establishment. She therefore qualifies her initial reluctance to comment by alluding to *"complications that go with that practice"*. When pressed to elaborate, she unexpectedly gives full credence to Khekhekhe's claims: *"I had an opportunity to observe it when I lived at my father-in-law's. Everything was working smoothly; there were no quarrels."* Does she therefore recommend a polygamous marriage to her sons?

"I encourage my boys to do as they wish. It will depend on whether they can afford it. I always tell them to be aware that these days money is very important, and if he decides on polygamy, he has to be able to afford that family."

After 32 years of marriage and bearing Mfanawezulu 14 children, MaMagwaza started to undergo divination training with Khekhekhe in 1996, joining a company of women diviners at Gilubuhle that included wives of her father-in-law and her husband's brothers. This apprenticeship came after a lifetime of having been "made sick" by her Magwaza family's ancestor spirits – an inevitable consequence of having ignored the call to become a diviner.

Opposite: **Qondokuhle on his way to collect medicinal herbs, 2002. When he was sick in December of the previous year, Khekhekhe prescribed collecting medicinal herbs as a cure. That is why Qondokuhle still goes out into the veld twice a week, unpaid, according to him.**
Photograph: Paul Weinberg.

Qondokuhle's guitar.

Phakamani, a nephew of Mfanawezulu, plays football between the huts of the main complex at Gilubuhle, 2001. Photograph: Paul Weinberg.

It is a "sickness" curable only by becoming an apprentice. Even before this, she had acquired some knowledge of medicine from assisting Mfanawezulu with his consulting, and today, *"many people come to consult me"*. She receives clients in one of the existing huts at Gilubuhle, but is having her own constructed for her – not a rondavel but a thatched dome, in the traditional Nguni style.

Being occupied in this manner helps to keep at bay the sting of having her husband and several of her sons – Qondokuhle among them – live away from her in the city. But she is resigned to this predicament which most rural black mothers share and regards it as inevitable if her children are to progress: *"I do understand that they have to get the education which we did not."* The young Baphendlile was denied schooling by a combination of her home's remoteness and her fate as first-born: *"The Mbongolwane area was not much developed then. Schools were very far from my home; you could not walk that distance, even to get education. To have gone to school, I would have had to leave home altogether, and go and live near the school. The problem was that I was the first child at home, so my parents needed me around to assist."*

The home she has made with Mfanawezulu on the hill behind Gilubuhle since 1994 is modest, a far cry from the plaster and whitewash, and showroom furnishings of the main complex below. Guests are received in her husband's rondavel, which is thatched and has an earthen floor, with low wooden beds and some rolled grass mats for the use of his sons. In their father's near-perpetual absence, this cool, dark room is their prerogative – hence the old car radio-and-tape running off a battery through two big speaker bins. Shoes are kept on top of the wall, under the inside eaves, with only one section of the lime-washed wall having any decoration. Some stickers from the "Arrive Alive" traffic safety campaign are stuck alongside an article from a local community news-letter dating back to 1993. It lauds Mfanawe-zulu's swift action when a pregnant passenger on his bus went into labour. The rest of the decor is clearly young men's doing: posters of youth-radio DJs dressed in smart outfits and elegant, young television personalities from an HIV-awareness show. Cut-outs of new-model luxury cars adorn the area above a gas lamp. Contemplating their future, the mother of nine boys and five girls echoes what parents everywhere believe: *"Education is very important ... I would like to see them well educated, so they can get decent jobs, and have nice homes – better than the one we have*

– in places of their choice. Although," she quickly adds, *"I prefer them staying in a rural area. That's how I grew up, and I like that lifestyle."* There is a nostalgic yearning when she reminisces about the seductive beadwork attire they used to wear as girls – heavy girdles and brilliant fabrics, lavishly decorated with glass beads bought at some store – all of which was lost in a fire at Ndulinde.

MaMagwaza is soft-spoken, not given to holding forth. She tries to be impartial, also when asked about township life: *"I do visit Inanda occasionally; in the past I used to go there when I was pregnant so I could be near clinics, and stay until the baby grows up. But life is expensive in towns, and a lot of money is wasted – though I must admit that I've never lived in town long enough to make a fair and balanced assessment. So, I won't force my children to come and live here [at Ngudwini]. That will be their choice. If they want to live in an urban area, that will be fine – I won't force them. For people who're born in modern times, the problem is that in order to live, money must be earned, and the jobs are in the cities."*

Whatever her regrets that there are no longer any real prospects on the land, she is quietly confident about the future of the country her children are inheriting: *"Life is much better today, because we're better informed about how the country is being governed. In the past, we didn't know what was happening. There is a big difference now because we have the right to vote, and we know who our leaders are. Things are changing for the better. It's becoming clear, and we're more aware about what is happening. For us, maybe, it's too late, but our kids will be in a better position."*

THE YOUTH'S CHOICE: THE CITY OR THE LAND?
Like most Zulu speakers, Qondokuhle is firmly rooted in a broad extended family. So extended and widely spread is his family, that while he can name uncles and aunts, he admits it is *"difficult to keep track of my many cousins; I don't even know the names of some."* And he is referring only to his father's brothers' children; his mother's relations are considered *izihlobo* – part of the family, but not of the *umndeni* (patrilineage). Not all members of the extended family on his father's side live at Gilubuhle any more: Qondo's two eldest siblings live at

Mangete in southern Zululand, not far from Mandeni, the nearest big centre to Ngudwini. Sipho, a school-going younger brother, lives with them, while Nduduzo, another older brother, lives in Eshowe.

When he moved to Durban more than a year ago, Qondo lost touch with all of them. But then, besides the six brothers with whom he shares his father's township quarters, he now has regular contact with his other siblings also living in the city – especially his half-brother Siduduzo in Umlazi, Durban's largest township, who is his age and also still at high school. *"He usually visits us, but when he doesn't for some time, we communicate by phone."* Sometimes, their sister Lalelile, who works in Durban, visits on weekends, keen to find out how the latest brother to arrive from Ngudwini feels about urban living.

Qondo's response is ambivalent: *"I learnt a lot when I arrived in the township last year: schools all over, so many within walking distance; water easily accessible, roads and toilets, sports fields in abundance. But so is crime – you need money every day; at Ngudwini, you can get by without being employed."*

Qondokuhle has made some friends, but like his father, he still regards Ngudwini – *"where you can get out into the veld for some fresh air"* – as his real home, and that is where he keeps the shot-put medals he won at his Phoenix school. The lure of the country has suddenly grown much stronger for him. Earlier the only real negative aspect to living in town concerned his first love – playing the "Zulu guitar." (*"Space is a big problem in town. There's not enough here. At Ngudwini, I can go to a separate house and be alone; there's privacy to play my guitar at night. Here I have to worry about neighbours being so close by. People so easily complain about noise."*) But recently matters suddenly became dramatically worse for Qondokuhle when he had to flee Durban after receiving serious death threats from a well-armed local gangster. Back home, he is not only able to devote undisturbed time to his music, he also feels much safer.

Besides music, Qondo considers two other career possibilities – vehicle mechanic or

Qondokuhle Mthethwa, 2002. Photograph: David Goldblatt.

joining the military (**"to protect the country"**). But that is for later. For the time being Qondo loves being a songwriter, with the ambition to record and perform his compositions in the melodic, plaintive "Zulu minstrel" or "walking guitar" style, maskanda (musician, derived from the Afrikaans, "musikant").

When his eldest brother Nsikayezwe sports a new baggy T-shirt with US rapper Tupac Shakur's portrait on the front, and Bob Marley's on the back, Qondo is not fazed by this widespread current passion for foreign imports, or by the preference for the local electronic dance-rap, kwaito ("big sound of the moment"). He still goes for the rural-acoustic tradition and describes both these sounds as *"for people who grew up in the townships"*.

Three of his songs tell of the broader tensions and preoccupations in his new high-density surroundings: *"You don't love me, it's my money you love"*; *"She [a new mother] hasn't given birth, she has discharged another gangster"* and *"Wake up, John, we're going to pray"*. This kind of reflection is well served by the maskanda style of music. Having originated in the early twentieth century, when courting youths took guitars, fiddles or "squeezeboxes" (hand-accordions) along on their way to romance girls at distant homesteads, maskanda now straddles the urban-rural divide. For Qondo, the music possesses the lyrical power he needs to express that feeling a rural person has of being torn between the pull of the familiar life on the one hand, and the draw of the new world on the other. "Maskanda *connects me with where I come from. I want to be educated, but not to forget my roots. I'm still attached to Ngudwini. I love the place where my umbilical cord is buried; I don't want to forget it. But I must also say that I love Inanda too."* Perhaps, then, from the songwriter among the many grandsons of inyanga Zizwezonke "Khekhekhe" Mthethwa – protector of the family name, Ngudwini's custodian of old Africa – may be expected songs that will recall to public memory how significant the role of his distinguished, yet side-lined family has been over two long, hard centuries of KwaZulu-Natal history:

"I encourage my younger brothers and sisters to be dedicated to their schooling, and choose careers. But I also advise them not to forget their roots; they must not forget respect, inhlonipho [traditional Zulu good manners]. I'm still young and have a lot to learn, but I believe you must still maintain connections with the real home in the rural areas. I'm proud of where I come from ..."

The **Nunn** family

Beyond the boundaries

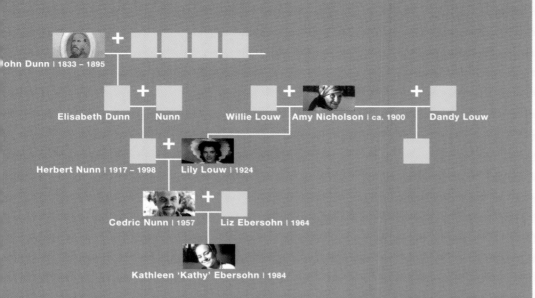

John Dunn | 1833 – 1895

Elisabeth Dunn + Nunn

Willie Louw + Amy Nicholson | ca. 1900 + Dandy Louw

Herbert Nunn | 1917 – 1998 + Lily Louw | 1924

Cedric Nunn | 1957 + Liz Ebersohn | 1964

Kathleen 'Kathy' Ebersohn | 1984

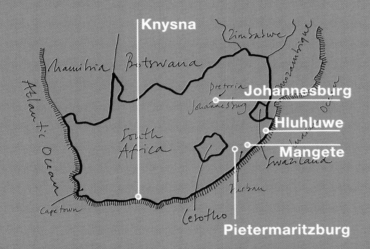

Knysna

Johannesburg

Hluhluwe

Mangete

Pietermaritzburg

This story follows the lives of five generations of the family of Cedric Nunn, a Johannesburg photographer, who traces his family tree back to four hunters and traders – Piet Louw, Arthur Nicholson, John Dunn and Herbert Nunn. From the mid-1800s, these traders set up trading posts deep in the heart of the Zulu kingdom, part of what today is known as the province of KwaZulu-Natal. According to local custom, they married numerous Zulu wives and aligned themselves to local Zulu chiefs. They are the first generation represented here.

The second generation is represented by Amy Louw (née Nicholson) who, throughout her life, which spans more than a century, has been the cornerstone of the Louws at Nongoma in central KwaZulu. Her daughter Lily Nunn represents the third generation. Lily lives at Mangete, close to the Thukela River in southern KwaZulu and fulfils the same role as her mother.

The descendants of the four traders – the Louws, Nicholsons, Dunns and Nunns – are united in the fourth generation, and are represented by one of Lily Nunn's sons, Cedric. On his mother's side, Cedric is related to the Louws and the Nicholsons, on his father's side to the Dunns and the Nunns. He has captured on film the lives of his mother and his grandmother and has on several occasions returned to manage the family store at Mangete. The fifth generation is represented by Cedric's daughter Kathleen, who at 17 is completing high school, and like her father has developed a keen interest in photography.

During the twentieth century, in an increasingly racially polarised South African society, the offspring of these traders and their Zulu wives formed the basis of a unique, racially mixed community that survived despite the ravages of apartheid. Like their forebears, many male descendants became traders or, later, shop-keepers, while female descendants fulfilled similar roles to those of their Zulu grand-mothers by providing a secure refuge for their children and grandchildren and, throughout the twentieth century, remained the cornerstones of their increasingly extended families.

In the frontier society of nineteenth-century colonial southern Africa, the road to prosperity lay in the control of land and the slow accumu-lation of wealth generated by the cultivation of livestock, especially cattle. The more rapid way to becoming rich lay in hunting and trading, especially in ivory, hides, arms and ammunition. Trade in colonial-style, Western goods, which gradually became necessities in pre-colonial black society, flourished.

In 1824, six enterprising Englishmen established a trading post at Port Natal (today Durban) with the express purpose to trade ivory and hides with the Zulu people of king Shaka. Soon, large numbers of black refugees, displaced by the wars of the Difaqane and stripped of their wealth and status, namely their cattle, sought protection from these armed traders. In return, the refugee women planted and tended crops, and the men worked as guides, hunters and carriers of supplies. In order to control this refugee community, the traders established themselves as headmen over a kraal and, according to Zulu tradition, took refugee women as wives. On the one hand, no other women were available at the trading post and, on the other, such unions made sense economically, socially, strategically and politically. In traditional Zulu society, the social standing of a man was measured by the number of cattle he owned, the size of his homestead, the size of the land allocated to him, the number of wives he had and the size of his following.

The English traders grew rich, especially in trading ivory for arms and ammunition – commodities that they could buy in the Cape Colony under the pretext that they were hunters. The white hunting and trading community expanded slowly but surely and, by 1838, prior to the arrival of the first wave of a few hundred Cape-Dutch-speaking white emigrant farmers (later called the Voortrekkers) in search of land in Natal, the white trading community had increased to 30 individuals. During the conflagration between the Zulu king Dingane, the successor of Shaka, and the emigrant farmers, the traders too were attacked and temporarily forced to abandon Port Natal. After the defeat of Dingane, however, they returned to resume their trading. In 1842, when Natal was annexed by the British Empire, the Cape-Dutch-speaking farmers left Natal in protest and a new wave of thousands of British settlers established a new farming community in Natal. With them they brought the social mores and practices of Victorian England and vigorously upheld cultural chauvinism and racist bias, condemning the social integration that had taken place at the trading post of Port Natal during the preceding 20 years. Being white and British and being constantly reminded of "Home" provided a sense of belonging to a newly established, insecure

Cedric Nunn, Kathy and Liz Ebersohn and Nikiwe Mpetsheni, 2002. Photograph: David Goldblatt.

white community that was not particularly prosperous, either as farmers or as traders. The settlers had not yet managed to exert their authority over the newly acquired colony and had as neighbours the huge, and for many, dangerous black population living in the Zulu kingdom. Like their Zulu neighbours, they also depended on the land for survival – a fact that made them all the more insecure. In this society, where white settlers kept their social

and other relatives joined the trading settlement at Port Natal in 1833, the year his son John was born. Like the other traders already established there, and according to Zulu custom, Robert Dunn became chief of a kraal. It is unclear whether Robert Dunn took a Zulu wife, but his father-in-law did and had a son by

Dunn grew up in a racially tolerant environment, where, from an early age, he learnt to speak fluent Zulu and was taught to observe Zulu etiquette, customs and traditions. Even as a youngster, he was highly proficient in riding, hunting and shooting and had what he called *"an apprenticeship in the hunting of*

distance from the black community, only a small number of enterprising traders, in a quest to get rich quickly, ventured into the Zulu kingdom to trade. Among them were John Dunn, Piet Louw, Arthur Nicholson and Herbert Nunn. Of these men, the best known was John Dunn, the hunter/trader who became political adviser to the Zulu king Cetshwayo and who took 48 Zulu wives in unions that proved to have been shrewd strategic and political decisions. Although much less is known about the three other traders, their lives followed similar patterns.

THE FIRST GENERATION: THE STORY OF JOHN DUNN (1833-95)

Robert Dunn, an eastern Cape Colony farmer turned hunter/trader and storekeeper, his wife, and six children, as well as his father-in-law

her. By 1839, Robert Dunn had made such profits that he could build a substantial home overlooking the harbour, which he called "Sea View". Whereas the settlement at Port Natal initially consisted of little more than a collection of traditional beehive huts erected by the Zulu refugees, interspersed with the traders' rectangular wattle-and-daub houses – described by visitors as being not much more than "hovels", Dunn imported enough materials to build a substantial wood-and-iron house. Here the family lived in relative splendour. The children had coloured nursemaids, who had been sent for from Port Elizabeth in the eastern Cape Colony, and were taught to read and write, presumably by their mother. John

John Dunn in a hut with his chiefs, circa 1873. Campbell Collections, University of Natal.

large game". In his autobiography, published in 1886, John Dunn reminisced about his childhood, and, if perhaps not entirely accurately, recalled: *"We often went out at night to get a shot at the elephants, which at the time used to come on to the flat, where the racecourse now is, and wander all about, often within a few yards of my father's house, Sea View, near Claremont [Durban]. The old house and the gigantic old fig trees have now vanished ..."* Tragedy, however, struck in 1847 when Robert Dunn was trampled to death by an elephant. John was 14 years old. His mother, rather than

Wonderboy Thokozani Nxumalo: John Dunn and
his first wife Catherine, Kathy Ebersohn and
her boyfriend Wandile Molebatsi, 2002. Painted
ceramic plate, diameter 38 cm.

remaining in the fledgling frontier village of Durban, returned to the greater comforts of the town of Port Elizabeth in the eastern Cape Colony, where she died three years later.

John had two choices, to return to the colony with his mother and sisters or to remain in Durban, where he would best be able to put to use his ability to speak Zulu, his knowledge of the countryside and his skills as hunter and shot, by acting as guide to the increasing number of hunting parties, traders and transport riders wishing to explore the interior of Natal. He must have realised that if he returned to more established colonial society with his mother, he would not be considered an adult but a juvenile with only some kind of apprenticeship to look forward to. As he had already served his apprenticeship, John chose to remain in Natal.

"I took to a wandering existence, having always been fond of my gun and a solitary life. In 1853 I was engaged, as was also my wagon, to go into the Transvaal ... On our return, when the time for my honorarium came, I was told I was not of age, and that by Roman-Dutch Law I could not claim the money. This so disgusted me that I was determined to desert the haunts of civilisation for the haunts of large game in Zululand."

When he disappeared into the hinterland of the Zulu Kingdom, John took with him 15-year-old Catherine Pierce, the daughter of his father's British retainer and a Cape Malay woman. Catherine later became John's wife and she, too, was faced with a choice: either the uncertain freedom and equality that life with John offered, or domestic service and subservience, the only possibility open to a girl of mixed parentage in white colonial society. The couple survived on John's skills as hunter and trader until he began to work for a retired British Army captain, Joshua Walmsley, who in 1852 had been appointed by the Natal authorities as Border Agent at the lower drift of the Thukela River, which separated the colony of Natal from the Zulu kingdom. Through Walmsley's patronage, Dunn was able to

Opposite top: **John Dunn talking to the Zulu leader Dabulamanzi kaMpande, 1873.** Campbell Collections, University of Natal.
Opposite bottom: **John Dunn with his chiefs, 1873.** Campbell Collections, University of Natal.

further his education and found employment as Walmsley's administrative assistant, training a corps of 40 to 50 Khoi and African policemen in the use of firearms and horses.

In December 1856, a civil war of succession broke out between the two eldest sons of king Mpande, Dingane's successor, namely Cetshwayo of the Usuthu faction and Mbuyazi, leader of the Gqoza. This was a traditional way of asserting and determining succession.

Cetshwayo defeated Mbuyazi at the battle of Ndondakusuka and became the most powerful claimant to the Zulu crown. Dunn fought on the side of Mbuyazi, most of whose troops were defeated or killed. Dunn himself had a narrow escape when he evaded the opposing army and managed to cross the Thukela River on horseback, thereby avoiding capture and almost certain death. Following the battle, old king Mpande pledged to allow Cetshwayo a considerable part in ruling the Zulu nation in return for Cetshwayo's promise to keep the peace. During the peace negotiations, John Dunn met with Cetshwayo and made such a favourable impression on him that Cetshwayo invited Dunn to establish himself in the Zulu

kingdom as his adviser. Since Dunn could read and write, spoke English and Zulu fluently, and was well-versed in Zulu etiquette and political strategy, he was entrusted with communicating with the Natal colonial government. Cetshwayo offered Dunn ten oxen, two wives from his own *isigodlo* (women's enclosure in the king's household) and a large area in the coastal region just north of the Thukela River over which he could act as chief.

Traditionally, marriage was an easy way of cementing political and economic bonds between clans in Zulu society. Since childhood,

Petros Gumbi: John Dunn and Dabulamanzi kaMpande, 2002. Ceramics, 27 x 33 x 26 cm.

John Dunn had seen how this system operated in practice and, having rejected his rather tenuous European cultural heritage, he took up the challenges of this way of life.

Dunn suddenly had the means to become a wealthy man, both in terms of Zulu custom and white settler society. He had been given cattle and selected land, including the Ongoye forest, which abounded with game. This provided the means to establish lucrative coastal routes for trade in ivory and hides.

"The finest bag I ever made was – one morning before 10 o'clock – twenty-three Sea Cows. One would think that, with all these carcasses, there would be great waste, but not a bit was lost. The natives [sic] around St Lucia Bay

used to come down in hundreds and carry every particle of meat away ... That season I killed to my own gun two hundred and three Sea Cows, besides a lot of other game, and was only away for three months from the day of starting."

Besides his wife Catherine, Dunn took a further 48 Zulu wives and for each wife he paid *lobola* of between ten and 15 head of cattle. These were shrewd moves: the women mostly came from clans living in the Zulu coastal region, the entire area through which his major north-south trade routes ran. So, by marrying five women from the Mzimela clan, four each from the Nzuzu and the Dube clans and three each from the Mthethwa, the Shandu and the Mdletxhe clans, he had succeeded in cementing exceptionally beneficial political alliances.

Dunn established settlements at Mangete, Emoyeni, Mtunzini and Qwayinduku, a summer retreat in the Ongoye hills, and ran his household affairs strictly according to Zulu custom. His own European-style house and quarters were placed in the middle of the kraal and his wives lived apart in their own traditional Zulu huts. His children lived with their mothers, and mothers and children were only allowed into his quarters at his behest. In addition, his household consisted of huts for his *izinduna* (headmen), guards, servants and visitors, and a large cattle kraal, stables for horses and a storeroom situated in the centre of his living area. In the 1880s, a magistrate's office and a school were added to the Mangete and Emoyeni settlements.

Catherine, who lived at Mangete, objected fiercely to Dunn's other marriages, so he tried to appease her by naming her his "Great Wife". According to Zulu custom, this accorded her status and privileges above all his other wives. As a result, her children saw themselves as superior to their other siblings, a situation that gave rise to considerable tension within the extended family. As in traditional Zulu society, Dunn's wives also enjoyed a measure of independence. Each received her own land to cultivate and a number of cattle were set aside for her daily use. The wives were responsible for their own children, except when it came to their schooling. To provide his children with a

Walking stick with female figure, made by Dandy Louw, Amy's second husband.

Western-style education, Dunn had schools built at both Mangete and Emoyeni and employed a teacher. In addition, Catherine was instructed to ensure that the daughters from all his marriages receive Western-style domestic training. Dunn did not, however, try to convert his Zulu wives to Christianity.

John Dunn's 48 wives were indispensable to the consolidation of his power base in the Zulu kingdom. They formed the bedrock of the various communities he established: they enhanced his status as head of a growing clan and their agricultural activity provided him with a substantial means of subsistence. His sons and daughters eventually numbered 117.

At his peak, Dunn was a wealthy hunter and trader; he was Cetshwayo's influential political adviser and ruled over a large tract of land and many people. He was not only envied for his economic success and political status, but Natal settlers and missionaries alike condemned his polygamy on moral, Christian grounds. He was alternatively referred to as a renegade, a degenerate and blight on white society.

By 1879, when the Anglo-Zulu War broke out, Dunn found himself in an unenviable position. He had enough knowledge of British military systems and power to realise that Cetshwayo would not be able to win a war against the powerful British empire and yet, having spent most of his life living according to Zulu custom in Zulu society, and owing his position of power and wealth to the goodwill of Cetshwayo, his loyalty lay with the Zulu king. However, he felt he had a responsibility to protect his family and followers – who now numbered about 6 000 – and, in the end, decided to side with the British, a decision that caused a break with Cetshwayo and caused him to be branded a traitor by many Zulus and even members of his own family. On 31 December 1878, to avoid the looming war, Dunn crossed the Thukela into Natal with 2 000 of his followers and 3 000 head of cattle leaving his homesteads north of the river to be looted and burnt.

After the Anglo-Zulu War, British authorities appointed Dunn chief of one of the 13 new regions into which the newly conquered Zululand had been divided. After the Zulu civil war of 1882-83 and the annexation of Zululand, his land was incorporated into the reserve

Amy Louw's stool.

Amy Louw's wooden bowl. According to Cedric:
"It was used for a long time to serve fruit and food."

territory and Dunn retained only limited control over the land around his homesteads at Mangete, Emoyeni and Qwayinduku.

John Dunn died in 1895 and, while Catherine Pierce was his main benefactor, his land was divided among all his surviving children. Each child, whether a son and or daughter, was given 100 acres, a bequest that was only ratified by an act of parliament of the Union of South Africa in the early twentieth century. It was also at this time, in the early 1900s, that the paths of Dunn's descendants crossed those of other white traders, such as Herbert Nunn, when their offspring united in marriage. Elizabeth, one of Dunn's many children by one of his Zulu wives, married John Nunn, one of the sons of Herbert Nunn. Since the 1860s, Herbert Nunn had been a trader in the district ruled by Hamu, a half-brother and supporter of Cetshwayo against Mbuyazi but who later sided with the British against Cetshwayo. Hamu's land lay in the far northwestern part of the Zulu kingdom, in the hills sloping down from the Ngome forest to the Mkhuse River. Much like Cetshwayo relied on Dunn for advice, Hamu relied on Nunn for support and advice in dealing with the colonial government in neighbouring Natal and, like Dunn, Nunn had established himself as a trader and a homestead chief with numerous wives.

THE SECOND GENERATION: AMY LOUW (1900-)
According to family legend, the trader Piet Louw was a friend of Dinizulu, the Zulu king who succeeded Cetshwayo. Louw, of Dutch descent, grew up in the Cape Colony and his parents were presumably part of the influx of Cape-Dutch-speaking emigrant farmers from the eastern Cape Colony. By 1888, Piet and his brother were running trading stores in the heart of the Zulu kingdom. Piet's store was located close to the Ceza mountain, and his brother's store was in the Mfubeni hills, some 16 kilometres away. As in the case of Dunn and Nunn, the Louw brothers had a foot in both the colonial and the Zulu worlds. They established homesteads for themselves with Zulu wives and began a local school for their numerous children. It was at this rural school, run by an English woman called Mrs Williamson, that Amy Louw (née Nicholson) met Willie Louw, a son of Piet Louw. Just after the turn of the century, it was exceptional for children living so deep in the rural areas of the Zulu hinterland to attend school and, regardless of race, only a limited number of children received an education.

Amy was the daughter of Arthur Nicholson, an English soldier who had elected to remain in

Zululand after the Anglo-Zulu War and had married Elina Mabaso, a local Zulu girl. They had eight children and Amy, the second eldest, was born in 1900. Arthur Nicholson was a road builder, bookkeeper and shopkeeper. Almost a century later, in 1998, Amy spoke of her father in an interview with her grandson Cedric: *"He was working in a shop; even in Ceza, we stayed in a shop too. You know, after the war was finished, then they told the white*

in quick succession. Willie and Amy Louw prospered, owning many cattle, donkeys and horses. All five daughters survived to adulthood, which was quite unusual for the time, given the proliferation of usually fatal childhood diseases. Lily, Amy and Willie's second daughter, was born in 1924, and

Granny Louw and her family first settled on top of the mountain, away from the river in the valley that was invested with malaria-carrying mosquitoes. It was a safe but uncomfortable location, for every day they had to haul water from the river down below. Willie died unexpectedly at the age of 34 and,

people to go back, those who didn't marry to [sic] an African, because most of them, they were married to Africans."
In the late 1910s, Amy went into domestic service, at first close to home and later in Durban, 350 kilometres away. At the age of 20, she returned, however, and married Willie Louw. Amy, or Granny Louw as she is now known, recalls that the marriage celebrations lasted four days, with an ox being slaughtered each day. All the members of the Louw family attended the service in the local Anglican church.
Willie Louw and his bride, Amy, built them-selves a house not far from Nongoma, to the south of Ceza. Here five daughters were born

remembers her father as *"a medium-sized man; quiet, very loving to his wife and children. We all adored him and only wished we were boys, because he longed for a son."*
When the youngest girl was about one-and-a-half years old, the family settled on land close to the village of Nongoma, where Granny Louw still lives today. They found the land at the confluence of the White Umfolozi and the Invuna River with the help of Granny Mabaso – the wife of Arthur Nicholson and Amy's mother – who had influential contacts close to the king. Since malaria was rife, the young

Amy Louw (seated) in conversation with a neighbour, 1988. Photograph: Cedric Nunn.

in accordance with local custom, Granny Louw married his younger brother Dandy James Louw. From Granny Louw's second marriage, three children were born: Vincent in 1938, Sheila in 1945 and Ronny in 1948. In addition to her younger children, Granny Louw also raised a number of her five elder daughters' children. When the threat of malaria was brought under control in the late 1930s, Dandy Louw moved his family to lower ground and erected a large

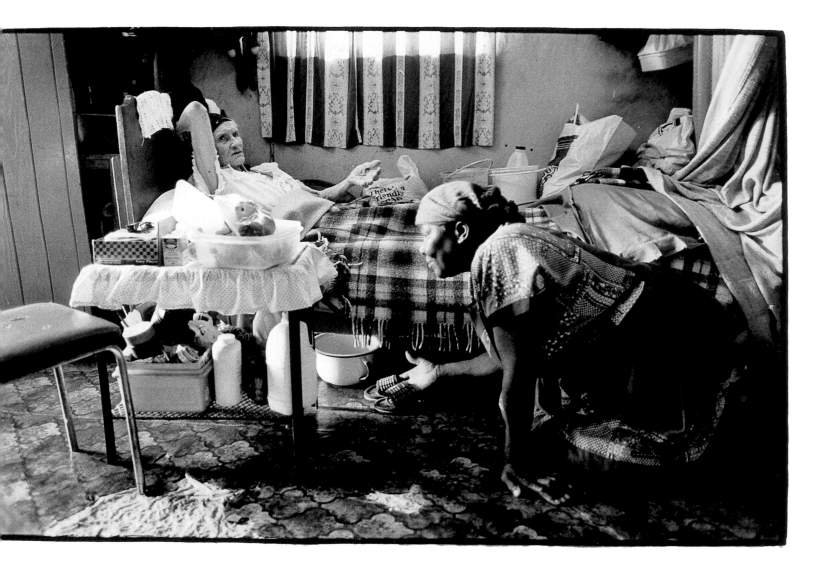

Amy Louw with her neighbour MaGwabe
Khumalo, 1999. Photograph: Cedric Nunn.
Left: Amy Louw feeding her chickens, 1986.
Photograph: Cedric Nunn.

house of stone and brick – the homestead of a prosperous farmer. Ronny vividly remembers living there:

"It had three bedrooms, with a big veranda, a dining room, kitchen ... there was the beer room. We weren't allowed there, unless you go to clean, like my mother went there, she was very good at brewing beer, she learnt from our clan when our kraal was here. My father had a plastered rondavel where he worked; he had a tree there that was his workshop, two trees. And there was a bench under the tree [and] that is where he mostly spent his time. I worked with him there, because he repaired ploughs. We had a kind of plantation and a garden for my mother, mulberry trees, banana trees and orange trees."

Dandy Louw died in 1963 and was buried at Ceza, where his brother – Granny Louw's first husband – Willie was also buried. Not long afterwards, in the mid-1960s, the widowed Granny Louw and her family – because of their mixed Zulu and English descent – were

classified "coloured" according to the new Population Registration Act. The Group Areas Act stipulated that only people belonging to the same race group could live together, so with its implementation the land on which Granny Louw's homestead stood was earmarked to revert to the local black people as grazing land. The homestead was demolished, but Granny Louw refused to leave the land and moved into a much smaller homestead higher up the mountain. It consisted of a number of rondavels and a small, three-roomed wattle-and-daub house. Although the arrangement – as well as these structures – were supposedly only a temporary measure, Granny Louw still lives there today. It has no running water and a pit latrine in the far corner of the yard. Close to the front door a scarlet bougainvillaea lends colour to the environment, while a bench made by Dandy still stands under a tree close by and

ploughs and other farm implements used by him can still be found stacked against the side of a small shed.

During the era of "grand" apartheid, forced removal and the destruction of homes – which Granny Louw personally experienced – was the fate of millions of black and coloured people in South Africa. From the 1950s onwards, the nationalist government segregated people of different racial groups and forced them to live in areas designated for their particular race group. Whereas these laws profoundly affected the lives of people in the urban areas, people in the rural areas did not altogether escape their impact either.

For the past thirty-odd years, Granny Louw has carried on living in her "temporary" homestead, surrounded by Zulu relatives, children and grandchildren. Rather than moving their almost 102-year-old mother elsewhere, daughters Lily and Sheila take turns caring for her. Each stays for several months at a time and then returns to her own home. Granny Louw's Zulu neighbours and relatives who live nearby visit her regularly. According to Cedric Nunn, Lily's son, his grandmother has a curious relationship with her neighbours. She is adamant that she has little in common with them. Yet, Cedric points out, there is little different about their abodes, the furnishings and what they eat. Her neighbours and friends never sit on her chairs, though, always on the floor, and preferably on the porch. If they do come into the house, they stand. Eventually, Cedric has come to understand: *"Though she was born to both a white and a black parent, she sees herself as apart, and according to her, her parents encouraged and expected such a view. She is not black and neither [is] she white, she is something quite apart. So she is not part of the considerable community in which she lives, not totally, that is, though she shares their confidences, hopes, fears and all the things that bind people together."*

THE THIRD GENERATION: LILY NUNN NÉE LOUW (1924-)

Lily Louw was born in 1924, the second eldest daughter of Amy and Willie. Like his father, Willie exerted himself to educate his daughters, and succeeded under much more difficult circumstances and at greater cost to himself and them. One of Lily's most vivid childhood memories is of having to leave home to go to boarding school in Durban, the only education available to girls of racially mixed parentage during the 1930s. Lily and her four sisters were sent by train to Durban, by then a bustling harbour town, where they boarded at the local orphanage and, because of distance and expense, rarely returned home. Travelling to school required a journey by ox wagon and an overnight halt in the veld before the village of Nongoma was reached. There the young girls embarked on the overnight train journey to Durban that included a change of trains. Finally, on reaching Durban, a rickshaw journey had to be undertaken, and still this was not the end of the road. Lily recalls: *"We would then struggle off [the rickshaw], each having a turn to carry the case, hating the first sight of the school, knowing it might be a long time before we saw home again. I was there*

for eight years and remember going home three times, the fourth time was when I left for good, in Standard Six."

After completing her schooling, Lily – like her mother – went into domestic service until she turned 21 and met her future husband, Herbert Nunn, at a family wedding. Herbert, one of four children, grew up in the Hlabisa district of northern KwaZulu. It was in this area, the territory of the Zulu chief Hamu, where his grandfather Herbert Nunn – after whom he was

named – had established himself as a trader in the late 1860s and became Hamu's political adviser. His father John Nunn, of the same generation as Granny Louw, had married Elizabeth Dunn, one of the many daughters of John Dunn.

Herbert and Lily were married in the Catholic cathedral in Durban in 1946. After the wedding, Herbert lost his job at the Lever Brothers soap factory due to a wartime shortage of raw materials. Herbert and Lily decided to raise their children in the country, so they returned to Lily's parents' home where Herbert was meant to farm the family land. However, because Herbert and his father-in-law's approach to farming clashed, this did not work out as planned and, through a local priest, he found work on the construction of the chapel at the

Nongoma mission. Lily and Herbert Nunn remained in Nongoma until their first child was born and then moved back to the Hluhluwe district in northern KwaZulu. Here Herbert found a job managing a shop deep in the rural countryside, since during the apartheid era it was impossible for men of mixed parentage to obtain licences to own and operate their own shops. During the 1950s, the Nunn family moved several times, but never left the district. They eventually settled in the small village of Hluhluwe itself and stayed there for quite a number of years. Herbert managed the general dealership, the only shop in the village, but –

Wedding portrait of Lily Louw and Herbert Nunn, 1946.

unlike his grandfather – he never owned it due to the laws of the land. Throughout these years, Lily worked in the shop alongside her husband whenever she could.

The Nunn family lived in a house attached to the shop, and six of their seven children were born there during their stay in Hluhluwe, between the late-1940s and late-1950s. At first, the children were sent to school in Eshowe, but in order to obtain a better schooling for their children, Lily and Herbert decided to send them several hundred kilometres away, to the Catholic school in Ixopo, south of Durban. Cedric, their second youngest child, vividly remembers his childhood in Hluhluwe and the increasing effects of apartheid on his life: *"I remember playing with white Afrikaans kids in the open lot next to my home and remember a white friend* who stopped visiting because his mother forbade him to play with that 'dirty boy'."

In the mid-1960s, Herbert Nunn, in an effort to gain his independence from employers, went to Mangete to lay claim to a portion of the Dunn land, which his wife Elizabeth could claim as a daughter of John Dunn. Lily recalls: *"They knew all along that they would be given land. They had been promised land for many years, that is why this place [the farm at Mangete] is called Endaweni, because she [my mother-in-law] always used to say 'endaweni', which means 'your place', and that is just to say that is where this place is, Endaweni. And we decided to call it Endaweni."*

Lily returned to her mother for about six months while Herbert was at Mangete, building a home for the family. It was a small house, which could barely accommodate the whole family and thinking back to their first attempt at making a go of the farm recently, Lily remained silent on the hardships they endured. Cedric, however, recalled: *"These were hard times for the family. I was fortunately much too young to experience the harshness of this time, though to this day the family talks in dread of that time. We lived on our smallholding in a two-roomed wattle-and-daub structure without water or electricity. Our main diet was the vegetables my dad grew, the staple of which was eggplant. Bathing happened in the river, and from the same river we daily drew water. My older brothers and sisters speak with horror of having to go over to the neighbours to collect milk or handouts. Dressed in their misshapen and cast-off clothing, they were the picture of poverty."*

After about two years, Herbert was offered a job as farm manager in the Pietermaritzburg area. He leased his land to a cousin and the family moved into a well-appointed house on the farm. Cedric remembers being overawed by the house's electric lights and indoor plumbing: *"The house seemed like the pinnacle of luxury and the few years we spent there were happy ones."*

Even while managing the farm at Pietermaritzburg, Herbert did not, however, give up his dream of farming for himself and at various times he enlisted the help of one of Lily's sisters as well as one of their daughters to share the development costs of the farm. After several years in the Pietermaritzburg area, Herbert returned to the Hluhluwe district, where he again managed a number of rural shops close to the game reserve. In the early 1970s, the family finally returned to live permanently at Mangete. Besides trying to make a success of farming, Herbert also

Studio portrait of Lily Louw. On the back of the photograph is written: *"To Dearest Mum & Dad, with all my love, from their loving daughter Lily. Taken Nov. 16th 1944 (Durban) at the age of 20."*

Opposite: **Lily Louw with her sisters Maggie (left) and Gladys, 15 March 1951.**

Lily Nunn entering the shop in Mangete, 1985.
Photograph: Cedric Nunn.
Opposite: **Herbert Nunn**, 1993. Photograph:
Cedric Nunn.

opened a shop at Endaweni. Times were difficult, Lily remembers.

"And those were hard years, you know, because we were running the shop. But I wasn't able to help in the shop then ... Our house was getting on gradually while we were living in it. Those were hard years, those were the hard years. It was a big house, it had four bedrooms, but it wasn't completed ... It was difficult. Water was a problem, because we had to fetch all the water from the shop."

Besides her own grandchild – the daughter of her daughter who had died – Lily's niece also lived with them and, later, Lily took in three children by the name of Fynn whom they had found abandoned in the area. At times, there were as many as 13 people living in the small house. Like her mother, Lily became the cornerstone of her extended family, caring and supporting those in need.

Although she herself remained reticent to talk about the hardships she had suffered, Lily's son Cedric filled in the silences. In 1984, on a quest for photographs for the forthcoming Year of the Woman, he returned to Mangete – and found his mother struggling to survive.

"I saw an image that radically altered my life. It was my mother walking through the door carrying two 25-litre buckets of water into the house. Her face was incredibly strained. She had just completed an eight-hour shift in the shop and was beginning another shift at home. The house she was entering was really just a shell. It had walls and a floor and a roof, but it ended about there. The floor was raw cement, uncovered. The walls were unpainted and the roof was without a ceiling. The house was without plumbed water and neither was it electrified. The shop was doing so badly that there was no hope of any of this changing soon. My father was ill. The strain and stress of holding all this together rested squarely on the shoulders of my mother."

Today, visitors arrive at the homestead by way of a dirt road that passes the shop – painted blue – and terminates in an avenue of tall, slim palm trees planted by Herbert, who died in 1998 after a long illness. A wide expanse of lawn surrounds the house, painted a soft peach colour, and surrounding it on all sides are the green sugar plantations that are the lifeblood of the farm.

THE FOURTH GENERATION: CEDRIC NUNN (1957-)

Lily was still living and working in Hluhluwe at the time she fell pregnant, but because she had returned to Granny Louw for the birth of her first child, Cedric was born in Nongoma

hospital. He recalls a happy village childhood that was rudely interrupted when he was sent away to school at the Mangete Government Coloured Primary School. Like his grandparents with their children, his parents strove to provide him with a sound education and, hampered by limited options imposed by apartheid legislation, he too was sent away for his schooling. Like his mother and

Lou-Anne, Cedric, Ginger and Gavin Nunn on the beach, circa 1970.

grandmother, Cedric remembers it as an unhappy experience: *"And most traumatically I remember being banished from home to the faraway place of Mangete. I was later to understand that this had more to do with the laws of the land than with any malicious intent on the part of my parents. I stayed with my father's sister, Aunt Aggie, and her family. My aunt lived about 250 kilometres from my home and I only saw my parents in school holidays. In Mangete, Aunt Aggie lived in an old wood-and-iron house on a smallholding, the closest neighbour being about a kilometre away. I became the eyes of my blind Uncle*

Reggie and had to remain in earshot to be at his beck and call."

Cedric looks back at the years on the farm in Pietermaritzburg as *"years of milk and honey"*, with idyllic holidays spent exploring on the farm. The return to the Hluhluwe district was good for him, as it felt like he was returning to home territory: *"As the farm [where the shop was] was on the edge of the Hluhluwe game*

reserve, days were spent roaming the bush, hunting birds and snakes, herding cattle to the dipping tanks with the workers, or just plain loafing in the hot sun and my father taught me to drive at the age of 12. Every holiday we were flooded with city relatives ..."

With his older brother, Cedric was sent to Ixopo to attend high school. At first they lodged in town, but later they became boarders at the school. After a hard time initially, he soon made friends. Being interested in art and music, his group of friends tried but failed to organise art classes, and neither did they succeed in introducing guitar music at their church services. So hearing about a local country-dance where a live band would be performing, the group of budding artists resolved to attend – despite a recent crackdown in discipline at school. *"We figured that they would never expect us to be as daring as to break out and attend the dance. We did and were promptly busted and expelled. We had to organise alternative accommodation for the last three months of the year and were not to return the following year. This signalled the end of my formal schooling career."*

At age 16, and fresh from school, Cedric started to work at the Amatikulu sugar mill as a pan boiler, a job found for him by a cousin, and this is where he spent the first two years of his working life. In the early 1970s, Cedric remembers giving – for a period of some two years – his entire earnings to his father who had just returned to Mangete, and taking only a small allowance for himself. His father had started a general dealership at Endaweni and was under considerable financial pressure.

By leaving school at 16 and earning a living, Cedric could thus contribute financially and so help to relieve the pressure on his family. He remained, however, undecided as to what he would do until he met Peter Mackenzie and was captivated by the photographer's portfolio. *"This was the cathartic experience I was waiting for. When I saw those photographs, I knew immediately and with absolute certainty that this is what I wanted to do with the rest of my life."* Mackenzie helped him to select camera equipment and began teaching Cedric the basics of photography. After a strike at the sugar mill, Cedric resigned and in 1980 decided to launch his career as photographer. Seeing very few prospects for what he called *"a so-called coloured photographer"*, he decided to travel abroad. With a friend's help, he went to London where – at an anti-apartheid art auction, presided over by the staunch anti-apartheid activist Father Trevor Huddleston – he met many South African artists in exile. Through this network, Cedric was welcomed and accommodated in all the countries in Europe he visited. On his return after nine months, he joined Afrapix Photo Agency in Johannesburg and found himself at the centre of the political upheavals

and increasingly violent anti-apartheid resistance that engulfed South Africa at the time. *"In 1983, the Sebokeng uprisings began, the United Democratic Front was launched and there was a frenzy of activity as labour and civics organised themselves around the country. Alternative publications sprang up overnight, and although their budgets were small ... we suddenly had clients and our photographs were moving and were being seen all over the country in relevant publications."*

It was in 1984, while visiting Mangete, that Cedric found his mother in dire straits and decided to suspend his freelance career as photographer in Johannesburg and return to Mangete to help improve the situation at home. But this, it seems, was not the only reason he decided to go home. On a more personal level, Cedric had to decide on the future of his relationship with Liz Ebersohn, the mother of their newborn daughter, Kathleen. As Liz was white and he was classified a "coloured person", they had not married. Shortly after he had returned to Mangete, Kathy and her mother joined Cedric, but the arrangement did not entirely meet with approval of his mother, Lily Nunn. Cedric, in his own words, explains: *"... [Lily] couldn't understand how it was possible that a white woman could come to live with a Coloured boy, never mind the conditions. I also think she was afraid about problems with the law. The Mixed Marriages Act [prohibiting marriages across the colour line] was still very real and enforced with zeal."*

At the time, Kathleen's mixed-race identity was kept secret and Cedric was not registered as her father for fear of having her adopted into a home for illegitimate coloured children. Liz and Kathy remained at Mangete for about a year and only returned to Johannesburg when it became clear that the relationship between Liz and Cedric was at an end. By the time Cedric left 18 months later, he had managed to treble the turnover of the shop, to electrify both the shop and the house, to install plumbing and indoor toilets and to do extensive renovations to the house.

Cedric's return to work as a freelance photographer in Durban coincided with the declaration of the country's first State of Emergency in 1985 and the eruption of the so-called Natal War. As a result, he found himself in the midst of the violence and had more photographic

work than he could handle. While at Mangete, his images of people's suffering had been used everywhere and four years after he had left Johannesburg, he returned and rejoined Afrapix, which had burgeoned in his absence. However, Cedric found that many of the new arrivals at the organisation did not share the political zeal of the early members, an issue that led to tensions and its eventual demise. Throughout the early 1990s, Cedric returned to Mangete at regular intervals to help with the running of the family business. In 1993, after convincing his eldest sister Beverley and her husband to move there, he once again returned to Johannesburg and bought an apartment in Yeoville. His first major photographic exhibition entitled *The Hidden Years* opened in Durban in 1997. Hosted by the KwaMuhle Local History Museum, it consisted of a collection of images dealing with the experiences of black people in KwaZulu-Natal against the backdrop of the struggle for democracy and change. At the show, he met Dawn, whom he married within a year.

Towards the end of the 1990s, Cedric became the part-time director of the Market Photography Workshop for two years, and no fewer than 16 graduates from the school found employment in the established media. Cedric continues to work as a freelance photographer.

THE FIFTH GENERATION: KATHLEEN EBERSOHN (1984-)

Kathy was born in Johannesburg in 1984 and her life to date has been characterised by numerous address changes. Not only has she lived in several suburbs of Johannesburg, but she also spent the first year-and-a-half of her life at Mangete and extended periods with her maternal grandparents in Knysna. In contrast to her father, her maternal grandmother and great-grandmother, she was, however, never sent away to boarding school. She started school in the early 1990s, at the time of the transition to a democratic South Africa, and is therefore one of the first generation of South African children who began their schooling in racially integrated schools. In fact, the high school, Sacred Heart College, she is attending was at the forefront of change since the mid-1970s and was one of the first schools in Johannesburg to accommodate children of all races.

After returning to Johannesburg from Mangete, Kathy and her mother lived with her maternal grandparents, where the toddler shared the house and attention of the adults with her cousin Sheena, two-and-a-half years her senior. When Kathy's mother met her future husband,

Neville, a man of Indian descent, she moved into a flat with him in Yeoville, a cosmopolitan suburb close to the centre of Johannesburg. Kathy moved with them and would intermittently see her father, Cedric, who came from Mangete to visit her in Johannesburg. However, since Kathleen found these visits very upsetting, her mother terminated the practice and, at age two-and-a-half, Kathy stopped seeing her father.

In 1987 Kathy's maternal grandparents as well as her cousin Sheena moved to Knysna and her mother married Neville, a step Kathy at first found difficult to accept: *"Simply, I wasn't willing to share her. When my mother married Neville, she had to go to Zimbabwe to do it because of the Immorality Act. I grew very attached to Neville."*

After an unhappy experience at a racist nursery school, Kathy was moved and put into a non-racial nursery school that catered for children from every conceivable background and celebrated every religious festival. Kathy does not remember much of this time – except that she had a boyfriend by the name of Mohammed who swore that he would marry her. The four-year-old Kathleen then went to live with her grandparents in Knysna for seven months. *"Life was never boring in Knysna. It was a place full of beauty, splendour and magical mystique. It was here that my belief in fairies, dragons, goblins, witches and all the supernatural originated."*

On her return, the family moved into a double-storey house in Fairview, an old residential suburb to the east of central Johannesburg. From Fairview they moved to Lenasia, an Indian township built in the apartheid era, some 30 kilometres south of the city. She loved the time she spent there and remembers how, during the Hindu festival Divali, people used to come round and give them sweet meats.

Kathy's mother's relationship with Neville deteriorated to such a degree, however, that the couple decided to separate, and Liz and Kathy moved into a flat with Liz's brother, Harry, who became almost like a brother to Kathy. She still saw her stepfather, but it was while she was living in the flat that she also saw her biological father, Cedric, for the first time in two years: *"It was the easiest thing in the world for me and very soon I had accepted him totally and completely."*

Cedric too, recalls the meeting with equal ease: *"I remember arriving at the Berea apartment that Liz shared with her brother Harry, to find*

Kathy with her grandfather Wessel Ebersohn in the Knysna forest, 1987.

her and Kathy locked in. Harry had left with both sets of keys and locked the gate behind him. I waited in the passageway for an anxious half-hour until Harry's return, with Kathy peering at me from a bathroom window. Kathy was an absolute delight and returned to my life as though she had never been away. She handled the reuniting far better than any of us. I was soon collecting her from her pre-school and then walking her home from her school."

Kathleen began attending primary school in 1991 when most of schools were open to children of all races, a development which, in retrospect, Kathy is very happy about since she believes that she would not have coped in a "single-race school". At school, she made new friends, many of which she has kept. She remembers meeting her best friend, Nikiwe Mpetsheni, on her first day at school, and today she and Nikiwe feel more like sisters than friends. Kathy's maternal grandparents returned to Johannesburg from Knysna when she was in Grade 3, and she was finally reunited with her cousin Sheena, who then attended the same primary school and who she today describes as her "surrogate sister". In 1994, however, Kathy's stepfather Neville, whom she was still seeing regularly, disappeared from her life for two years, and she found his absence very upsetting.

In reviewing her life so far, Kathleen singles out three people who, to date, have had a marked influence on her life. They are her mother and her friends Nikiwe and Wandile. Her mother, however, has remained her stabilising influence, and Kathy credits Liz as the constant force in her life: *"She gives everything she has to give and truly appreciates me for all my quirks, misunderstandings, slow learning and irritations. I cannot imagine a time or space without her ... Without her, I would not have the intricate montage of beauty diversity and 'realness' that has become my life."*

Even though she did not much enjoy her last two years at primary school, it was at this time – when she was in Grade 6 – that she went overseas for the first time. In addition, she was elected captain of the swimming team in her last year of primary school and became a student librarian in the school library, as well as being elected a school prefect. Kathy started her high-school career at Sacred Heart College in 1998 and found it a stimulating challenge, making a number of new friends with both girls and boys. Wandile, especially, has had a great influence on her life.

Kathy and Cedric in Magaliesberg, circa 1988.
Photograph: Anna Zieminski.

Liz's sister Thurza, her daughter Sheena, Liz,
Kathy and Cedric, 1984-85
Right: Kathy and her great-grandmother, Amy
Louw, 2001. Photograph: Cedric Nunn.

Kathy and Wandile, 2002. Photograph: Cedric Nunn.

Kathy, 2002. Photograph: David Goldblatt.

In addition, she developed a keen interest in photography, having received her first camera from her father Cedric at the age of 14. Although she has completed a course in photography, she feels that she has learnt more from her father than any course could teach her. In 2001, she started the first school newspaper, called *Untitled*, and has supervised the publication of two issues. She has also been involved in a photography club, serves on the school's matric yearbook team, and has been elected to be part of the Learner Leadership Council.

Kathleen is fortunate. On her father's side she has not only grown up knowing her grandmother Lily, but at 18 – unlike many teenagers – she knows her 102-year-old great-grandmother at Nongoma well. Here and at Mangete, Kathleen relates to relatives across four generations: a great-grandparent, grandparents, great-aunts and uncles and cousins, who watch her development at school and as a photographer with keen interest. During her visits, she also moves easily from the urban sophistication of Johannesburg to the simplicity of the rural, farm existence of her great-grandmother and adapts to life where running water, electricity and indoor plumbing are not a given.

The **Rathebe** family

I have seen it all

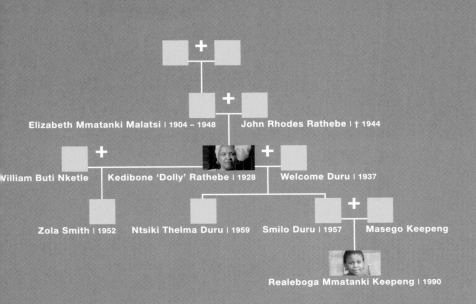

Elizabeth Mmatanki Malatsi | 1904 – 1948   John Rhodes Rathebe | † 1944

William Buti Nketle   Kedibone 'Dolly' Rathebe | 1928   Welcome Duru | 1937

Zola Smith | 1952   Ntsiki Thelma Duru | 1959   Smilo Duru | 1957   Masego Keepeng

Realeboga Mmatanki Keepeng | 1990

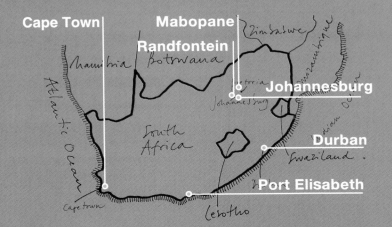

Cape Town   Mabopane   Randfontein   Johannesburg   Durban   Port Elisabeth

In July 1886, an Australian prospector by the name of George Harrison discovered gold in considerable quantity on the farm Randjeslaagte in the Transvaal Highveld, in an area known as the Witwatersrand. The news spread fast, and soon prospectors, miners and fortune seekers were flocking there from different corners of the country – and the world. By December of that year, a small town of tents and shacks had mushroomed into what was to become Johannesburg. In the first ten years, the population of the original mining settlement grew from a few hundred to 120 000 people and, within 50 years, became one million. Many of the mineworkers were Africans, drawn from all over the region by the opportunities offered by the growing city. Finding work there provided some escape from the poverty in the rural areas decimated by the Runderpest of 1895 and 1896 that had destroyed nearly 90 per cent of the cattle in southern Africa.

AROUND THE GOLDEN CITY

Elizabeth Mmatanki Malatsi was born in 1904 near the small village of Boons, a farming area some 60 kilometres northwest of Johannesburg. The farm on which she and her 11 siblings were raised belonged to her parents, who were relatively well-off, selling vegetables and other foodstuffs to the markets of the growing "city of gold". As a child, Mmatanki worked in the fields – at the time, education was not deemed necessary for young black girls – but when she grew older, she decided, like many other young women, to find a paid job in the city. She moved there and settled in Madubalaville, the African township outside Randfontein, not far from Boons and 45 kilometres west of Johannesburg. She became a domestic worker and while she was visiting friends, she met a young man, John Rhodes Rathebe, named – ironically – after the British imperialist Cecil John Rhodes.

John Rathebe had been born in Phokeng village, a stone's throw from Rustenburg, 110 kilometres to the northwest of Johannesburg. John's family, too, was relatively well off, and while other parents struggled to provide their children with an education, his were able to put him through high school, whereafter he became a teacher.

Lured by the prospect of better pay and better living conditions, John Rathebe moved to Johannesburg where, as a migrant worker, he initially stayed at the Crown Mines dormitories for single men. Miners were not allowed to bring their wives and children, so John had left

his family in Rustenburg and only visited them over holidays, and occasionally on weekends – a common routine for many migrant workers. It is here that Mmatanki Malatsi and John Rathebe met and fell in love. Although he had a spouse back home, John Rathebe moved in with her. In 1928, a daughter was born to them, whom they named Dolly Kedibone.

"It was in Madubalaville that my mother gave birth to two girls and a boy who all unfortunately had died at infancy. Hence it was something of a miracle when I was born healthy on 2 April 1928. My mother was so relieved that she gave me the name Kedibone, which means 'I have seen it all'."

It was also in Madubalaville that Mmatanki's family converged, albeit scattered across the township. While her mother was at work, Dolly was initially cared for by her grandmother Dorothy. But Dorothy died when the little girl was only two years old and her uncle, Joseph, who worked in the local mine, assumed responsibility for her well-being and so became an important father figure to her. Although he lived in the mining compound, Joseph made sure that Dolly never went to bed with an empty stomach.

REMEMBERING SOPHIATOWN

In 1887, property investor Herman Tobiansky bought a tract of high-lying land some way out of Johannesburg with the intention of developing it into a white residential suburb. Although 88 white families had moved there by 1910, the establishment of municipal sewerage works and a refuse dump nearby discouraged further investment and white people became more and more reluctant to settle on the land. As a result, Tobiansky divided the area into 1 694 plots and allowed Africans to buy property, offering them freehold title deeds to the land. He named the area after his wife Sophia and streets such as Toby, Edith, Gerty and Bertha after himself and his daughters. Sophiatown developed in a special way. Because it was not allocated by the government as a "location" for black people, it grew naturally: people moved there with their families and set up their own businesses. It thus became a close-knit, vibrant – and often violent – community, and home to people of different ethnic and cultural backgrounds. Over the years, the township grew into a landscape of solidly built brick houses, interspersed with flimsy, ramshackle, corrugated-iron hovels.

Masego Keepeng, Smilo Duru, Mmatanki Keepeng and Dolly Rathebe, 2002.
Photograph: David Goldblatt.

With time, it degenerated into a slum because of the number of corrugated iron shacks that sprang up in backyards (many shack dwellers falling prey to unscrupulous landlords). Sophiatown – affectionately known as Kofifi to its inhabitants – nevertheless had great advantages, not the least of which its proximity to the centre of Johannesburg. Less than five kilometres away, it was much closer to town, and the jobs it offered, than the official black townships.

Dolly was still an infant when her mother, Mmatanki Malatsi, settled as a subtenant in a house in Ray Street. At first, because her mother worked during the day, she was left in Madubalaville, but when she was old enough to attend the pre-school owned by Mama Mkajane in Ray Street, she moved in with her mother. Dolly afterwards attended St Cyprian missionary school – adjacent to her old pre-school – and sang in the school troupes – even though the sedate, well-organised music of school choirs was not quite to her taste.

She also went to Sunday school and was an ardent Girl Guide. She loved camping, going on parade and just hanging around the streets of Sophiatown in her smart, always-neat Girl Guide uniform.[1]

Although Dolly did not see much of her father, as he now stayed with his own family, John Rathebe never deserted either her or her mother. He would often visit, never hiding the fact that Dolly was his daughter. He was *the best man I ever met,"* she says. Sadly, he died in 1944 after a long illness.

For many years, Dolly's mother was employed as a domestic worker by a Jewish family in Saxonwold, and Dolly would visit her at work every weekend and, occasionally, after school on weekdays. Mmatanki Malatsi, in the meanwhile, was not coping well as a single parent and, after some time, fell in love with and married John Nge Matiwane, who worked in a hardware store. The couple moved to a bigger house in neighbouring Western Native Township with Dolly, where Dolly's aunt Dorah Maleshane Kgomane joined them.

This was the beginning of a traumatic time in Dolly's life.

"This stepfather ruined our lives as he ill-treated my mother and always beat her up for no apparent reason. Every time he came back home drunk he would assault my mother and

John Rathebe in Robinson, Randfontein, at the beginning of the 1940s. According to Dolly Rathebe he was always very well dressed.
Opposite: Studio portrait of Dolly Rathebe, Sophiatown, 1947.

*chase her down the street. I would also run
away and sleep with neighbours. In the
morning, I would go back home and prepare
for school."*

In 1943, when Dolly was just 15 years old, her
mother fell ill and Dolly left school to take care
of her. Because her stepfather had run off with
another woman, Dolly had to support the two
of them.

*"My mother became very unstable emotionally
and took ill often. As a result, I could not
further my studies after passing Standard Six.
Not able to bare this domestic torture and
abuse, my mother moved out and went to stay
with a cousin of hers, Emma Mokgosinyane, at
Matta Street in Western Native Township. I was
only 15 years old and terribly traumatised."*

Dolly went to stay with her best friend, Dorah
Mahibila, who lived in Paul Malunga Street in
the same area. Dorah's mother took good care
of her young house guest and even though
Dorah had a small child, the two young girls
got along well, sharing household chores,
running to town on errands and doing small
jobs to earn extra money.

Like most other girls her age, Dolly enjoyed the
street life of Sophiatown: she often visited
shebeens – illegal drinking places, often at
private houses – and regularly attended night
vigils, where family and friends and other
community members met prior to a burial to
sing songs all through the night in memory of
the departed. Dolly always joined in, quite
unaware of the singing talent she was
displaying.

At the cinema Dolly was introduced to
American music.

*"I had already begun singing in school choirs
where I excelled with Tandi Klaasen, then
known as Tandi Mpambani – as Tandi Klaasen,
she became a great songstress in the early
fifties. She and I were tigers when it came to
singing. But what encouraged me were stars
like Sarah Vaughn and Ella Fitzgerald, whom
we saw in the movies."*

In fact, two of Hollywood's most successful all-
black musicals, which both date from 1943 –
Stormy Weather and *Cabin in the Sky*, with
Lena Horne and Ethel Waters – were to shape
Dolly's musical destiny.

*"My mother used to sing at home. She was
also in my uncle's band and when I first heard
Stormy Weather, it was sung by my mother.
Every time I sing it, it reminds me of her
because it was her favourite."*

In the townships, music was everywhere – on

Dolly Rathebe early in her singing career.
BAHA archives.

the street corners, at bus terminals, at parties and at home – and the predominance of American music inevitably lead to it being adopted and fused with traditional African forms, such as *isicatamiya* (performed mainly by Zulu migrant workers) and *famo* (sung by the Basotho from Lesotho), in particular at mining compounds around Johannesburg. Later, this gave birth to *marabi* music, which in turn was amalgamated with urban rhythms, resulting in the popular *kwela* music of the fifties, in which the penny whistle played a key role.

In 1949, Dolly's life changed dramatically. After a long life of abuse and suffering, her mother was admitted to Baragwanath Hospital, in what is Soweto today, from where she was transferred to Bongweni Mine Hospital in Randfontein. Here she died on 9 April 1949 at the age of 45 years.

'I lost a friend. She was a beautiful woman, who dressed smartly – a religious person; she loved cooking and singing. She pampered me with love and was killed by this horrible stepfather."

Dolly is extremely proud of the fact that she could pay, entirely on her own, for her mother's funeral.

JIM COMES TO JO'BURG

And then, almost simultaneously, Dolly's fortune changed. A popular jazz group, the Harlem Swingsters, were performing at a picnic. Dolly and some friends from Sophiatown and Western Native Township attended, and when they played *Tamatie Sauce* (sic), a township favourite, Dolly was literally swept away by the rhythm. Completely impromptu, she began singing along with the band. Unbeknown to her, Sam Alcock, a talent scout from Orlando East, was among the crowd, on the lookout for a young female vocalist to feature in a film about to be shot in Johannesburg.

"I was 21 years old and I was wearing sneakers – takkies, in township jargon. I sang like hell, doing the jitterbug, and people gave me a rousing ovation … [Sam] approached me and invited me to come for auditions at the Bantu Men's Social Centre [BMSC]² in Eloff Street in Johannesburg. I was reluctant because I did not have fancy clothes. Besides, I was only 21 years old. [But] Sam Alcock begged me until I agreed."

When Dolly turned up for auditions the following day, she was even more intimidated by the presence of the Pitch Black Follies, another famous jazz band from Sophiatown led by Motsieloa. Emily, Motsieloa's wife, was also present, as were Snowy Radebe and Lindi Makhanya.

"These women were the top female singers in the 1940s and I was thoroughly intimidated by their presence. Unlike them, I did not have shoes but was wearing my usual takkies and a swing skirt [a pleated skirt that got twirled into a circle while dancing the jitterbug]. My knees simply wobbled. I thought I had no chance. I felt like a nobody, especially after Mrs Emily Motsieloa, who was playing the piano for those auditioning, discouraged me. She dismissed me like a dirty little township wench. I told my friend Dorah that we should go, but Sam Alcock insisted I stick around."

Jacob Moeketsi, the brother of the famous saxophonist Kippie Moeketsi, agreed to accompany Dolly.

"I chose the song Salt Lake City Blues, *which I had heard sung in the musical* Cabin in the Sky. *When the pianist gave me a key, I did miracles and shocked everyone, including the older female singers who had looked down upon me. I sang the shit out of the song. Because I was an orphan at the time I challenged established female singers at those auditions, I sincerely believe that God, my late mother and my ancestors gave me strength."*

Afterwards Eric Rutherford, the producer, walked over and hugged Dolly, excitedly telling her that she had got the part.

"I just cried like I have never done before when he told me that."

Jim Comes to Jo'burg, directed by Donald Swanson, was the first feature film to be shot on location in South Africa and the first to present black actors in the leading roles. Dolly played the part of a nightclub singer. Just like in her favourite musical, she majestically glides down the stairs, resplendent in a glittering gown, and belts out the song *Salt Lake City Blues*, changing some of the original lyrics to "Oh! I came to Jo'burg, the Golden City". Shooting the film was not without complications, however. Once Dolly was absent for two weeks because a friend jealous of her success had stabbed her. In addition, the crazy consequences of some of the apartheid laws

disrupted filming, the pass laws and Separate Amenities Act in particular. To facilitate matters, Dolly, for part of the time, stayed in the posh white suburb of Houghton, at the house of Gloria Green, whose family was paying most of the production cost. But there was no escaping the discriminatory laws: *"I thought I'd take a walk down the road one evening – I was arrested for [not carrying a] pass. The filming had to be stopped again. They just took me, and I slept in jail."*[3] The film company reported to the press that Dolly *"was fined 15 shillings in the Native Commissioner's Court, in Fordsburg"*.

Completed on a small budget, and shot partly on location, partly on a set that depicted an imaginary bar called the Ngoma Club, *Jim Comes to Jo'burg* became the most successful production of its time in South Africa. Despite the simplistic and romantic, politically ignorant plot, the film was nevertheless an important symbol of African potential. To most black Africans, the film presented not only entertainment but also a political statement that they were just as good as anybody else.

On 25 October 1949, the Johannesburg newspaper, *The Star*, reported: *"History was made at the Rio non-European cinema, Market Street, last night when "South Africa's first full-length entertainment film featuring non-European South Africans" had its world premiere."*[4]

A week later, the *Rand Daily Mail* reported: *"Daniel Adnewmah (Jim) and Dolly Rathebe, who played main parts in* Jim Comes to Jo'burg *are already important people. Admirers follow and ask for their autographs. Dolly's hairstyle, designed for her part in the film, is copied everywhere in the townships. It is 'cottage loaf' drawn together with a filet of native beadwork."*[5]

STARDOM

Although it was not a financial success, the movie certainly proved to be a popular success, and Dolly's life changed dramatically: *"I became the first African female film star. I became a celebrity overnight and people greeted me everywhere, while others hugged and kissed me."*

Soon after the release of *Jim Comes to Jo'burg*, Dolly was signed to co-star with Tommy Ramokgopa in another feature film, *Magic Garden*, shot on location in Alexandra township, north of Johannesburg. But the success of *Jim Comes to Jo'burg* was not to be repeated, and *Magic Garden* was not even shown in South Africa until ten years later. Dolly, however, had by now made her name and was using her voice to establish a career. She was a lead vocalist with both the Harlem Swingsters and the Inkspots, many of whose members had performed in *Jim Comes to Jo'burg*.

As a result, Dolly began to perform regularly in white nightclubs in Johannesburg, and was making plenty of money. Whereas once she wore sneakers and cheap skirts, she now was able to afford designer clothes and expensive shoes. Regarded as the sexiest woman to hit Sophiatown, Western Native Township and adjoining Newclare, she had many suitors clamouring for her attention. In fact, she is reputed to have had such sexy and desirable thighs that when men greeted one another and wanted to emphasise that all was tip-top or "sharp", they would say: *"Is Dolly se boude [thighs]"*. In time, the expression was shortened to "Is Dolly".

One man – William Buti Nketle, a member of the notorious Americans gang, a smart dresser popularly known as "Toweel", finally swept her dolly off her feet.

The Americans was initiated in 1945 by George "Kortboy" Mpalweni, a boxer and knife expert, who banded together some of his boyhood friends, including William Buti Nketle. Together they formed a gang that stole mainly from the South African Railways trucks that delivered expensive clothes and shoes to boutiques in Johannesburg, and because the gangsters prided themselves on the American designer clothes they wore, they called themselves the "Americans".

Their modus operandi was simple and effective: while deliveries were made at a store, one of the gangsters would go up to the Afrikaner who usually guarded the SAR truck and distract him by offering to sell him a fake watch. While they haggled over the price, the other members would quickly unload several boxes of clothing and cart them off on bicycles or in a car. Alternatively, the white guard was teased and harassed and while he was chasing after the cheeky "kaffir", part of the consignment would be stolen.

With their efficient operation, the Americans had lots of money, which they spent on refining their image. They behaved like aristocrats, changing clothes three times a day and never wearing a shirt twice. They cruised around in an open coupe, which belonged to a Chinese friend.

Dolly was madly in love with her handsome Toweel Nketle and together they moved to number 17 Meyer Street, Sophiatown. But Toweel's mother and many others frowned upon the relationship: a woman in showbiz was

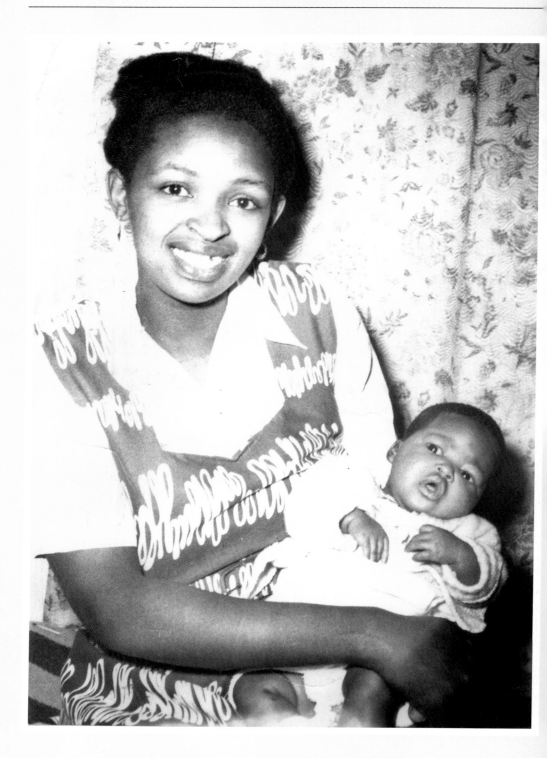

regarded as a "tiekie-line" – as cheap.
"She did not like me one bit and told him I would never give birth to children. But Toweel and I were so much in love that he told her that he loves me and only me and that he would never marry any other woman but me. He was my main man and he taught me so much about love and life. When I gave birth to our daughter Zola on 17 May 1952, it was the crowning of our love."
Dolly was crazy about her little angel, but found it extremely difficult to raise her daughter the way she would have preferred to, especially

Dolly with Zola when she was three months old, taken at her "coming-out party", 1952. It was the custom to show off a new baby to friends and family as soon as it was nice and chubby. Opposite: **Dolly Rathebe in the "Jazz Train" to Durban, 1955.** Photograph: Bob Gosani. BAHA archives.

without the support and advice of a mother.
"I did not know anything about raising a child. Once Zola became very sick and I did not know what to do. On the advice of neighbours and friends, I took her to the clinic where I was

given medicine to treat her. But she did not get well and seemed to be getting worse. As her situation deteriorated, everybody thought that she was going to die. A friend introduced me to a faith healer who stayed in our neighbourhood. I went to this old woman who sprinkled water on her as she prayed continuously. After a night of prayer, we woke up the next morning and my baby was cured. It was a miracle."

THE ROUGH LIFE

As the lover of Toweel Nketle, Dolly naturally often consorted with members of the Americans and even took part in the battles they waged with other gangs, such as the Berlins, the Skietmekaars and the Corporatives. She was always in the forefront, and because of her courage, they nicknamed her "Kitty Collins", after the character Ava Gardner played opposite Burt Lancaster in *The Killers*.

"I was an integral part of the Americans and used to hide their guns in my gumboots when we were going to fight other gangs. I was a gangster's moll and I could deliver a crushing blow with my fists. As a result, the guys had another name for me: 'Mawisa' – the knocker … I might have been beautiful and sexy, but I was a toughie and did not tolerate nonsense. Even girls who dared to have an affair with my man felt my wrath because I would knock them out. I was a fighter and I was not afraid."

Music was never absent from this rough life, and the Americans often visited shebeens, where they shared in the township's lively lifestyle. Because the apartheid laws prohibited black people from drinking what was regarded as "white people's liquor", shebeens were illegal, but as they formed the social nucleus of township life, they could not be eradicated. Dolly's favourite shebeen was Sister Nobeni's Place in Gibson Street.

"But I also liked going with the guys to Back o' the Moon and 39 Steps because the jazz was hot there. We were the envy of the town, doing the jitterbug to the strains of jazz music. Some of the Americans, especially Kortboy, were rather good at doing the jitterbug. It was exciting when the mood was high and big fat Mason Dubaduba Libalele – a well-known bus

Dolly Rathebe, 1953. Photograph: Jürgen Schadeberg.

inspector – had everyone clapping when he was doing the jitterbug."

In the end, Dolly's relationship with Toweel Nketle did not work out, and she left him and moved to Orlando, and later to Alexandra. Zola was left in the care of Toweel's mother, who raised her. Not long afterwards, Toweel

disappeared from the scene when the members of the Americans were picked up one by one by the police. Dolly would later learn that he was serving time at Leeukop Prison.

AFRICAN JAZZ

Although Dolly's film career had come to an end, her fame as singer was gaining momentum. Before Miriam Makeba joined the group, Dolly was the lead singer with the Manhattan Brothers, with whom she recorded her first album. Other engagements followed.

"Life was hectic for me because I also toured South Africa's major cities with the Harlem Swingsters with Dorothy Masuka, sharing top billing with her."

Dolly was then contracted by Alfred Herbert, an inventive organiser of numerous music events and at the time the driving force behind South African jazz. It was Herbert who taught her the finer tricks of the music trade. In 1954, Herbert arranged an extended series of jazz concerts that would be launched as the African Jazz Parade the following year and end in Kenya as the African Jazz and Variety Show years later. In the interim, the show became

Sam Nhlengethwa: Dolly Rathebe, 2002. Paint and textile on paper, 75,5 x 73 cm.

somewhat of an institution, performing to full houses at theatres in Johannesburg and touring all the major cities of South Africa and the neighbouring countries.

The musicians all travelled by train and would stop along the way to perform. Inspired by the successful "Jazz Train" in the United States, a special tour was arranged to Durban. This "Jazz Train" boasted the who's who of South African jazz and music. Packed with fans, performers and hangers-on, it left Johannesburg for Durban on a Wednesday morning in June 1955.

The African Jazz and Variety Show regularly performed and, although it toured with a variety of performers who came and went, the main attraction remained the sultry voice of Dolly Rathebe. By 1956, taught to her by Herbert's mother Sarah Silva, she even began to sing in Yiddish, because an important and influential part of the jazz-loving public were Jewish.

At the time, audiences were still mixed in terms of class and race and even though apartheid policies were being implemented, music somehow managed to escape the forced racial divides in the country. But not for long ...

MUSIC AND POLITICS

In the 1950s, the lives of black South Africans were increasingly affected by the ever-stricter enforcement of segregation. One tragic result was the destruction of Sophiatown. By now, the area was entirely surrounded by white suburbs and the government had repeatedly threatened to remove the "black spot". While Dolly was away on tour, it finally happened. On 10 February 1955 the Johannesburg municipality started to demolish houses. In just four years, the vibrant, ethnically integrated community of Kofifi was removed and resettled along ethnic lines far from the city centre in Meadowlands, a part of what later became known as Soweto. The apartheid laws, designed to keep black people out of white neighbourhoods at night, demanded that no African could be in a white area after 9 p.m. This "white by night" rule hit performing artists particularly hard: they earned their livelihood in the evenings and obtaining a permit to move around was neither fair nor practical. One night as Dolly was returning from a show with the Manhattan Brothers, the Flying Squad suddenly flashed into view and forced them to pull their car over. The police could find no dangerous weapons or illicit liquor, so the officers demanded to see their night passes. Dolly and her friends didn't have passes, so they were locked up for the night.

Top: **Dolly Rathebe posing for an advertisement of Max cigarettes, 1951. Photographer Jürgen Schadeberg:** *"I took this picture at Werner Studios in Johannesburg to promote a cigarette brand. This was one of the first images of black people being used in commercial advertising."*

Bottom: **Dolly Rathebe, 1952. Photographer Jürgen Schadeberg:** *"This photograph was taken on a mine dump to give a beach atmosphere. [Suddenly] We were surrounded by at least a dozen white policemen ... The police did not ask us any questions but proceeded to arrest us. Dolly explained to me that we were being arrested under the Immorality Act."*

Opposite: *Drum cover, 1955. Dolly photographed by Bob Gosani.* BAHA archives.

DRUM

Registered at the GPO as a newspaper.

Exclusive
Pictures of
Seretse Khama's
Children!
—see inside

KARG SAYS:

"MEET THE GREAT
CHONG INSIDE!"

ZZ STARS AT THE BEACH!
—page 38

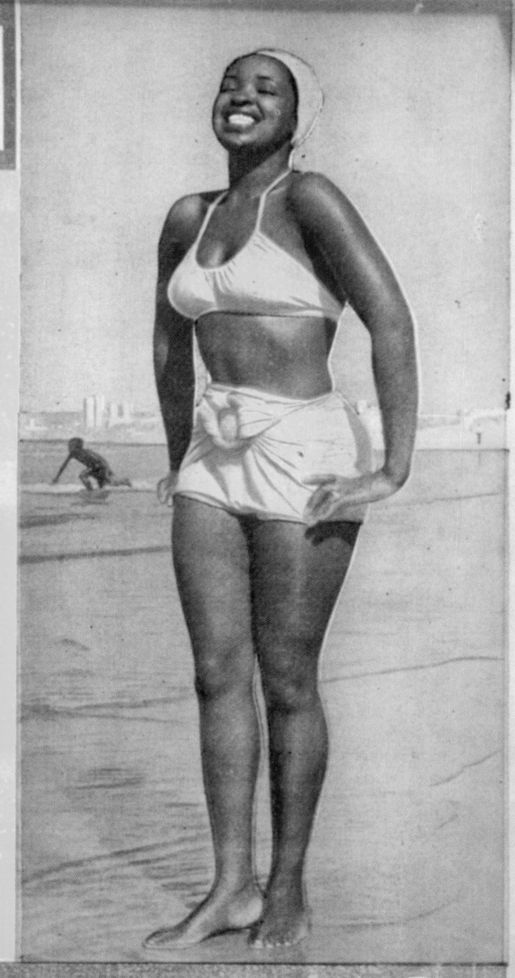

Africa's Leading Magazine

6d

JULY, 1955

Thelma and Smilo Duru, circa 1963. Dolly
carried this photograph with her for many years.

GROUP PORTRAIT SOUTH AFRICA

popularity, products aimed at the African market – Karoo Cream (a skin lightener!) and Max cigarettes among others – became associated with her image. Black pin-up stars were becoming a phenomenon, and Dolly recalls an incident in February 1952 when she was invited for a photo shoot by Jürgen Schadeberg. The pictures were published in 1954 in the magazine *Africa* but, by looking at the demure beauty on the double spread inside, few readers would have suspected the drama that had accompanied the photo session. Schadeberg remembers the incident well: *"Apartheid insanity multiplied. I arranged a series of photo shoots with Dolly requiring a beach background. We drove to a mining dump near Kensington. Upon arrival, one of the residents was watering his lawn. Dolly and I climbed out of the car and begun walking towards the dump to find a suitable spot. We did a series of shoots and suddenly I realised we had company. We were surrounded by at least a dozen white policemen who all spoke Afrikaans. I had just arrived [from Germany] in Johannesburg and Drum was my first real job ... and Mr Bailey gave me a break. Dolly was only in her bikini. The police did not ask us any questions but proceeded to arrest us. Dolly explained to me that we were being arrested under the Immorality Act, where sexual relations between Africans and white people were legally prohibited."* Dolly remembers: *"They took us to the Jeppe police station, all along harassing us. But after a few hours, they let us go without charging us."*

The days of integrated audiences were now gone. Yet, in 1956 the Johannesburg City Hall presented a series of concerts featuring both black and white artists. Although no performing group was racially mixed and the audiences were segregated – there were shows for "Europeans only" and shows for black music lovers – the line-up of artists included both black and white bands. Billed as "Township Jazz", the large music show repeatedly filled the hall to capacity. Perhaps the black audience went for the same reason as photographer Bob Gosani who said: *"Doggone, man, let's go see this Township Jazz thing. And I've never been inside the City Hall anyhow. And I live in Sophiatown and pay rates and taxes and whatnot."*

A WELL-KNOWN FACE

Despite the troubled times, Dolly's fame continued to grow, much of it due to the remarkable development of the black printed media in South Africa. In fact, the boom time for African musicals coincided with an era of outstanding African journalism, the best of which appeared in *Drum* magazine. Under the banner of *African Drum*, the publication had a rather lame start in March 1951. However, as soon as Jim Bailey took over as publisher a few months later, things changed rapidly. The magazine was renamed *Drum*, and Bailey appointed Englishman Anthony Sampson as editor and German Jürgen Schadeberg as chief

Label on a Dolly Rathebe vinyl record. The music was written by Welcome Duru, whom Dolly married in 1957.

photographer. Then he recruited a large staff of African writers and photographers. Soon an atmosphere of excitement and creativity enabled great talents to bloom. Journalists, among them Todd Matshikiza, Henry Nxumalo, Lewis Nkosi and Can Themba, and photographers, the likes of Peter Magubane and Bob Gosani, quickly rose to prominence. *Drum*'s strength lay in investigative journalism – it revealed shocking aspects of apartheid and provided a platform for new black leaders; but it was also a fun magazine that presented urban black culture as vital and attractive. Dolly's life and music was thus a natural subject for *Drum* and comparable magazines, such as *Zonk*, and she was splashed on the cover of both magazines. Because of her

MARRIED LIFE IN PORT ELISABETH

In 1956 Dolly fell in love with Welcome Duru, a fellow artist eight years her junior, who with his brothers and friends had formed his own

Drum cover 1957. Dolly photographed by Jürgen Schadeberg. BAHA archives.

**Robert Lungupi: Radio with portrait of Dolly
Rathebe, 2002.** Wood and paint,
29,5 x 51 x 15 cm.

own. Memorable, too, was the "Tribute to Dolly athebe" concert at the Johannesburg Civic heatre on 11 August 2001. Arranged in her onour by Miriam Makeba, with Hugh Masekela

that they were planning to make a tribute to me, it was a very emotional experience and we all cried."

It was as if Dolly's musical career was being

Sam Nhlengethwa: Dolly Rathebe, 2002. Paint and textile on paper, 152 x 95,5 cm.

as musical director, the show was a complete sell-out. *"When Miriam Makeba, Faith Kekana and Mara Louw came to my house to tell me*

born again. Once again she was being booked for performances week in and week out. Today, Dolly is content with her life. She has four grandchildren, and all three her children live in their own homes and provide for themselves. Her daughter Zola lives in the former "coloured"

area of Eldorado Park, south of Johannesburg, happy with the identity she had taken from her mother during their Cape Town stay. She is married and works for the Johannesburg Municipality. Thelma lives in Mohlakeng, and Dolly has become a mother to Thelma's sons with whom she shares the family house. The only grandchild who might have inherited Dolly's singing talent, however, is her grand-daughter Mmatanki, the daughter of Smilo.

LOOKING TO THE FUTURE

Smilo Duru, 45 years old, is Dolly Rathebe's only son. He was two years old in 1957 when his mother left his father, Welcome Duru, in Port Elizabeth to return to Johannesburg. *"Although I grew up in Mohlakeng in Randfontein, where my mother placed me in the care of her uncle Joseph Malatsi, I never lost contact with my father. Most importantly, I have never for once forgotten that I am a Xhosa by birth, which is why in 1979, at the age of 22 years, I returned to the Eastern Cape to be circumcised. It is the Xhosa culture and I felt compelled to attend the ritual after which a boy is certified a man."*

The circumcision ritual was performed in the outskirts of KwaZakhele, a black residential area near Port Elizabeth.

While his mother pursued her singing career, Smilo attended school in Mohlakeng and later matriculated in Lesotho.

"My aim was to pursue a BA degree in com-merce, but a riot broke out at the Moshoeshoe Two High School in Matsieng because of many problems, including bad food which we were served. The school management blamed the disruptions on us students from South Africa. They called in the soldiers and we had no option but to flee from Lesotho."

Smilo joined his mother in her house in Elsies-rivier in Cape Town for some time.

"I did not stay there long because our house in Mabopane was already under construction. But there were a lot of problems by the construction people who could not account for lost building material. Matters came to a head when, after completing the two backyard rooms and a garage, they rented them out without our know-ledge. My mother asked me to return and live in one of the rooms while monitoring the building process. But first I had to evict the people who had been staying in the rooms illegally."

Since his mother returned to her completed house in Mabopane in 1981, Smilo Duru has been in and out of jobs.

"At some of the jobs I have had, I was retrenched, which is why I am committed to helping my mother with her businesses in

Smilo and Dolly at the grave of Dolly's mother, 2001. Photograph: Motlhalefi Mahlabe.

GROUP PORTRAIT SOUTH AFRICA

although the children at school call her Lebo – was still very young, and she grew up with he mother Masego. Masego lives in Mabopane, i a new residential area built for government officials, teachers and nurses. The houses are very clean and neat, but rather impersonal, an small and constructed very close to one another.

Masego is a qualified nurse and works in the intensive-care unit at Rankua Hospital. She often works night shifts and is therefore not able to take full-time care of her daughter. Fo this reason, Mmatanki spends most of her tim with her aunt, Maria, her mother's sister who also lives in Mabopane, but a considerable distance from Masego. Mmatanki regularly visits her grandmother Dolly over the weeken and here she often sees her father, who spends much of his time at his mother's place Because the schools in Mabopane lack quality teaching and equipment, Mmatanki attends Oostend, one of the oldest schools in Pretoria Oostend, which recently moved into new buildings, is a Christian school, with mostly Afrikaans-speaking white teachers, while most of the learners are black. The school is very regimented: all the pupils line up after the bel rings and have to walk in neat rows to their classes.

Going to school in Pretoria means that Mmatanki makes the long trip to town by minibus every day; she only returns at about four in the afternoon to her home in dry and dusty Mabopane with its neat little shacks on the hills, its more solid brick houses and dirt roads; Mabopane, which is no longer part of a apartheid homeland, but which is still very much a black African town, invisible from the nation's administrative capital; Mabopane, which Mmatanki hopes to leave behind one day, to go and live in Johannesburg, a city of dreams, but now no longer out of reach.

Leftt: **Dolly Rathebe and Smilo** (right), **Thelma** (left) **and family at Thelma's house in Mohlakeng, Randfontein, 2001.** Photograph: Motlhalefi Mahlabe.
Opposite: **Mmatanki, 2002.** Photograph: David Goldblatt. Opposite top and middle: **Mmatanki a school, 2001.** Photograph: Motlhalefi Mahlabe.
Opposite bottom: **Mmatanki with friends, in fro of her mother's house in Mabopane, 2001.** Photograph: Motlhalefi Mahlabe.

Klipgat, a stone's throw away from our home in Mabopane. She has already built a hall where old pensioners are now able to receive their pension money in a covered place. My mom intends partitioning the place to have a phone section, a small grocery shop and a beer distri- bution outlet. I am going to help her ensure that her business becomes a success."
Smilo married Masego Keepeng in 1988. They have one child, a daughter, Realeboga

Mmatanki Keepeng. She was was born on 18 March 1990, just a few weeks after Nelson Mandela was released from prison, and was only four when the first democratically elected black government came into power in 1994. Her parents separated when Mmatanki – as most people call Dolly's granddaughter,

The **Plaatje** family

Completing the circle

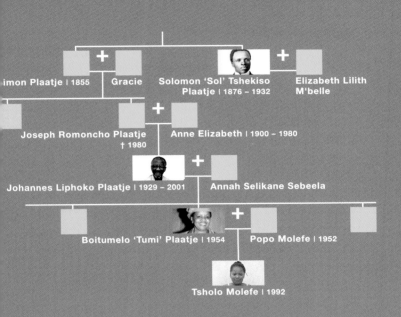

imon Plaatje | 1855   Gracie   Solomon 'Sol' Tshekiso   Elizabeth Lilith
                                  Plaatje | 1876 – 1932   M'belle

Joseph Romoncho Plaatje   Anne Elizabeth | 1900 – 1980
        † 1980

Johannes Liphoko Plaatje | 1929 – 2001   Annah Selikane Sebeela

Boitumelo 'Tumi' Plaatje | 1954   Popo Molefe | 1952

Tsholo Molefe | 1992

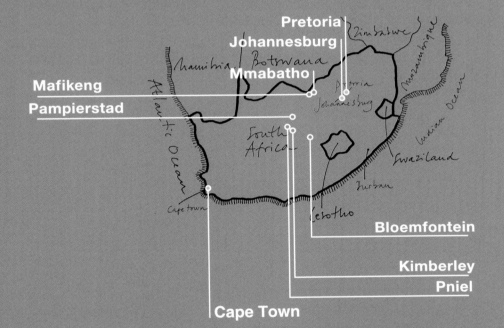

Pretoria
Johannesburg
Mmabatho

Mafikeng
Pampierstad

Bloemfontein

Kimberley
Pniel

Cape Town

In the 1980s, at the height of Chief Lucas Mangope's reign as President of the "independent homeland" Bophuthatswana, the new capital Mmabatho was home to the high and mighty of this apartheid-created puppet state. Today, Mmabatho is little more than a suburb of Mafikeng in North West Province. Here, concealed by tall trees behind high security fences, stands the house that was at that time the residence of South Africa's ambassador to Bophuthatswana. At the entrance, a sentry stands guard and has announced the arrival of all visitors before he is permitted to open the gates. The house is now the official residence of the North West Premier, Popo Molefe.

Popo Molefe shares the house with his wife Boitumelo Plaatje and daughter Tsholofelo. As the front door is opened, visitors are ushered into a wide passage. Doors lead off to various parts of the house, and immediately ahead is a spacious and elegantly furnished living room. Perched on one of the leather settees and smiling benignly is Tsholo, the couple's only daughter. Tsholo's family and forebears have an illustrious history of political involvement. She is the daughter of one of the most distinguished leaders of the Black Consciousness Movement of the 1970s, who in newly democratic South Africa was appointed the first premier of North West Province. She is also the great-grandniece of Solomon Thsekiso Plaatje (1876-1932): journalist, political activist and temperance organiser in South Africa during the early twentieth century.

A HAPPY CHILDHOOD

Solomon Tshekiso ("Insight") Plaatje was born on 9 October 1876 of Barolong parents, strict Lutherans who had settled as farmers on the Pniel mission station between Kimberley and Barkly West, where Plaatje spent "the best and happiest days of his childhood". At the time, it was not unusual for families growing crops and raising livestock frequently to move in search of better opportunities, so when Solomon was just seven or eight years old, his parents left Pniel for Mayakgoro, some 100 kilometres to the north, along the Harts River. Solomon's father, Johannes, made this decision and his mother, Margaret, was extremely reluctant, even resentful of having to leave. Their eldest son, Simon, a strong-willed man of about 28, chose to remain at Pniel with his wife, Gracie, and their daughter, Lydia. Born in 1855 and nearly 21 years older than Solomon, Simon insisted that his younger brother should remain

with them in Pniel. So the young Solomon was left in the care of Simon, who raised the boy as his own.

The Berlin Missionary Society (BMS) had started the mission station in Pniel in 1845. Set in attractive surroundings, the church, school buildings and missionaries' houses lay close to the banks of the Harts River, and it was from here that a succession of missionaries were sent to do evangelical work among the Koranna people, who had settled in the region. Their aim of converting the Koranna clans met with a varied and largely unremarkable degree of success and, by the 1860s, the mission was on the verge of collapse. A series of severe droughts had forced many of the inhabitants to leave; others had stayed, because the discovery of diamonds and the growth of related industries in and around Kimberley had unexpectedly created an excellent market for African farmers growing food crops.

The BMS thus decided to make land available to families in the congregation willing to give their labour and expertise in growing crops and raising livestock. Solomon Plaatje had fond memories of this period in his life. In 1914 he wrote: "*In rainy seasons ... the river used to overflow its high banks, and flood the surrounding valleys to such an extent that no punt could carry the wagons across. Thereby the transport service would congregate for weeks on both sides of the river until the floods subsided. At such times the price of fresh milk used to mount to 1 shilling per pint. There being next to no competition, we boys had a monopoly over the milk trade. Mother and our eldest brothers had leather bags of gold and did not care for 'boys' money ... we had hardly any use for money, for all we wanted to eat, drink and wear, was at hand in plenty.*"[1]

His brother Simon occupied an eminent position in this prosperous mission community and was of great assistance to the various missionaries. In 1882, the BMS sent Ernst Westphal to Pniel and he, succeeding where many of his predecessors had failed, turned the fortunes of the mission station around. As Westphal's daughter later remarked, the European diamond diggers were wont to ignore the legal and moral conventions of the mission and it took Simon's ingenuity to resolve some of the difficult situations that arose. It was for this reason that Simon accompanied Westphal on his visits to some of the BMS outposts. Because of the close relationship that

Popo Molefe, Tsholo and Tumi Plaatje-Molefe, Mafeking, 2002. Photograph: David Goldblatt.

developed between his brother and the missionary, young Solomon endeared himself to Westphal and his wife Elizabeth.

A HUNGER FOR KNOWLEDGE

The arrival of Ernst Westphal gave the young boy the opportunity to acquire an education that would prove most valuable to him later in life.

Westphal had been sent to restore the confidence of the mission station's converts as well as to transform the school. He did the latter remarkably well. When Dr Heinrich Wangeman, Director of the BMS, visited Pniel, in 1884, as part of his extensive tour of southern Africa, he was *"struck by the children's keenness, tidiness, punctuality and discipline and compared them favourably with children of the same age whom he had seen in schools in Germany"*. Observing their ability in Mathematics, Scriptures and Languages (mainly English and Dutch), Dr Wangeman was convinced that *"he had never seen a better-run school anywhere in either Africa or Germany"*.[2]

Solomon Tshekiso Plaatje was probably the first pupil from the Pniel Mission School to reach Standard Three and, having attained the highest level of education available at the school at the time, was appointed – despite his youth – a pupil-teacher. Apart from the formal education received at the school, Solomon also benefited from regular lessons with Westphal's wife, Elizabeth. Elizabeth Westphal had been a teacher in Westphalia, Germany, before she joined her husband in South Africa, and was fascinated by the challenge of teaching him. According to Erna Westphal, the couple's daughter, the young boy approached her mother and specifically requested to be taught English, German and Dutch. Soon he was familiar with the writings of both Shakespeare and Sir Walter Scott and had learnt to play the piano and violin and was training his singing voice. He remained at Pniel as pupil-teacher for two years, but in early 1894 decided to venture further afield, taking up a job as a letter carrier in Kimberley.

MOVING TO THE CITY

In the early 1870s, Kimberley was a rapidly expanding mining town, buzzing with activity and resembling "an insane asylum turned loose on a beach". By the 1890s, the town had however changed considerably. It had become relatively settled, as many of the small-scale

Sol Plaatje, circa 1900. Historical Papers Collection, University of the Witwatersrand Library.

Johannes and Annah Plaatje, shortly after their
wedding, circa 1955. In the 1990s, their
daughter Tumi had two separate photographs
enlarged, joined together and air brushed.
*"My heart aches when I look at this photograph,
such young and innocent people."*
Next pages: **Penny Siopis: Panorama of the
Plaatje family, 2001-02.** Oil paint and video
projection on paper, 300 x 500 cm.

three sons: their daughter Boitumelo (Tumi), born in 1954, is the eldest. The eldest son, Goode, was born in 1957 and a daughter, Ditshane, was born in 1959, followed in 1962 by another daughter, Maria. Sons Thekiso and George were born in 1966 and 1969 respectively.

Johannes enjoyed the pleasures of family life, loved soccer and rugby and had a passion for education. He believed that one is never too old to learn and proved his point when he matriculated at the age of 44. (Although he had been teaching, he qualified as teacher with only a Junior Certificate, an acceptable qualification for African teachers at the time.)

Still, life was not always easy for the family of Johannes Plaatje. After the implementation of the Group Areas Act of 1950, Johannes witnessed the forced removals of black residents from the Kimberley area of Green Point – which was declared a coloured area – and the subsequent closure of the Green Point Secondary School, which was re-established as the Tidimalo Secondary School in the suburb of Vergenoeg in Kimberley in 1967.

Discipline, commitment and dedication to his work saw Johannes appointed Headmaster of Boitshoko Primary School in Kimberley in 1976, a post he held until his retirement in 1993. He was a rigid disciplinarian and, even at the height of the school boycott of the 1970s and 1980s, he still managed to maintain strict discipline at Boitshoko Primary.

Most people remember Johannes as a no-nonsense headmaster. Of all the anecdotes about his exploits as educationalist, one stands out for the many teachers who have served under him: Johannes Plaatje prescribed a uniform for his teaching staff! Male teachers had to wear grey flannel trousers, white shirts and blue blazers; female teachers a blue skirt, white blouse and black shoes. When confronted by teachers who were opposed to the wearing of a uniform, Johannes offered one of two options: either respect his wishes and wear the uniform or find employment elsewhere. What infuriated many of the teachers was that this ruling did not emanate from the education authorities, but from their headmaster himself. The education authorities could, in fact, do nothing to persuade Johannes to relent on this ruling.

Apart from his work as teacher, Johannes Plaatje was an ardent music lover – the family organ and gramophone at Plaatje's Hoogte no doubt must have offered much inspiration. His

Tumi Plaatje photographed by her father in Kimberley, 1957.

The coffin with the body of Johannes Plaatje in St Martin's Church, 11 March 2001.
Photograph: Ruth Motau.

ove for music could, however, not be sepa-
ated from his religious convictions, and as
ounder and master of St Martin's choir, his
obituary read: *"As a Lay Preacher and elder in
he Church he brought creativity and innovation
o St Martin's Parish. He guided his fellow
parishioners and inspired them with his
mastery of the Gospel of God. He was active in
he parish partnership and led a delegation to
Kassel in Berlin [in] 1992, promoting German/
South African partnership. His outspokenness
in favour of the truth created a situation of no
ove between him and some senior church
elders. Yet he remained steadfast in his faith in
God."*[12]

Johannes was well informed, but only became
politically active after his retirement. During the
first democratic elections of 1994, he served as
an electoral officer of the Independant Electoral
Commission and, as member of the ANC's
Galeshewe Branch Two, distinguished himself
both as a dedicated ANC canvasser for votes
and a party agent in the months leading up to
the 1999 elections. His death was a great loss
to his community and family, among them his
daughter Boitumelo.

BOITUMELO PLAATJE

Johannes's eldest child Boitumelo ("Joy")
Plaatje was born in 1954, and the first few
years of her life were spent with her paternal
grandparents Joseph and Annie at Plaatje's
Hoogte. When she was five, she joined her
parents in Kimberley and started school there.
*'My classroom was a tree. I started school
under that tree, Sub A. Sub B and Standard
One; I had school inside the church. I started
school when I was five; my father smuggled me
in. The only time we had school inside the
church was when it rained.'*
Tumi was close to her father: *"We always
talked a lot together, about history, about life in
general. He used to expose me to many things;
he took me to the aerodrome, which was still
there, to show me aeroplanes, and took me to
the McGregor Museum, and to the Big Hole,
the open diamond mine. He also made me read
much – poetry, history books, the newspaper.*

*Tumi outside the nurses' flats in Bloemfontein,
1973. "Those were the good old times. I was still
training to be a nurse. That was then the best
job there was."*

He bought the Daily News *every day, and said,
'If you cannot read the paper every day, then
buy the* Sunday Times.' *I learnt a lot from him."*
In the early 1960s, Boitumelo still regularly
visited her grandfather at Plaatje's Hoogte.
Although ageing, Joseph continued to work as
a sharecropper/labour tenant. The convenient
relationship between the African labour tenants
and the mission station had survived for over
50 years after the passing of the Native Land

*Tumi as nurse, Bloemfontein, 1978-79. "I was
then working in intensive care. You can see that
I was tired. We worked very hard."*

Act so despised by his nephew Sol. In 1967,
however, Joseph Plaatje finally fell victim to the
Act, when he and his family were ordered by
government decree to terminate the contract
they had entered into with the missionaries and
move from Plaatje's Hoogte. In this way, the
Plaatje family was finally removed from their
fertile land, because it had been declared a
"white spot", and relocated to Pampierstad, a
typically desolate, barren reserve set aside for
Africans 120 kilometres west of Kimberley.

Joseph and his family had no choice but to
sever their long-standing ties with the land
completely.
Thirteen years later, in 1980, Joseph's wife
passed away after a long illness, aged 80. Soon
afterwards Joseph, also aging and somewhat
frail, moved in with Johannes's family in
Kimberley. Shortly thereafter, he too died.

CHOOSING A CAREER

Tumi Plaatje completed her high-school
education in Kimberley, and then proceeded to
Pelonomi Hospital in Bloemfontein where she
trained as a nurse – undoubtedly inspired by
her mother who was an assistant nurse:
*"I was always admiring my mother who was a
nurse. I listened to her stories about the
hospital, the patients. I developed that caring
attitude. I thought I must follow in her footsteps. There were also some nice old nurses at
the clinic, Nurse Betty, Nurse Martha, and
others, looking nice in their white uniform.
They were very popular."*
Boitumelo was only 17 when she enrolled for a
nursing diploma at Pelonomi in 1971, and these
were exciting years for her: discovering the
world, working hard, making friends, and
enjoying life in a big city.
Political and social realities could naturally not
be avoided. When Steve Biko was killed in
detention in 1977, Tumi and 14 of her closest
friends decided that they had to attend the
funeral, but, like thousands of other people
from all over South Africa, were prevented by
massive police deployments from reaching King
Williamstown in time for the funeral.
A second major political event made its
influence felt soon afterwards: in 1978, Bloemfontein was drawn into the student unrest that
erupted in Soweto in 1976. Henceforth,
Boitumelo's involvement in politics deepened
and her resolve to challenge the system
hardened. She did not, however, allow political
involvement to stand in the way of her
obtaining various nursing qualifications. While
working at Pelonomi, she temporarily left to
qualify in midwifery in Port Elizabeth in the
Eastern Cape, afterwards returning to resume
her work. A few years later, she studied
Intensive Care at UNISA in Pretoria, and then
moved to Johannesburg, to work in private
clinics on a freelance basis. Salaries here were
much higher and registered nurses were in
considerable demand, but it was a difficult time
for Boitumelo. She lived in a flat in Meadowlands township while the political struggle was
intensifying. She remembers well the general
repression that followed the ANC bombing in
Church Street, Pretoria. It became too much,

and in 1984, Tumi returned to Kimberley, where she worked in a medical laboratory. But in 1987 she found herself back in Johannesburg – this time with her close friend Notuba, "seeing the way forward".

UNEXPECTED RETURN TO MAFIKENG

In 1990, Tumi Plaatje met Popo Molefe, who had entered resistance politics in the 1970s as an activist in the Black Consciousness Movement. Along with many of his generation of activists, he switched allegiance to ANC-aligned organisations in 1990 and, after the launch of the United Democratic Front in 1983, was elected General Secretary of the UDF. He served in this position at first above ground, then – after the declaration of the State of Emergency – largely underground and ultimately in prison, from which he was released in 1989. When the UDF was dissolved in 1991, Popo Molefe and many of his UDF comrades were well on their way to prominence in the recently unbanned African National Congress.

Tumi had been married before, but the marriage she entered into at the age of 19 and from which a son was born, was not successful and after only four years the couple parted ways in 1978.

Popo had also been married before and he, too, has children from that union, but on 1 June 1991, soon after they had met, Popo and Tumi were married. On 10 November 1992, Tumi gave birth to the couple's first child and only daughter, Tsholo. Tsholo was born prematurely, and was precariously small. Now, when Boitumelo looks at her she says, with tears in her eyes, *"It is a miracle she has grown so big. She looked so fragile one had to cover her up with a blanket before carrying her. We called her Tsholofelo, which means 'Hope'."* Tsholo was born at a time when South Africa was going through a great deal of uncertainty about the future. The spectre of a major civil war was looming large, and what is now the North West Province produced some of the most dramatic political confrontations of the period.

Under apartheid government's policy of so-called separate development, Bophuthatswana was declared the "homeland" of all Setswana-speaking South Africans. When Lucas Mangope, as leader of this homeland or bantustan, as it was also called, accepted Pretoria's offer of "independence", the new capital Mmabatho – just north of Mafikeng – earned the dubious privilege to host a South African ambassador. But in the process, the Tswana lost their South African citizenship. Only after the first democratic elections in 1994 were the bantustans dismantled and South African citizenship restored to their subjects. The North West Province was created as one of nine new provinces, with Mafikeng as capital, and Popo Molefe, convicted for treason in the 1980s, became the first premier. So it happened that Tumi and Popo Plaatje moved to the town where Sol Plaatje was based from 1898 to 1910. It is one of the ironies of South Africa's recent history that Molefe, one of the most distinguished leaders of the internal resistance against apartheid, would find himself living in the residence that once housed the South African ambassador to Bophuthatswana. Moving to Mafikeng was reassuring for Tumi, because she felt she could take a cue from the brother of her great-grandfather:

"Sol Plaatje's work was not finished – not that I want to compare myself to him! It was a difficult time. I didn't know what to do; there was no job description. What should a first lady do? I don't like that name First Lady; I always call myself First Servant. I am much involved in women's affairs, also women in detention. I go to prisons, talk to the women there, give them hope, tell them [that] crime does not pay."

Tumi is a staunch member of the Methodist Church and its Mother's Union, a powerful organisation that meets once a week to pray. As First Lady, she has a full agenda, yet she is a councillor with the Mafikeng municipality, concerned with Municipal Health, Social Welfare and Recreation.

TSHOLO IN KIMBERLEY

Thsolo was born prematurely and, after spending a month in hospital, was taken by Tumi to her parents, who helped her care for the tiny baby. Tumi was worried about the health of her little girl, but leaving her with the

Tumi at the Miss Beauty Pageant in Bloem-fontein, circa 1972.

Popo Molefe and Tumi Plaatje on their wedding day, 1 June 1991.

The **Steyn** family

A family and their farm

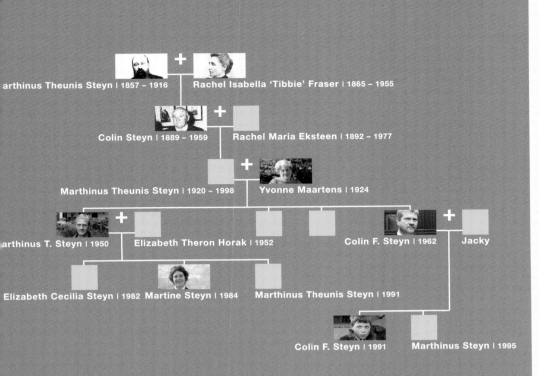

Marthinus Theunis Steyn | 1857 – 1916 + Rachel Isabella 'Tibbie' Fraser | 1865 – 1955

Colin Steyn | 1889 – 1959 + Rachel Maria Eksteen | 1892 – 1977

Marthinus Theunis Steyn | 1920 – 1998 + Yvonne Maartens | 1924

Marthinus T. Steyn | 1950 + Elizabeth Theron Horak | 1952   Colin F. Steyn | 1962 + Jacky

Elizabeth Cecilia Steyn | 1982   Martine Steyn | 1984   Marthinus Theunis Steyn | 1991

Colin F. Steyn | 1991   Marthinus Steyn | 1995

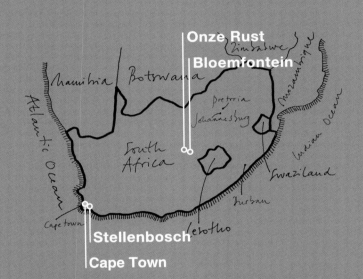

Onze Rust
Bloemfontein

Stellenbosch
Cape Town

A family farm means that when you plant a tree, you can watch it grow.
Onze Rust in the Kaalspruit district near Bloemfontein has belonged to the Steyn family for more than a century. President Marthinus Theunis Steyn bought the land shortly after he was elected president of the Republic of the Orange Free State and the blue gum trees he planted in 1897 are still there.
Years later, his grandson – also Marthinus Theunis – hammered a fence-pole into the ground. It started growing. His wife, Yvonne, planted the giant plantain shading the house and veranda. She says, *"I dreamed that one day it would look like this. But I never thought I would live to see it."*

The blue gum trees at Onze Rust were young saplings in 1899 when President Steyn decided to join Transvaal president Paul Kruger and *"fight for freedom and fairness"*.
The Bloemfontein Conference, a last attempt to heal the rift between the Boer republics and the British, had ended in disaster and Kruger's ultimatum, demanding the withdrawal of British troops from the ZAR (Zuid-Afrikaansche Republiek), was ignored. Steyn commanded his troops in full support of Kruger and on 11 October 1899 the two Boer Republics declared war with Britain. The Anglo-Boer War would last until 1902, claiming the lives of 6 189 men from Boer ranks, as well as 27 927 white men, women and children and between 14 154 and 20 000 black South Africans in concentration camps.
During the first six months of the war, Steyn stayed on in Bloemfontein as head of state and commander-in-chief of the Free State Council of War, but the Presidency was hurriedly evacuated early in March 1900 when it became clear that the British were preparing to invade the city. As a result, President Steyn fled to the north to join the Free State regiment of General Christiaan de Wet, where he was increasingly viewed *"as the soul of the Boers' struggle for freedom"*.
On 13 March, only 12 hours after his departure from Bloemfontein, the British forces under Commander-in-chief Lord Frederick Roberts and General-Major John French occupied the city. Roberts moved into the Presidency and, on the following day, had a celebratory breakfast on the *stoep* (veranda) of the Onze Rust *opstal* (homestead), enjoying the luxury of fresh milk and cream. On 24 May 1900, the former Boer Republic was officially annexed to the British crown.
When Mrs Rachel Isabella Steyn (known as Tibbie) was captured in Fouriesburg and asked

advocate, Colin travelled extensively and, in 1919, Emmie was married and left home. Tibbie wrote that she was *"reduced to the companionship of a housekeeper"*. Later that year, Colin married Rae Eksteen and Tibbie persuaded the couple to move to Onze Rust. Her grandson, Marthinus Theunis Steyn, was born in 1920 and in 1924, Tibbie's daughter Hannah moved back to Onze Rust after the suicide of her husband. The farm was once again home to a family.

Difficult times lay ahead, however. Before their wedding, Rae made Colin promise to have only a *"certain limited number of drinks a day"* and in 1921 she again pleaded with him *"not to sadden and disappoint her in this respect"*. It also worried her that he worked too hard. In 1928, Colin suffered what his mother Tibbie called a *"nervous breakdown in a serious degree"*. He refused to eat or speak. After 17 days in a clinic and a suicide attempt, it was decided that Tibbie's daughter, Tibbie Jnr (Isabella) van der Merwe, and her husband would move to Onze Rust and that Colin would stay in their house in town. When he showed no signs of improvement, Colin's sister Gladys took him to Santpoort in the Netherlands and Hamburg in Germany for treatment. Colin's illness lasted almost four years and, as a result, the Steyns were left without an income. For the second time, it seemed as if the farm would have to be sold, but the crisis was warded off when Colin's wife, Rae, accepted a teaching position at Oranje Meisieskool (Girls High) and Tibbie received news of a state pension. She wrote, *"It is a sweet thought that now I will be able to stay on Onze Rust, so full of sacred memories for me, for as long as I live."* Colin finally returned to Onze Rust in 1931 and seemed much better, winning his first case in the Supreme Court of Bloemfontein in August of that same year.

Studio portrait of Marthinus and Tibbie Steyn's five children, 1903. From left to right: **Hannah, Emmie, Colin** (standing), **Tibbie** and **Gladys.**

The period leading up to the Second World War was one of political strife among Tibbie's children.[3] Colin was Bloemfontein's Member of Parliament when, in 1939, Smuts decided to support Britain in the Second World War. Colin backed him, and became Minister of Justice in Smuts's war cabinet, both his sons fighting for the Allied Forces. For this, he was harshly

Portrait of Colin Steyn as Barrister of the Middle Temple in London, England, between 1910 and 1920.

criticised by veterans of the Anglo-Boer War, who were vehemently opposed to the decision to fight alongside their erstwhile British enemies.

During the war years, the house at Onze Rust became more and more dilapidated and the farm seemed unkempt. In 1943, Tibbie Jnr married her second husband, Cornelius Visser, and the couple settled at Onze Rust. The

house was once again full of people, but there was *"never any [money] to spend on the house"* and one of Tibbie's grandchildren, Nerina Ferreira, called it *"nobility falling apart"*. For Tibbie, it was, however, more important that the house be a welcome haven for her many grandchildren. When Colin's sons used a .22 rifle to mark a bedroom wall with their initials, Tibbie admired the fact that they were *"such good shots"* and refused to have the damage repaired. However, when the British monarch George VI and his family visited South Africa in 1947, Tibbie was too ashamed to receive them at Onze Rust and insisted on going to Colin's house in town.

The first badly needed repair work was done when Colin's oldest son, Marthinus Theunis, returned from Italy after the war and moved to Onze Rust. He was sworn in as an advocate in 1948, married Yvonne Maartens in 1949 and, in 1950, the couple's first child, Theuns, was born. Tibbie was present when the baby was christened at Onze Rust and wrote at the time, *"[Marthinus] Theunis works hard and everything is starting to look pretty."* It was the beginning of a new era for Onze Rust, but Tibbie was not to witness it. She died in 1955 and was buried next to her husband at the foot of the Women's Monument.

Marthinus Theunis Steyn, grandson of President Steyn and the third patriarch at Onze Rust, became a senior advocate in 1965, the first administrator-general of South West Africa in 1977 and a judge in the Bloemfontein Appeal Court in 1988. He had been born on the farm in 1920 and died there in his sleep in 1998. The historic old homestead is now home to his widow, Mrs Yvonne Steyn, his youngest daughter, Willemien Steyn, his youngest son, Colin Steyn, and Colin's wife Jackie and their two children.

Workers whose families moved here in the time of President Steyn also live on the farm. The effect of HIV/Aids in the past few years has, however, been devastating and the oldest black and Griqua families on Onze Rust have virtually been wiped out.

COLIN
State Advocate Colin Steyn – the son of Marthinus Theunis (Theuns) and a great-grandson of President Steyn – is a robust, volatile

man who still recites an Old-Dutch prayer when he says grace at meals. We meet for the first time in the Bloemfontein courtroom where he is prosecuting a gang accused of a series of murders and rapes. *"I'm going to get them,"* he grins when the court adjourns. *"First, I'm closing all the escape routes. Then I'll drive a wedge between the accused and their advocates."* His eyes glitter dangerously. *"I'll slide between them like a hot iron."*

Law is in his blood – it comes from his father, grandfather and great-grandfather. When he poses for a photograph, debonair in his black robe, his posture is reminiscent of the Anton van Wouw statue of President Steyn on the campus of the local university.

"It is in this very courtroom that General Christiaan de Wet was tried for treason after the Rebellion and sentenced," he says and launches indomitably into a spirited account of one of the many stories in his arsenal. He is a raconteur, a war veteran and a historian who never loses sight of the life of his forebears. He is reminded of them every time he enters the rambling old farmhouse at Onze Rust. Their pictures remain on the walls, their books on the shelves and many of their personal belongings in the old rooms.

The writer and historian Karel Schoeman writes that in the first half of the previous century the house was already a place where *"the deposits of lives led over half a century accumulated undisturbed. There were important and valuable remainders as well as trifles. Mrs Steyn had a keen historical aware-ness and saved everything, and in the big house there was enough room to keep it for posterity: books with inscriptions, letters, photographs, portraits, menus, newspapers and newspaper clippings, photo albums, collected autographs, bundles of telegrams, ribbons and bows, cards, deeds, documents, clothes and household articles were packed into cupboards and drawers and trunks in such a disorderly way that, for the greater part, nothing could be found again, and 50 years of South Africa's history became entangled in the goings-on of every new day, part of a living texture, to such an extent that no one was fully aware of the riches. A brass bedstead was dredged from the dam years later and Emily Hobhouse's wedding dress that she never wore was stored in the cellar but could not be found again."*

It is decades later and even more layers have been transposed onto the palimpsest of the Steyn family history. New pictures of the great-grandsons and their children hang on the walls, but the house, the cellars, the outbuildings and

storerooms still contain a plethora of relics and remnants.

The study is almost exactly as it was in the days of President Steyn. It is a typical late-Victorian room with a cast-iron fireplace, the president's old desk and the sombre-looking wheelchair in which Steyn spent the last years of his life. The bookcases are stacked with dusty legal volumes; biographies of people such as Bismarck and Garibaldi; works by Goethe, Schiller, Vondel, Busken Huet and Milton and even a copy of Percy Fitzpatrick's *Jock of the Bushveld*. The walls are crowded with framed portraits of the five men who preceded Steyn as president of the Orange Free State, President Paul Kruger, General Koos de la Rey, the doctor who treated Steyn in Amsterdam after the war, the first cabinet of the Union of South Africa, and generals Botha and Herzog with the theologian Sarel Celliers between them *"to keep the peace"*.

The picture of Ruiter, a Griqua man who served with Steyn in the war and saved his life, has been hung in a place of honour above the fireplace. Some keepsakes include the little Bible that Steyn carried with him during the war and signatures of all the representatives of the National Convention, all the members of the Union's first cabinet and all the men who helped translate the Bible into Afrikaans. Sometimes, things are lost in this labyrinthine house, only to be discovered again at a later stage. A few months ago, Colin Steyn found two cardboard boxes in an old armoire when looking for something completely ordinary. It was the ashes of two of his ancestors that had been misplaced years before. The boxes were neatly labelled in his father's hand, tied with ribbons, and have now been locked in a safe so that the family will remember to scatter it when they have time.

For Colin, this does not seem strange. He is used to encountering evidence of past lives in the house. When he was 14 years old, he discovered his grandfather's Boer War rifle[4] in the cellar.

"We were playing hide-and-seek and I crawled under a bed, where I found a gun rolled up in a carpet. I went to my father and said, 'Look! Look at this.' And my father looked at it and said, 'My God, it's your Oupa's [Grandfather's] Boer War Mauser. I last saw it in 1933 when I was your age.'"

That was the start of a fierce, life-long interest in the Anglo-Boer War. Today, at the age of 3[?] Colin Steyn is chairman of the board of the War Museum for the Boer Republics in Bloemfontein and chairman of the South African Weapon and Ammunition Collectors' Society for people who share his passion for vintage rifles. He hosts regular *"commemo-ration shooting competitions"* on the farm for participants who dress up in Anglo-Boer War uniforms and shoot with old Martini-Henrys, Lee-Metfords and Mausers at gas cylinders painted to look like Tommys (British soldiers). The shooting days are held at his "fort", with its replicas of old field guns, a lookout tower, ammunition kists (chests) and mock graves. There is also a British blockhouse dating back to 1901 that he fetched with a truck from its original site between Bethulie and Burgersdorp. In the cellar, he has a large collection of Anglo-Boer War memorabilia, including a stretcher *"soaked with English blood"* and the Orange Free State flag that his great-grandfather took with him on commando. (*"I found it in Aunt Hannah's trunk in the stables."*)

The cellar is also a testimony to the lasting influence of the South African "Border War" on Colin's life. Ironically, his father was adminis-trator-general in South West Africa in the 1970s when South Africa would not implement United Nations resolutions for Namibian independence. When Steyn Snr returned to South Africa in 1979, protracted negotiations about the status of South West Africa and the worst years of the Border War (in which liberation movements such as SWAPO fought against South Africa's occupation of South West Africa) lay ahead.[5] Colin was conscripted in 1983.

He says he was comforted by the thought that his great-grandfather and grandfather had survived the Anglo-Boer War and his father the Second World War. *"My father came to see me off at the station where his father had seen him off when he left for Italy during the Second World War. He looked at me and said, 'This is the exact same spot where Grandpa Colin said his farewells to me in 1943. Come, Boeta, come and stand here – this is where we must say*

Theunis and Yvonne Steyn with their three eldest children, Isabel, Theuns, and Willemien between the parents, at Onze Rust, circa 1960.

tance – was one of the reasons for staying in South Africa and not emigrating to Australia. He says, *"I realised that I would have no roots there. That I would have to explain myself all the time. I would have to tell strangers who I was and where I came from and it would mean nothing to them."* He was eventually reconciled with his father who, before his death in 1998, wrote Theuns back into the will and appointed him head of the Onze Rust Trust, which today owns and manages the farm.

It was the beginning of an uneasy, schizophrenic relationship for Theuns between his city life in Cape Town and regular 1 000-kilometre trips to Onze Rust where his mother, sister, brother and sister-in-law live. His attempts to manage the farm and make it profitable have brought him into conflict with the members of his Free State family. *"He*

Advocate Colin Steyn, 2001. Photograph: David Goldblatt.

arrives here once in a blue moon and tells us what to do," grumbles his mother, Mrs Yvonne Steyn. On the other hand, Theuns is resentful about having to carry all of the responsibilities while the others enjoy the privileges of life on the farm. *"All of them think they are the bosses. But I'm the one footing the bills, writing the cheques. They don't realise that there's no such thing as a free lunch."*

On the farm there is a room Theuns still thinks of as his own. His brother Colin is amused by this. *"It's his room when he's here. When he's not here, it's everybody else's."* So, in a way, Theuns has become a visitor on his family farm. Colin says, *"I feel sorry for Theuns. I think he is besieged by regrets because, now that he's getting older, he misses the Free State. There was a time when he wanted nothing to do with the farm – but now he wants to come here more often, he wants to bring his son. And suddenly he realises that it's complicated. He's built a life for himself in Cape Town. His wife*

Colin Steyn on a captured Russian tank, after the battle of Cuvelai, 7 January 1984.

and his daughters are sophisticated city people. They live in a completely different world."

For Theuns, Colin's world seems like a *"make-believe world"*. He says, *"Colin is like my father. My father had the ability to withdraw into his own world. He would hide in his library or the room where he kept and played with his model trains. If the lights in our house went out, he would light a candle and carry on reading. Someone else would sort out the problems, pay the bills. Not him. And now Colin has the cellar where he keeps his war memorabilia. And the small shack where he builds his model airplanes. Like my father, he too is continually escaping."*

Next pages: **Colin Steyn with his son Colin in clothes dating from the Anglo-Boer War. The army camp has been reconstructed behind the farm house on Onze Rust.** Photograph: David Goldblatt.

Marthinus Theunis

The very different relationships the brothers shared with their father, Judge Marthinus Theunis Steyn, lie at the heart of these different approaches to their family history.

For Theuns, his father remained *"an enigma"* right to the end. He seemed *"a little bit like Father Christmas. He laughed a lot, he was never cross and he was very loving. But you never knew what was behind his public facade. There was always a veil. And when you wanted to talk to him or really needed him, he was gone. Sometimes, I would go and look for him in the study. He would never make me feel unwelcome or ask me to leave, but he was impenetrable – and eventually I would give up."* The age difference of 12 years also meant that the two brothers did not share a childhood and Colin says he knew a father very different to the one Theuns had known.

"When I grew up, my father had more time and was much calmer. One of the reasons for this was that he stopped drinking when I was a baby. He often told me how, one day when I was asleep in my cot, he picked me up and looked at me, and looked at my mother who was sleeping in her bed, and realised that a drinker does terrible things to his family. He decided then that he would never drink again. He was 45 years old. Like me, he had learned to drink as a soldier."

The fact that both Colin and his father were war veterans also brought them closer, says Colin. Theuns says, *"Colin grew up in a time when the Afrikaner in general and my father in particular became more militaristic. I had grown up in the hippie era and avoided the military and everything associated with it like the plague."* It seems that the two sisters, Isabella and Willemien, had a less complicated relationship with their father. Like Theuns, Willemien also uses the image of Father Christmas when speaking of her father – but without irony. Isabella says, *"He was a fun father, a warm person who always hugged us. He loved pranks and he was bigger than life, an exciting man and an exciting father, who made life interesting for us with his hobbies and the stories he told."*

After spending a few years abroad, Isabella worked as her father's private secretary when he was administrator-general in South West Africa. She remembers how they would sit for

Top: **Theuns Steyn in front of Onze Rust, 2001.**
Photograph: David Goldblatt.

Bottom: **Theuns and Elize Steyn during a cycling trip around the Cape peninsula, 2001.**
Photograph: David Goldblatt.

hours under a tree in the veld, patiently waiting for the opportunity to speak to one of the local chiefs. *"It was a time when the Afrikaner was very arrogant, but my father was different. He taught me how to resolve conflict, how to break through suspicion and hatred and win someone's trust. He gave me peace of mind about the future."*

When she returned to South Africa in the 1980s, she embarked on a career in labour relations. *"Establishing democratic systems in the work-place was the predecessor of social democracy in South Africa. In those years, I used much of what my father taught me in Namibia."*

In spite of their conflicting memories, all four children speak of their father with respect. As jurists, Theuns and Colin admire his verdicts, known not only for their legal acumen but also for their carefully crafted language. *"To hear him returning a verdict was like listening to poetry,"* wrote a journalist in a tribute that appeared after Judge Steyn's death in 1998. Willemien and Colin shared the house with their parents for many years and Colin says he was deeply affected by his father's death. *"I never said goodbye. Shortly before his death, I left for a circuit-court case in Virginia. I kissed him and told him that I loved him, all the time thinking that I would see him again. Two nights later, they called and told me he was dead. I got in my car and drove back. The road was long. I tried to think. And then, when I was already close to the farm, when I passed Leeuberg and saw the blue gum trees on the mountain, and the autumn sun making dark shadows under them, I realised that my father had been a big tree and that all of us had been sitting in the shade. And suddenly the big tree that grew in the garden was gone."*

His father's death was *"a traumatic experience"*. It also sparked the beginning of what Colin calls laconically *"the debate"* with his own ten-year-old son Colin, who won't yet admit that his grandfather is dead.

THE CHILDREN

"I don't like homework. I don't like school. I don't like the city. I don't like the shops ... One day, when I grow up, I want to farm at Onze Rust; I want to feed the cattle, plough the lands and sow the crops ... I don't want to be unhappy." The school essays written by Colin

Top: **Yvonne Steyn in the garden of Onze Rust, under a tree she planted herself, 2001.** Photograph: David Goldblatt.
Bottom: **Young Colin with his grandfather's collection of model trains at Onze Rust, 2001.** Photograph: David Goldblatt.

Jnr show that the farm is the epicentre of his life. He seems a serious child with a morbid interest in the most gruesome details of his father's war stories. He is also devoted to the memory of his grandfather.

Jackie says, *"When Collie was born, my father-in-law was overcome with joy. So he took my son and basically claimed him for himself. It was difficult for me because it was my first-born. But I realised that my father-in-law had more time on his hands and that he would not live long."*

Judge Steyn and his grandson were inseparable. They spent their days together and slept in the same bed until shortly before Steyn's death from cancer. Colin Jnr refused to attend his grandfather's funeral and is fond of returning to the cellar where the two of them spent many hours playing with a collection of model trains assembled over decades. It is a room so cold and eerie it chills you to the bone and when the boy comes here, he likes playing a tape-recording of his grandfather telling blood-curdling folk stories. The narrative is often interrupted with the injunction: *"And what happened then, Collie?"* It is easy to imagine that the grandfather is speaking to his grandson, but in fact the recording dates back to the 1960s, when Colin Snr was a young child and ill in bed with 'flu and his father entertained *him* with stories. Colin Jnr refuses to play with the most beautiful of the miniature train engines, a gleaming red one called Big Boy. *"Oupa says I shouldn't."*

Jackie has stopped confronting her son about his grandfather's death. *"I don't want to keep telling him that his grandfather is dead. I respect his way of seeing things and I know that time will heal the wounds. The healing process has already started. Grass is growing where before there was only a bare patch of earth."*

The brothers are different, and so are their children. Colin Jnr's older cousin Martine (the youngest daughter of Theuns) lives in Cape Town and, even though she was named after her grandfather, he does not loom so large in her life.

In fact, her ancestors are not something she thinks about very often. She hasn't read any of the books written about her illustrious great-great-grandparents and she hasn't studied news clippings about her famous grandfather, Judge M.T. Steyn. *"I've leafed through some of the stuff and I have a vague idea where every-*

Top: **Marthinus Steyn Jr in his room in Cape Town, 2001.** Photograph: David Goldblatt.
Bottom: **Martine in her room, Cape Town, 2001.** Photograph: David Goldblatt.

Four generations of the Steyn family at Onze Rust, 1950.
Tibbie Steyn with her great-grandson Marthinus Theunis on her lap, with at the back:
her grandson Theunis (left) and Colin, her son and Marthinus Theunis's father.
A portrait of Tibbies Steyn's husband, Marthinus, can be seen on the wall behind them.

one fits in, but it's not something I'm obsessed about."

Posing for a picture, looking at the camera in a brave, experimental way, she seems determined to have adventures, to be unconventional. Unlike her great-great-grandfather, who actively identified with the Afrikaner movement, she thinks that if she becomes a writer or journalist, she'll write in English *"because then my options won't be limited"*.

She broke with another tradition when she decided not to study law like her sister, both her parents and three Steyn generations before them. *"There was no pressure on me,"* she says. *"My parents are cool about it. They'll let me do what I want."* And recently, when she had to apply for a university residence, she chose a different one to her sister's. *"My father wanted me to apply for the residence where my sister stays because he says that's how you build tradition and so on, but I think we should each do our own thing and have our own life."*

THE WOMEN

Martine is the youngest in a long line of formidable Steyn women. Her father jokes that *"the Steyn men have a gene that comes to their rescue time and again – the gene that makes them marry strong women."* It started with the president who had a great love and respect for women. He was the founder of the Oranje Meisieskool and of the Oranje Vrouevereniging (Women's Society), and was instrumental in the decision to erect the Women's Monument in Bloemfontein, an impressive sandstone shrine sculpted by Anton van Wouw as a tribute to the Boer women and children who died during the Anglo-Boer War. When, after the war, the Union government had to decide about voting rights for women, the British feminist Emily Hobhouse declared that Steyn was *"a splendid champion for our cause"*. The president died while addressing the Oranje Vrouevereniging and lies buried at the foot of the Women's Monument. His wife was comforted by the thought that, in his last moments, he was *"surrounded by women"*.

Much has been written about Tibbie. It has been said that *"without the Anglo-Boer War her life would probably have been a footnote in the annals of history"*. The war made her realise that she *"would have to fight her own battles and have to overcome difficulties"*.

She identified closely with the Afrikaner cause, refused to go into exile and became an example of the adamant resistance of Afrikaner women against British domination. When she was interned in Bloemfontein, Lord Kitchener of Khartoum, commander of the British troops

The christening gown in which various generations of the Steyn family have been christened. It was given to Tibbie Steyn by the well-known British activist Emily Hobhouse in 1920, shortly before the birth of Colin and Rae Steyn's first child. Before that the gown had been used by the Hobhouse family for a considerable time already.

Opposite: Claudette Schreuders: Bust of Tibbie Steyn, 2001.

Jacaranda wood and enamel paint,

58 x 47 x 25 cm.

during the second half of the Anglo-Boer War, branded her one of *"the worst of a number of irreconcilable woman"*.

She drew strength from her lifelong friendship with the staunch feminist Emily Hobhouse and, when she was reunited with her husband after the war, she was no longer *"the delicate and dependent wife [Theunis] had left behind"*.

In Europe, she took control of the family and their finances and was such a help and comfort to her husband that he later said, *"Tibbie was everything to me in all respects."*

She was 51 when her husband died and, after a marriage of 29 years, lived for another four decades. Theuns and his siblings grew up with a story of how, one day when their great-grand-mother was seriously ill, a servant saw the ghost of the president at the foot of her sickbed, beckoning to his wife to join him. *"But she just gently shook her head, turned her back on him and suddenly her breathing was steadier."*

Tibbie lived to receive the British Royal family at her son's house in Waverley Road on their official state visit to South Africa in 1947 and in 1948 – when she was 83 years old – she was sent to the Netherlands to present a gift from the South African government to Queen Wilhelmina.

Theuns calls the story of Tibbie and his great-grandfather *"a true love story"*, but his grandfather's wedding to Rachel Maria (Rae) Eksteen in 1919, he adds mischievously, *"was the result of intimidation"*. He remembers his grandfather Colin as *"a small, rotund, bald man who never stopped laughing. Whenever I saw him, he showered me with gifts and laughed. He was the little man who handed out gifts and left exorbitant tips – to the chagrin of my Granny Rae."*

It was, however, Granny Rae who stole the show. She was a flamboyant and eccentric character who insisted on speaking only English after meeting the British Royal family in 1947 and tried to persuade her sons to marry girls from English families. Theuns says, *"She tried to teach me that I would never be a true gentleman if I could not speak English."*

His sister Isabella remembers that Granny Rae habitually wore a turban decorated with a striking piece of jewellery and that she often took her to the theatre.

After her husband's death in 1959, Rae assembled a sizeable fortune. Theuns says, *"She had a little notebook and wrote down every damned expense in that book. If I wanted to go to the toilet and asked for a penny, she would say, 'Now, look, my boy. We're having tea now and you need a penny for the toilet. I'm jotting this down in my book so I can keep track of my money.'"*

She saved enough every year to travel for

three months on a luxury ocean liner. *"Every year, when the Free State winter arrived, she would pack 18 big suitcases and embark on a three-month-long journey around the world. One suitcase contained all her pills and medicines and the other 17 her clothes. She would show me her suitcases and say: 'This one is for Hawaii, that one for London and that one for New York.'"* Theuns saw her for the last time when she invited him and his wife Elize for breakfast on the *Windsor Castle*.

It would be the *Windsor Castle*'s last run to Southampton and Granny Rae's last voyage. She died in 1977.

The younger Steyn women followed the brave and flamboyant example set by Rae and her contemporaries. Rae's daughter-in-law, Yvonne, was a better farmer than her husband, Judge M.T. Steyn. Yvonne was also in charge of the family's financial affairs. *"My husband couldn't work with money. So one day I said to him, 'I think that from now on you should leave our financial affairs to me.' He seemed relieved. He just wanted to read his books in any case."*

As a Victorian, Tibbie was amazed by the political outspokenness of her daughter Emmie, and cautioned her: *"I don't wish you not to have your own opinions, but in expressing them be careful what language you use."* Emmie paid no heed to her mother's words and Tibbie was horrified about her impetuous behaviour in parliament: *"Emmie always enters as if the House belongs to her, takes her seat*

Martine's fourth birthday at her preschool, Cape Town, 1988.

reserved for the members' wives and, if that happens to be full, she is off to the prime minister's bay."* Tibbie was also shocked when her daughter Gladys quit her job as head of the Oranje Meisieskool, declared that *"nothing will ever induce her to marry"* and moved in with Dr Nell van Heerden, the first female medical doctor in South Africa.

In 1921, Emily Hobhouse wrote to Tibbie to console her: *"But, you know, in Europe it is an everyday matter this coupling up of young women who have struck out for themselves and do not marry. They find thus the companionship they need and one usually, I notice, takes the more masculine, the other the more feminine role. Thus they secure nearly (not quite) the best of both types of life – having complete independence coupled with companionship ..."*

The relationship between Nell and Gladys was later broken off, and Gladys became only the second woman in South Africa to obtain an LL.B. qualification, the first female advocate in the Appeal Court in Bloemfontein and later became involved in politics. More recently, Martine's mother, Advocate Elize Steyn, was appointed senior counsel and acting judge at a relatively young age.

Martine's aunt, Isabella, speaks with great admiration of her female forebears. She chuckles about her grandmother, Granny Rae, who she says was visionary, her aunt Gladys, who was a suffragette, and her niece Nerina Ferreira, who was *"seriously wild"*. *"I didn't care what anyone thought of these women. I thought they were great and inspiring."*

Theuns says the Steyn women have always saved the day when the men, for some reason or other, could not live up to the expectations or demands of patriarchy. *"It is like a relay race,"* he says. *"When we are tired, they take the torch and run with it. At the moment, the Afrikaner is tired. He is resting and rejuvenating himself. We have made many contributions and many mistakes. It is now the time for input from others. And if it is once again the turn of the women in my family to carry the torch, so be it."*

He says he feels disempowered by the realisation that, as a white Afrikaner male, the tide has turned against him. *"I won't be able to make a political contribution in my lifetime. I accept it only because it is partly the result of things my people have done, and I am putting all my energy into business and the legal profession. All that is left for me is to do my job as best I can. And if that is interfered with, I shall probably have to leave the country. For the women, it is different. They have been co-opted by the* ANC. *Their time has come."*

But his youngest daughter, Martine, seems hesitant when you ask about her expectations and dreams for the future. *"I'm just living from day to day. I don't have an end goal, I don't plan ahead. I don't know yet where I'll be in 15 years' time or even where I want to be."* Martine nevertheless knows where she comes from – a family even older than the trees that grow on Onze Rust.

Martine in her school uniform, Cape Town, 2001. Photograph: David Goldblatt.

The **Le Fleur** family

The dead bones of Adam Kok

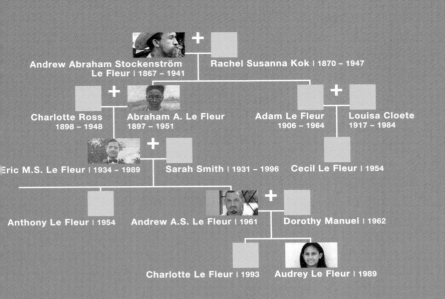

Andrew Abraham Stockenström
Le Fleur | 1867 – 1941   Rachel Susanna Kok | 1870 – 1947

Charlotte Ross
1898 – 1948   Abraham A. Le Fleur
1897 – 1951   Adam Le Fleur
1906 – 1964   Louisa Cloete
1917 – 1984

Eric M.S. Le Fleur | 1934 – 1989   Sarah Smith | 1931 – 1996   Cecil Le Fleur | 1954

Anthony Le Fleur | 1954   Andrew A.S. Le Fleur | 1961   Dorothy Manuel | 1962

Charlotte Le Fleur | 1993   Audrey Le Fleur | 1989

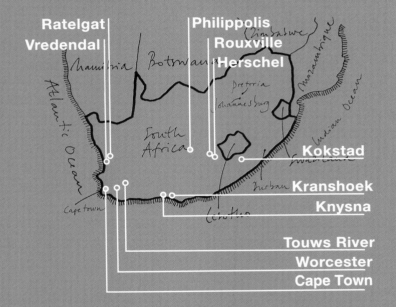

Ratelgat
Vredendal

Philippolis
Rouxville
Herschel

Kokstad

Kranshoek
Knysna

Touws River
Worcester
Cape Town

"And there on the mountain ... the voice of God called from a bush burning with the fire of the sun, Andries Abraham Stockenström Le Fleur, and I said, Lord I am your servant, and the voice said, These are your people who have lost their land, who have become tenants on their own Griqua farms. It is you who must restore to them their dignity."[1]

Many of Andries Abraham Stockenström Le Fleur's family and followers firmly believe in the veracity of the event described here by a great-granddaughter in a recent novel, ostensibly quoting from her forebear's diary. Since this memorable day in May 1889, when the voice of God called him to restore their lost land and dignity to the Griqua people, four generations of the Le Fleur family, the Griqua Independent Church and the Griqua National Conference of South Africa have drawn inspiration from legends and a mythology that have developed around the person and work of "Die Kneg" – the Servant of God or The Prophet – as he is reverently referred to by his followers.

FROM ORANGE FREE STATE TO NO-MAN'S-LAND

Andries Le Fleur was born on 2 July 1867 at Herschel, a village on the northeastern border of the then Cape Colony, and raised in the district of Rouxville in the Boer Republic of the Orange Free State.

Andries's father, Abraham Le Fleur, became a burgher of the Orange Free State before the Griquas of Adam Kok III trekked over the Drakensberg to No-Man's-Land in the early 1860s. Like most other burghers, Abraham was a stock farmer, but for a while he served as secretary to the Griqua Chief, *Kapteyn* Adam Kok III (1811-75), who was based at Philippolis. Secretary Le Fleur accompanied the Chief and his Griqua Reconnoitring Expedition to so-called No-Man's-Land in southern KwaZulu-Natal, but remained on his farm in the Orange Free State when 3 000 Griquas trekked over the Drakensberg in 1861-62 to the rolling grasslands of present-day East Griqualand. The desire to trek stemmed from the untenable situation that arose when the Voortrekkers took charge of the wider Philippolis area following the signing of the Bloemfontein Convention between the Boers and the British in 1854. As a way of resolving the conflicting claims over ownership of farms between Free State Boer settlers and westernised Griqua landowners, the Governor of the Cape Colony, Sir George Grey, promised Adam Kok III the frontier area east of the Drakensberg. There, the Adam Kok III Griquas hoped they would be granted an opportunity to make a new beginning in nation building.

Oral tradition has it that Abraham baptised his son Andries Abraham Stockenström with good reason: the middle name was in honour of himself, while the first and last names honoured a request made to him by Andries Stockenström, a controversial former frontier administrator of Dutch descent who once farmed near Graaff-Reinet. During the Eastern Cape frontier conflict of the early 1850s, Abraham and his Xhosa-speaking interpreter-cum-bodyguard saved Stockenström's life and, in appreciation of the avowed heroic deed, Stockenström handed Andries's father a £5 note with the words: *"Abraham, as daar eendag 'n seun uit jou huwelik kom, gee hom my naam, en as hy 'n papbroek is, slaan hom dood, want 'n dapper man soos [jy] kan nie 'n lafhart seun hê nie. Ek gee jou dus hierdie vyf-pond noot om in daardie verwagting te doop."*[2] Stockenström died three years before the birth of the boy. By virtue of his father's status in the pre-dominantly Cape-Dutch-speaking community of Rouxville, the young Andries received the same rudimentary Christian school education as the children of the white farmers.[3] Yet Andries never felt that he was one of them. Later, he would remark: *"Although we received Burger treatment from the Dutch people as free as themselves, we recognise that we are a different race."*[4]

At his Rouxville home, the young Andries was made to believe that the Griquas of Kokstad were a proud people. Although they had lost their land in the Free State, they had re-established themselves in No-Man's-Land beyond the Drakensberg, where they were once again an independent people in charge of their own destiny. There, *"Adam Kok III ruled with the aid of a written constitution that gave him executive and legislative councils ... He ran an administrative system which maintained control over and empowered him to tax African communities within the territory."*[5]

In 1884, Abraham Le Fleur and 17-year-old Andries finally joined the East Griqualanders. Father and son were, however, ill prepared for what they found. Little did they realise that most of the hope that inspired the Griqua Trekkers of 1861 had been dashed by the late 1870s. At the insistence of settlers and white land specula-tors, No-Man's-Land had been brought under Cape magisterial rule from 1874 onwards and formally annexed to the Cape Colony as East Griqualand in 1879. A rebellion broke out in 1878 following the arrest of a member of the Kok clan in Kokstad, but the uprising was easily put down. During the same year Adam

Dorothy, Andrew, Craig, Audrey and Charlotte Le Fleur, 2002. Photograph: David Goldblatt.

Kok's nephew, Adam "Muis" Kok (1832-78), rose to some prominence in the rebellion, but following the 1874 ruling, the death of Kapteyn Adam Kok III in 1875 and the annexation of No-Man's-Land in 1879, confusion and panic reigned in East Griqualand. This must have prompted the widowed Lady Kok to approach Andries's father in Rouxville.

The young Andries was deeply distressed when he found the proud people of his imagination with "no status as a people".[6] Adam Kok III, who

who acted as their coachman – already displayed extraordinary insight into colonial frontier politics at this early age.

THE VOICE ON THE MOUNTAIN

Before he rose to prominence in the next century, the most defining moment in the life of Andries would have been his encounter of 9

times his name was called and then the voice told him that the donkey was just behind the koppie. The voice identified itself as God and told Andrew [Andries] to 'gather the dead bones of Adam Kok' [versamel die dooie bene van Adam Kok]. Andrew doubted the voice as he himself was not Griqua, but again the voice instructed him to collect the bones.

had left no children, had by then been dead for nine years and Adam Muis Kok for six. The loss of Adam Muis, whom some had regarded as the Kapteyn's (Chief's) successor, had left the Griquas at Kokstad extremely vulnerable.

The Le Fleur family settled at Matatiele, about 60 kilometres west of Kokstad, and for some time Abraham Le Fleur operated as "store-keeper, baker, butcher and carrier"[7] from nearby Ongeluksnek on the Lesotho border. Occasionally, the young Andries would accompany his father and Lady Kok on official business. According to family lore, Andries –

May 1889 on Mount Myanyane near the Telle-brug border post in southern Lesotho, almost halfway between Ongeluksnek and Rouxville. What happened that fateful day was narrated many years later by Marie, wife of Die Kneg's great-grandson Anthony Le Fleur:

"Andrew's father was a wagon-maker and one day he sent his son, Die Kneg, out to look for a donkey. For three days, Die Kneg searched and then he heard a voice call his name. Three

Andrew Abraham Stockenström Le Fleur with followers in prison at Kokstad before he was sent to the Breakwater Prison in Cape Town, 1898. Cape Archives Photo Collections.

He wondered what his father would say, but the voice told him that Lady Kok would die at 8 a.m. the next day as proof of God's words. Andrew told his father, who inspanned the oxen and went to Kokstad. Sitting outside her home where Lewis Stores is today] was Lady Kok, clearly in good health. Five minutes before 8 a.m. she experienced a pain and by 8 a.m. she was dead. Then Andrew's father believed him, or the Bible explained, only God could predict someone's death."[8]

After this revelation, Andries – who anglicised his name to Andrew at about this time[9] – started to "devote all his energies to the task of righting the wrongs the Griquas had been done".[10] In 1895, he joined the Griqua Independent Church, founded according to Griqua folklore, by the father of the Griqua people, Adam Kok I (circa 1710-95). Conventional wisdom, however, attributes the founding of the Kokstad-based Church to the Edinburgh-born missionary, the Rev. William Dower of the London Missionary Society, who came to work among them in the late 1860s at the invitation of Adam Kok III. Dower was also the one who advised Kok to move his Griqua laager from Mount Currie to establish a rather more respectable European-like town, Kokstad, a few kilometres down the hill in 1871. By the 1890s, Dower was still resident in Kokstad, but attending more to the spiritual needs of the white population of the region – perhaps due to his diminishing influence on Griqua affairs after the arrival of the Le Fleurs, who did not get along with him. In 1897, Andrew married Rachel Susanna Kok (1878-1947) who happened to be Dower's domestic worker. But more important to him could have been the fact that she was the youngest daughter of the late Adam Muis Kok. The marriage paved the way for Andrew to become more accepted within the ranks of the town's political fraternity. According to one of Andrew's sons: "Met troue van Kapteins kind en deur Volk se verkiesing is Hy Le Fleur toe aan geneem as leier."[11]

Through his marriage and the lack of interest in Griqua politics on the part of his wife's brothers Lodewyk and Jimmy, Andrew managed to sway many Griquas to look up to him as inheritor of the Kok "kapteynskap" (chieftainship)[12] – in some circles a development already evident from 1894. During the late 1890s, he increasingly positioned himself as their leader. He embarked more vigorously on a crusade to return East Griqualand to Griquas self-rule (as it was before 1874) or to retain its status as a colony – under direct British colonial rule, however, instead of an annexed territory under

the administration of the Cape Colony or Natal. With his rallying call "Griekwaland-Oos vir die Griekwas en die Swartes" (Griqualand East for the Griquas and the Blacks),[13] Andrew unleashed strong reaction from both the Cape colonial government and the people on whose behalf he believed he acted. He was betrayed, caught and eventually handed over to the colonial authorities. Before the magistrate at Kokstad sentenced Andrew to 14 years' hard labour for sedition in April 1898, he concluded: "It was a foolish rebellion ... [Y]ou allowed yourself to be persuaded, and you had a great deal to do in persuading others, in taking part in what I may term a mad rebellion. A number of men went out on the veld with a few assegais, a few quince sticks, some peach sticks and expected that they were going to carry on war against the Government, which can command hundreds of thousands in the field. A more ridiculous thing I don't think I have ever heard of ... You were the ringleader. The sentence of the court must deter any one in the future from taking up the position you now occupy."[14]

The Rev. William Dower described him as a person who "suffered grievously from head swelling" and of whom it could be truly said that "die gode diegene wat hulle wil vernietig, eers mal maak" (those they wish to destroy the gods first make mad).[15] Andrew's first-born, Abraham Andrew (1897-1951) – whom Dorie, as he fondly called his wife Rachel Susanna, "brought with bitterness into life"[16] – was only 14 months old when his father entered the Breakwater Prison in Cape Town. Instead of 14 years, he was eventually incarcerated for only five.

The legend about Andrew's release from the Breakwater Prison reaches back to the night before his trial commenced in Kokstad. In a letter "to my Wife Rachel (Dorie)" written years later, Le Fleur reminded her of the vision he had had that night: three heavenly messengers appeared to him in his Kokstad prison cell, comforting him with the words: "We are sent to go before you. We are the three men you read [about] in the Bible who met father Abraham when he took his son to Mont Moira as an offering to God. And we are commanded to go before you, fear not ..."[17]

Many months would, however, pass at the Breakwater Prison with no hope and only despair about Dorie and his child "suffering a

bitter life" in Kokstad, more than a 1 000 kilometres away.

Within the extended Kok family there was much unhappiness about the misfortune Andrew had brought on Rachel Susanna and some advised her to break with him. At the time, one of her relatives wrote to the Kokstad Advertiser that "Le Fleur took advantage of ignorant Griquas by making use of their grievances, namely, the land question, in which he had misled them by taking the steps with which the public are acquainted, leaving a blot on the Griqua nation in general ... I think and trust that the Government will put a stop to this kind of thing, as we got quite well enough of the Le Fleurs."[18]

In response to the rumour mongering in East Griqualand and the embarrassment his incarceration was causing her, Andrew Le Fleur suggested to his wife from prison that she should consider instituting legal proceedings for a divorce. She would rather leave it in the hand of the Lord, she responded: "Nee, Andrew. Ek sal alles oorlaat in die hand van die Here."[19]

Years later, Die Kneg revealed that, in his moments of despair in Breakwater Prison, a mysterious voice gently reprimanded him in a whisper: "You have no right to think that ... I will show you, you have no right to think that you have a long term of imprisonment."[20]

Even today, every generation of his family and many of his followers unquestioningly believe in Andrew Le Fleur's early-twentieth-century prophecies about his own release and the release of other prisoners on the occasion of King Edward VI's coronation. In January 1901, when the death of Queen Victoria necessitated preparations for the coronation of her successor-son some months later, the Breakwater Prison was awash with hope and expectation. Each of the 889 prisoners looked with excitement to their possible release. Only 13 were pardoned – the precise number Die Kneg had predicted. It is said that sceptics were amazed when two white and 11 coloured and black convicts received their freedom in August of that year.

At the beginning of 1903, The Prophet predicted his own release: he would be discharged at a specific time on the first Friday of April, with the officiating warden saluting him, he said. After much ridicule from the wardens because of his perceived madness, it happened exactly the way he had predicted it would. In the words of his grandson Eric, the following happened: "Die dag van 3de April het aangebreek en die prisoniers het gespot en gesê: Ons sien jou vanaand onder 'n skaterlag. Om 10.30 v.m. lui die telefoon en die bewaarder kom aangehard-

oop en sê Le Fleur, man, ek het nou 'n oproep
ehad, hulle kom jou haal om twee-uur. Nee
an, sê Le Fleur, ek gaan om drie-uur hier uit.
g man, wat maak dit saak watter tyd jy hier
itgaan, maar jou woord het waar
eword en nou weet ek dat jy 'n
Godsman is.
Om 2-uur lui die telefoon weer en
ie bewaarder sê aan Le Fleur:
Hulle sal jou om drie-uur kom haal
vant daar is 'n oponthoud. Ek het
ou mos gesê ek gaan drie-uur uit,
vant God bepaal alle tye.
Om vyf voor drie kom Sir Peter
aure en Sir Thomas Graham aan
n gee 'n nuwe pak klere aan die
ewaarder om aan Le Fleur te
orhandig.
lokslag 3 n.m. stap die Sirs met
e Fleur in die middel en die
ewaarder moet op aandag staan en
alueer en Gods kneg het na die
ewaarder se kant geloer en sy oog
eknip en die bewaarder het sy
voorde onthou, dat hy hom sal
alueer wanneer hy uitgaan.
oe hulle by die hek kom, het Die
neg die twee Sirs gevra om 'n
omblik stil te staan en het op sy
nieë God gedank en sing die vers
O, God my God van alle vorste Heer
k sing verheug U grote naam te eer
k sal die roem steeds van U Majesteit
erhoog tot in die eindloos Ewigheid.' "21
ndrew's discharge papers were marked
a Christian and a Gentleman".22

N SEARCH OF A PROMISED LAND

ndrew Le Fleur was released on condition
hat he would not return to East Griqualand, so
ne of his first tasks was to bring his wife and
on to Cape Town.
fter he had set up a home for his family, first
n rural Goodwood on the Cape Flats and later
n the Cape Town suburban of Wynberg,
ndrew Le Fleur began working unrelentingly
o "gather the dead bones of Adam Kok".
He earned his daily living by working as a
lacksmith and wagon-maker, like his father,

nton Kannemeyer: Portrait of Andrew Abraham
tockenström Le Fleur, 2002. Paint and ink on
aper, 42 x 30 cm.

Abraham, before him. At the beginning of this
second phase of his life, three more children –
Dorothy, Adam and Annie Maria – were born in
relatively quick succession. Thomas, the last-

The Le Fleur family, circa 1908. From left to
right: Rachel Susanna holding Adam, Dorothy
and, behind her, Abraham Andrew, with on the
right, Andrew Abraham Stockenström Le Fleur.
UNISA collection.

born, came only after Union, during the First
World War.

About this time, Andrew Le Fleur started
creating his own social and political movement
for the development of a special brand of
Griqua respectability among the marginalised
coloured people of the Cape and East
Griqualand. Le Fleur began focusing his mind
increasingly on two issues of great concern to
him: the promotion of temperance, and the
founding of a Griqua Independent Church –
unaffiliated to the Kokstad-based Church of the
same name – as a counter to the European-
controlled mission churches.

A mixture of strong influences determined the
strategy Le Fleur would follow to promote

temperance and probity among his people and to
achieve the upliftment of the coloured under-
class: his Christian upbringing in the agrarian
Republic of the Orange Free State; his late-nine-
teenth-century interaction with the Rev. Dower;
his prophetic visions during the late-1880s, and
the "ideology of segregation [that] dominated
much South African thought in the
early twentieth century."23

The Native Land Act, passed in
1913, prevented the further purchase
of land by Africans in "white" areas,
while at the same time recom-
mending the acquisition of more
communal land for the indigenous
peoples of the Union of South
Africa. When during the turbulent
years of the First World War (1914-
18) requests were made for "state-
aided Coloured land-settlement
schemes",24 Le Fleur must have
realised more acutely than ever
before the need for a material base
from which to promote his dream of
restoring pride and dignity among
people of colour. It seems Le Fleur
started to consider the idea of a land
settlement trek not long after Union
had become a political reality in 1910.
The first trek happened in 1917. By
this time, he was entitled to move
around the Union of South Africa as
freely as he pleased. His prime target
audience for the Griqua Trek of 1917
was the descendants of the Adam Kok III
Griquas of East Griqualand who had trekked
from Philippolis to No-Man's-Land in the early
1860s. Without much persuasion, he apparently
succeeded in gathering a large number of
people to trek with him to Touwsrivier, a small
town in the southwestern corner of the arid
Great Karoo.

They travelled by road as far as Maclear, and
from there Andrew Le Fleur chartered a train to
take them and all their possessions the rest of
the way.25 More than 800 Griquas followed Le
Fleur in the hope and belief that a prosperous
farming community could be established at the
"God-forsaken spot" of Smousbosch and nearby
Driekoppen near Touwsrivier. From there, they
would send their produce by rail to Cape Town,
some 180 kilometres away, and to Johannesburg
in the far north. But within three years the
project had failed miserably, "thanks to the
hostility of the Karoo climate, financial management, and the Spanish flu" of 1918.26 Deeply
disappointed, some Griquas found work on the
farms in the area while the majority drifted down
to Cape Town, "where they joined those already

in employment, who lived in Plumstead, Wynberg, West London [Athlone], Kensington, and other places on the Cape Flats."[27]
In a subsequent government enquiry into the Touwsrivier Trek fiasco, the magistrate of Kokstad commented: "*Le Fleur is a man with a considerable amount of ability and exercises a great deal of influence over the Griquas, and*

But Andrew's soldier-brother, Thomas (not to be confused with Die Kneg's son Thomas, who shared his uncle's name) held an opposing view, believing that Andrew was living in a fool's paradise when he took upon himself the

have been about Andrew Le Fleur, for many o[f] the rural poor in the Western Cape and the shanty-dwellers of the Cape Flats, Die Kneg remained their man of destiny and the one Go[d] had ordained to lead them to a Promised Land[.]

some of those who had suffered through him gave the information obtained in a very unwilling manner."[28]
Various charges of theft, forgery and fraud were put before Le Fleur. In his own defence at the trial, he said in December 1920:
"*The Griquas are a people who, if away from the dark life of East Griqualand, are most worthy of respect, and I can assure you they have proved, midst the many trials and temptations, first they can fight against the drink even better than any European people ... [T]heir migration ... has made them a people from the very lowest degradation ... to the best respected coloured people at the Cape, and every European feels that when he is speaking to a Griqua he is speaking to a man.*"[29]

The Le Fleur family, circa 1924/25. Front, left to right: Adam J. Le Fleur, A. Kok. T.L. Le Fleur, Rachel Susanna Le Fleur, with Ray Le Fleur in front of her, and C.C. Le Fleur, with A.A.S. Le Fleur on her lap. Back: D. Le Fleur, Andrew Abraham Stockenström (Opperhoof) Le Fleur, Polly Kok, Abraham Andrew Le Fleur and A.M.L.E. Le Fleur.

task of ameliorating the lot of the Griquas, "*who ... were too lazy to work, and had many other bad habits*".[30]
However, no matter how negative some members of his family and community might

in the fullness of time. After the First World War, Le Fleur had reason to believe that the time had finally come to encourage and lead his family and followers towards realising his dream of a Promised Land through job-creation projects and fresh land-settlement schemes in and near the Olifantsrivier Valley between Vredendal and Klawer on the border of Namaqualand, almost 500 kilometres from Cape Town.

ON THE MOVE
Some historically significant developments preceded and accompanied the move to an entirely different part of the country. Firstly, in

919, Die Kneg launched his predominantly
emale Griqua choirs. The response of the
ublic was overwhelming. In due course,
Griqua praise-and-worship choir singing was
aking place on the streets of many South
African towns and hamlets, and the charac-
eristic Griqua choir attire became a distinctive
performing feature of the Le Fleur mission
o regenerate *"the dry and dead bones of
Adam Kok"*.

A second, related development, was the
publication of *The Griqua and Coloured
People's Opinion*. From his office in Caledon
Street, District Six, Cape Town, Andrew and
his eldest son, Abraham, tried to distribute the
newspaper containing mostly notices and
reports of his travels and work, and also of the
leadership of the Griqua National Conference
of South Africa (GNC) and Griqua Independent
Church (GIC). The paper was launched about
two months before Le Fleur founded his own
church on Easter Sunday, 1920. For the official
launch of the Griqua Independent Church –
unaffiliated to the Griqua Independent Church
in Kokstad – more than 800 faithful followers
gathered in the Maitland Town Hall. This was
perhaps the greatest moment in the life of
Andries Abraham Stockenström Le Fleur after
the 1917 Griqua Trek, and it was here that the
members of the GNC confirmed his position as
their *Opperhoof* (Paramount Chief). Through
the joint structures of these two bodies, Andrew
wished to attract people of colour, scattered
throughout the country, away from the "foolish
doctrines" of the European missionaries. As an
alternative, he offered an independent, Griqua-
oriented Christian belief system and church
structure headed by the Le Fleur family.
Structurally, the two bodies are difficult to
separate because of the integrated nature of
their operation. Die Kneg was supreme head of
both institutions. Half a century later, Die
Kneg's youngest son, Thomas, recalled the
religious significance of that special day in the
history of their family and *volk*:
*"Dit kon niks anders [as 'n Gods Sending]
gewees het nie wanneer ons daaraan dink dat
die Manne wie hulle dienste geoffer het in 1920
meestal in die groep van ongeletterdes geval
het. Nogtans was hulle so besiel met daardie
geleentheid om ook 'n geringe bydrae te kan
doen aan hierdie Heilige Taak dat baie van
hulle op hoë ouderdom geleer het om [te] lees*

*en skryf binne 'n paar weke vanaf hulle instal-
lering as Leraars en Predikers."*[31]
Andrew Le Fleur sent these newly ordained
preachers, until a few weeks before still
illiterate, throughout the country accompanied
by choirs of young girls, to awaken his people
to their own nationhood. As founder of this
reformist movement, he personally led the first
choir on foot from Cape Town to Port Elizabeth
and back.[32] He created a tremendous
impression. The Griqua preachers served as
rondreisende organiseerders (travelling
organisers) whose duty it also was to keep the
various congregations and communities in
touch with Le Fleur's GIC. They went from town
to town, preaching and propagating their
leader's view that all people of mixed blood are
Griquas: *"dat alle Kleurlinge wat uit die
vermenging van blanke en nie-blanke bloed
gebore is, Griekwas is."*[33] Fellow Griquas
believed, however, that intermarriage with
"natives" deprived the Griquas of their national
identity: *"dat ondertrouery met die naturel die
Griekwa se nasionale identiteit ontneem."*[34]
Finally, the favourable outcome in September
1921 of the Touwsrivier Trek trial, in which
Andrew was held not responsible for the
disastrous Griqua Trek of 1917, was seen by
many as divine intervention, and their leader
gained further influence from his acquittal.
By this time, many of Andrew's following of
contract workers, who were based at Steilhoogte on the Olifantsrivier near Vredendal,
had completed the construction of the water
canal system from Clanwilliam to Koekenaap.
Some now returned to their places of origin,
disillusioned with Le Fleur. Many, however,
remained behind in Namaqualand and moved
around with him, entirely under his spell.
Despite being accompanied by their families,
they moved to, among other places, the
inhospitable Ratelgat and Klipgat on the farm
Soutfontein, about 20 kilometres from
Vredendal. Soutfontein was part of the larger
farm Beeswater, where Andrew's successor-
son Abraham later founded his well-known
Griqua settlement in 1942.
The people who settled at Steilhoogte, Ratelgat
and Soutfontein were mainly of Nama origin,
coming from the mission reserves of Steinkopf,
Komaggas and Leliefontein further north.[35]
They were Namaqualanders from whom Le
Fleur and his agents had collected money

during and after the First World War for the
purchase of, inter alia, the three farms north of
Vredendal. For some of them, the trek with Le
Fleur to these labour-and-land settlements was
a deep disappointment. The farms, bought with
a deposit only, did not have the capacity to carry
the many people who came to settle there. As a
result, a number of people returned to the
coloured reserves from where they had come,
resentful of the money and livestock they had
entrusted to the *Opperhoof* and lost. During all
the time that he toured the country to promote
his vision and mission of restoring the dignity of
his Griqua people through self-help schemes
and new settlements, Die Kneg's wife Dorie
remained in Cape Town with the children.
To be more mobile, Andrew eventually acquired
a motor vehicle in 1926. When he was in the
southern Cape, the Opperhoof stayed either in
his clay house on the farm Jackalskraal near
present-day Kranshoek, or in the small cottage
on the Robberg Peninsula at Plettenberg Bay.
On 11 June 1941, Andries Abraham Stockenström
Le Fleur died in the cottage. For many, his
death was unexpected, but others claimed he
had prepared himself, bidding acquaintances
and family a final farewell on his way from
Ratelgat via Jackalskraal to Robberg. On 2 July,
three weeks after he passed away, he was
buried a few metres from the cottage. The
official reason given by the GNC for this late
burial was that the date of his burial should
coincide with Die Kneg's date of birth. For other
followers, however, there is a more mythical
explanation: the body remained warm until the
Plettenberg Bay police ordered that it be
interred. The police sergeant's strict order left
them with no option but to accept the inevitable
reality of Die Kneg's death – although some of
his followers still persisted in believing that he
would soon return to life.
Andries Abraham Stockenström Le Fleur's
grave is revered as a most sacred site to this
day. The only other site afforded the same
sacred status by the GNC is at Ratelgat on the
N7 Route, about 20 kilometres north of
Vanrhynsdorp. Here Die Kneg often went into
retreat for spiritual meditation over protracted
periods in the 1920s and 1930s. An obelisk has
been erected there on the site of his old
cottage. At these two sites, family and
followers believe he pronounced most of his
prophecies about the future of his people and
the country. Some of these prophecies
accurately predicted that there would be a
second world war; that a new government
would come to power in England after that war;
that the British royal family would visit South
Africa shortly after the war; that India would

RACHEL SUSANNA KOK
Dorie

YOUNGEST DAUGTER OF ADAM "MUIS" KOK.

MARRIED TO ANDREW ABRAHAM STOCKENSTROHM LE FLEUR WITH WHOM SHE HAD FIVE CHILDREN.

SHE REMAINED MARRIED TO "DIE KNEG" DURING HIS IMPRISONMENT, DESPITE PRESSURE FROM HER FAMILY TO FILE FOR A DIVORCE.

THE GRIQUA CHOIR UNIFORM

KNOWING THAT HE MIGHT BE FURTHER PERSECUTED FOR REBELLIOUS ACTION AFTER HIS RELEASE FROM PRISON, "DIE KNEG" DECIDED TO USE YOUNG WOMEN INSTEAD OF MEN TO SPREAD HIS MESSAGE OF HOPE AMONG THE COLOURED POPULATION.
THE CHOIRS WERE THUS SET UP AND WOMEN, UNDER THE LEADERSHIP OF **DORIE**, WERE RECRUITED.

"DIE KROONMOEDER", AS SHE WAS LOVINGLY REFERRED TO, DIED ON THE 16th OF JUNE 1947 AT KRANS-HOEK.

ventually be freed from the British; and that Cape Town would get a new harbour and that the city's central railway station would be rebuilt. In respect of coloured and Griqua politics, he prophesied that a Coloured Council would be established (this happened in 1943); that the Griquas would go to Geneva one day (the first statement by the GNC at the 15th Session of the United Nations Working Group on Indigenous Peoples of the World was read there in 1995); that the current incumbent, Andries Abraham Stockenström Le Fleur II,

Abraham and Charlotte Caroline (née Ross) in Johannesburg on 4 June 1934. Abraham and Charlotte had four sons and two daughters, of whom Ray, mother of well-known author Zoë Wicomb, was the eldest.

According to family lore, Eric's mother received a telegram from her father-in-law on the day of his birth, informing her that the newborn baby should be brought to him at the sacred site at Ratelgat in the Cape. Die Kneg wanted him there for a presentation and dedication ceremony, as was the Griqua custom. About

Prophet, who had not yet been told of their misfortune on the road, welcomed the travelling party with the words: *"Waarom twyfel julle?"* (Why are you doubtful?) Baby Eric was clearly immune to poison. At the dedication ceremony, Abraham's brother Adam was instructed to bring Eric back to the Prophet at Ratelgat when he turned 12, *"want hy is die Nuwe Dag se Man"* (because he is the Man of the New Day).[36] Adam was unable to honour this command, because Die Kneg died when Eric was only seven. He, however, did present the 12-year-old boy at Die Kneg's grave at Robberg. Dorie, Andrew's wife – known to the *volk* (people) as *die Kroonmoeder* (the Crown-mother) – died six years later, on 16 June 1947, at the Kranshoek Griqua settlement founded by her eldest son, Abraham, the year her husband died.

would eventually become the leader. In respect of the future of the country, Le Fleur noted that *"the black man would be in power in South Africa one day"*.

Most of the predictions said to have been made by Die Kneg have come true. In addition to these general prophetic utterances, a further prediction is held dear only by the Eric Maxwell Seth Le Fleur section of the Le Fleur family. It pertains to the chieftainship of the Griquas of the GNC. At the centre of this issue is E.M.S. Le Fleur, youngest son of Die Kneg's building-contractor son Abraham. E.M.S. Le Fleur, more commonly known as Eric, was born to

Conrad Botes: Portrait of Rachel Susanna (Dorie) Le Fleur, 2002. Paint and ink on paper, 42 x 30 cm.

A wreath-laying ceremony at the monument in remembrance of A.A.S. (Die Kneg) Le Fleur at Kranshoek, 2001. The anniversary of his death is commemorated here each year. Photograph: Paul Grendon.

three months later, the mother, accompanied by the baby's uncle, Adam Le Fleur – Die Kneg's second eldest son – and a few followers, took the infant, as Die Kneg had instructed them, by truck to Ratelgat. On the way, a miracle occurred: everyone who had drunk milk from a can, earlier used on a farm in the Calvinia district to hold poison, became gravely ill. Strangely, this happened to everyone except the baby, who had also drunk of the milk. Still very worried that the baby might soon show signs of poisoning, the party arrived at Ratelgat. The

HOOF ABRAHAM

Abraham, eldest son of Die Kneg and father of Eric Le Fleur, became *Hoof* (Head) of the Griquas four days after Andrew was buried. At the time of his father's death, Abraham was not as actively involved in the Paramount Chief's nation-building endeavours as he had been in earlier years. It was his younger brother, Adam, who from very early on had played a key role in family affairs, carrying out the administrative work of Die Kneg. Already in 1926, the GNC had appointed Adam as their General Secretary, a position he held until 1943. In the early 1940s, Hoof Abraham put him in charge of the new settlement of Beeswater where he went to live – partly for health reasons. Adam became popularly known as *Bestuur* (the one who personified the total management of the settlement). As a token of respect, all GNC people later addressed him as Bestuur.[37] Little is known about the early life of Hoof Abraham. He was born at Kokstad on 10 March 1897, at a time when his father was constantly fleeing the long arm of the law for instigating a Griqua rebellion against the Cape colonial rule. When his father, a tall man with penetrating blue eyes, saw him for the first time, little Abraham was already six months old. Only at age seven, when he and his mother moved to Cape Town after the release of his father from the Breakwater Prison, did he grow up with the guidance of both parents. It seems that Abraham, about 20 years old at the time, started practising the trade of builder seriously when his father initiated the Griqua Trek to Robberg in the late 1920s. He was also a fairly good cricket player, and in character "hoflik, simpatiserend, vaderlik en geesdriftig ... besiel met 'n diepe insig van alle sake in die lewe" (polite, sympathetic, fatherly and zealous ... preoccupied with a deep insight into all aspects of life).[38]

The two brothers Abraham and Adam seem to have come to a practical arrangement after the death of their father. Hoof Abraham took responsibility for matters of a temporal and secular nature, while Bestuur took charge of the spiritual welfare of the Griqua people of the GNC and GIC.

This arrangement left Hoof Abraham free to focus on the economic development of the Griquas. His endeavours were relatively successful. He managed to gather together Griquas dispersed in the Northern Cape and to establish the Beeswater settlement in 1942. Almost hundred families from Namaqualand and elsewhere settled and established a subsistent agricultural community on the farm while many men worked on the construction of the Lower Olifantsrivier water canal. The canal system was, however, developed largely for white farming and poor-white poverty alleviation, which excluded the Beeswater community. Kranshoek in the southern Cape is another Griqua settlement that came into existence during the reign of Hoof Abraham. The establishment of the Historical Monuments Commission of the GNC, soon after Die Kneg's death, was also one of his significant initiatives. With his eldest sister, Ray, as an efficient Secretary, the Commission completed the Robberg Monument, where the body of Paramount Chief A.A.S. (Die Kneg) Le Fleur was interred in September 1942.[39]

Like his father, Hoof Abraham simultaneously held the positions of Chief of the GNC and President of the Griqua Independent Church (GIC). Unlike his father, however, Hoof Abraham did not move from place to place, but settled at Kranshoek after he took office and moved the headquarters of the GIC and GNC there from Cape Town in April 1948. The execution of the work of the Church and the Conference was, however, left in the hands of his brother Adam. Many people speak with great admiration of the relationship between Hoof Abraham and Bestuur, who had to move from Kranshoek to the drier climate of Beeswater because of his asthmatic chest. In the months following the death of Hoof Abraham, who died of a heart attack on 13 July 1951, Bestuur acted as regent. A few days after Bestuur died, the *volk* buried him next to his mother Rachel Susanna's grave at the Griqua Monument at Kranshoek.

The Hoof Abraham's eldest son, Andrew Abraham Stockenström Le Fleur (born 1923), was living in Cape Town at the time of his father's death. Apparently, he was not as

Hoof Abraham – Abraham Andrew Le Fleur, 1950.

Opposite: **Conrad Botes: Portrait of Abraham Andrew Le Fleur, 2002.**

Paint and ink on paper, 42 x 30 cm.

ABRAHAM ANDREW LE FLEUR
HOOF ABRAHAM

BORN IN KOKSTAD ON THE 10th OF MARCH 1897, THE OLDEST SON OF ANDREW ABRAHAM STOCKENSRÖM LE FLEUR.

AT THE AGE OF 20 HE STARTED PRACTISING TRADE AS A BUILDER, WHICH TOOK HIM AS FAR AS PORTUGUESE EAST AFRICA.

THE BUILDING OF THE PRIMARY SCHOOLS IN THE EARLY 1940s AT BOTH BEESWATER AND KRANSHOEK ARE ATTRIBUTED TO HIM.

HE TRAINED MANY GRIQUA BOYS IN THE BUILDING TRADE AND CARPENTRY.

LIKE HIS FATHER, A.A.S. LE FLEUR, HE HELD THE POSITION OF NOT ONLY CHIEF OF THE MODERN GRIQUAS, BUT ALSO PRESIDENT OF THE GRIQUA IN- DEPENDANT CHURCH.

GOD IS LIEFDE

AFTER HE TOOK OFFICE, HE MOVED THE HEADQUATERS OF CHURCH AND CON- FERENCE FROM CAPE TOWN TO KRANSHOEK WHERE HE DIED ON 13 JULY 1951.

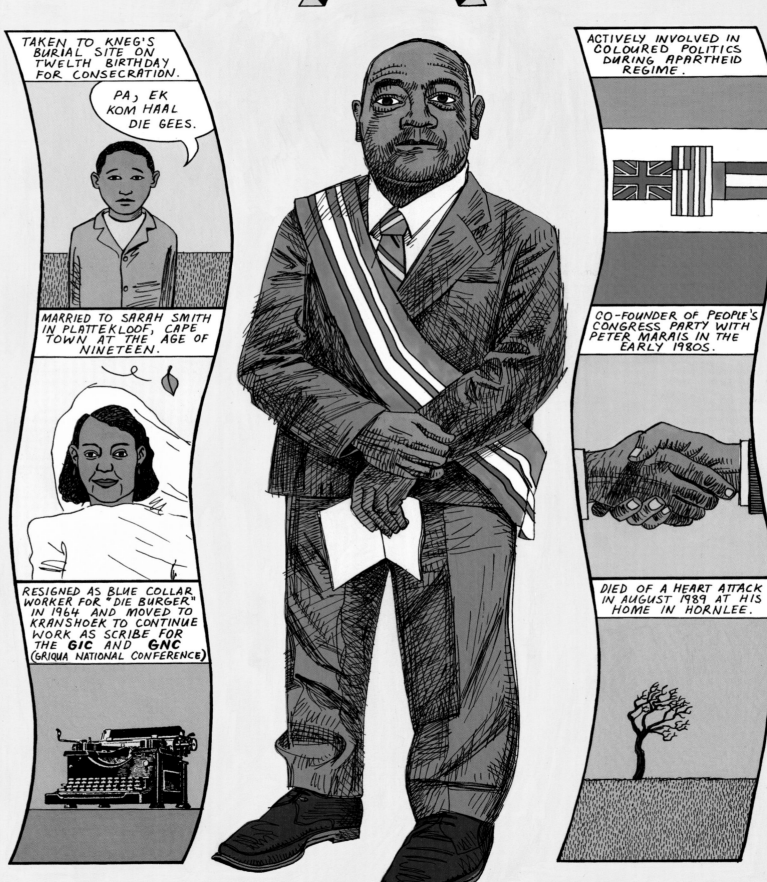

chooling, that the young Andrew discovered that there was a different – and much wider – world beyond Kranshoek. For the first year, before his family moved to Knysna for reasons of safety and to provide a more stable environment for him and his siblings, Andrew was extremely lonely. As a teenager in search of an identity, he suddenly found himself in an alien social environment for which his Griqua upbringing had not equipped him well. In fact, all through his four years at Knysna High School, he was painfully aware of their otherness as a Griqua family midst an apartheid community that viewed itself as coloured, despising not only Africans but reacting even more negatively to anyone calling him or herself Griqua.[52] "Omdat ek uit 'n Griekwa-gemeenskap afkomstig was, moes ek ook weer hier die spot en verwerping van medeleerlinge en selfs onderwysers ervaar omdat ons anders was en het ek soms my herkoms ontken omdat dit my soveel probleme besorg het en omdat ek aanvaar wou word."[53] What really confused Andrew at that stage was his own father's involvement in state-sponsored coloured politics on the one hand and, and on the other, his advocacy of the Griqua cause from their house in the coloured township of Hornlee. The student unrest of 1976, during

which black youths revolted against the use of Afrikaans at school, and which is seen as a decisive moment in South Africa's history, hardly impacted on the consciousness of the 15-year-old Andrew and his community in the tranquil coastal town of Knysna.

This, however, changed in 1980 when Andrew enrolled for a B.Juris degree at the University of the Western Cape (UWC). The university,

established in 1960 by the Nationalist government for persons classified as coloured, was in the midst of a tempestuous transition to becoming a student-led African National Congress front of struggle against the apartheid regime of P.W. Botha. It was an entirely new experience for the great-grandson of Andrew Abraham Stockenström Le Fleur. For most of his student years, Andrew remained inactive in student politics, and concentrated instead on his studies, the main purpose for which his parents had sent him to UWC. He did, however, occa-

Top: **Dorothy and Andrew Le Fleur with Audrey (left) and Charlotte, probably 1994.**
Bottom: **Audrey with her parents at her primary school graduation and the presentation of merit certificates, 2000.**

sionally take part in social programmes, such as the handing out of blankets to black squatters on the Cape Flats. In addition, he worked in the Department of Law's legal-aid clinic.

Andrew graduated at the beginning of 1986 and, after doing some menial work, successfully applied to replace Worcester's first state prosecutor of colour, who had resigned. He saw his appointment as a serious challenge, "aangesien dit in die jare van hoog apartheid was en dit duidelik was dat ek nie as enigste sogenaamde 'kleurling' welkom was in 'n oorwegend wit omgewing nie".[54]

He set himself the goal, however, of showing his superiors in the Department of Justice that through hard work he would not fail his profession. He started his new job in Worcester on 1 July 1986 and, a little more than a year later, married the daughter of his landlady. His new wife, Dorothy Manuel – born in Knysna

Top left: **The meeting at Ratelgat was well attended.**

Bottom left: **Andrew and Cecil Le Fleur in discussions at Ratelgat, 2001. Plans are afoot to create a "Khoi cultural village" here.** **Photograph: Paul Grendon.**

on 20 August 1962 – left the Roman Catholic Church for the GIC.

Andrew excelled at his work and was promoted to state prosecutor when Nelson Mandela was released from prison in 1990. From time to time, Andrew was commissioned to act as

magistrate and, in March 1992, he was appointed magistrate of Worcester. Since 1996, he has distinguished himself by repeatedly receiving a merit award for outperforming his colleagues of equal status in the magisterial district. Considering his background, it is not surprising that Andrew initiated projects within the historically disadvantaged communities to develop a better understanding of the country's legal system: *"Ek was ook verantwoordelik vir die stigting van die 'Peace Committee'-strukture in die swart woongebied Zweletemba, wat daartoe gelei het dat daar 'n beduidende afname in misdaad plaasgevind het."*[55]

In the sphere of social welfare, Andrew's voluntary activities include projects concerning street children, youth programmes and child and family care of the local Kibbutz El Shammah organisation, sponsored mainly by the Israelis. He is also interested in sport. At the beginning of 2001, he acted as team tour manager when Boland played rugby against the Indigenous People's teams in New Zealand. Andrew's enthusiasm for sport is somewhat at variance with Die Kneg's general perception that Griquas are too serious by nature to be interested in such trivial pursuits:

"In ooreenstemming met die Griekwa se ernstige lewensuitkyk, is hulle vermaaklikheid beperk to sangbyeenkomste waar geestelike liedere voorgedra en deur die koor gesing word, voetbal vir die seuns en korfbal vir die dogters. 'Annerlike' plesier het hulle nie."[56]

Andrew also plays a role in the Knysna-based GNC. As *Volks President*, he is responsible for coordinating civic matters pertaining to the Griqua communities. Under his guidance, the GNC was granted a subsidy in 2000 in terms of the government's Land Reform policy to obtain, for agricultural development, a farm of 40 hectares adjacent to the Kranshoek settlement. He is also a member of the National Khoisan Council, a temporary forum initiated by the government to discuss the constitutional political future of traditional leaders. As part of the research process on the issue, Andrew contributed a report entitled *Die Geskiedenis en huidige stand van die Griekwavolk*, which he submitted to the Department of Provincial and Local Government in 1999. In memory of the broader vision of his namesake, Die Kneg,

Top: **Audrey Le Fleur** (standing on the right) at a LoveLife manifestation, organised to create an awareness of HIV/Aids among children, 2001. **Audrey participated in a play.** Photograph: Paul Grendon.
Bottom: **Audrey at school in Worcester.** Photograph: Paul Grendon.

Andrew seems to remain committed to the cause of the Griquas and, by extension, Khoisan revivalism in post-apartheid South Africa.

THE VISION OF THE NEW GENERATION

Andrew's eldest daughter, Audrey, was born in March 1989, and her younger sister, Charlotte, almost four later. Their mother's two older children from an earlier relationship, Melany and Craig, have also adapted well to their upbringing according to Griqua customs and practices. For most of her infant years, Audrey stayed with her grandma Sara in Knysna, as is quite customary in Khoisan and coloured households. Another reason why Audrey lived with her grandma after the death of her grandfather in August 1989, was that her parents in this way wished to compensate the widow Sara Le Fleur for the loss of compan-

The Le Fleur family at the Griqua National Conference in Ericaville, The Craggs, Plettenburg Bay, 2001. Photograph: Paul Grendon.

ionship she had suffered. However, in 1994, when the time had come for Audrey to attend nursery school, she returned to her parents' house in Worcester. Today, Audrey hardly remembers those years in Knysna. What she does recall, however, is how respectable and neat her grandma always was – but nothing aimed at instilling in her a proud Griqua consciousness.

Audrey's grandma died in her second year of primary school. Six years later, she still vividly recalls how brave she was on her first day at "big school": *"Daardie oggend was ek baie braaf en het sonder my ouers langs my sy skool toe gegaan omdat hulle moes werk. Ek het die ander kinders dopgehou terwyl hulle*

aan hulle ouers geklou en gehuil het. My eerste skooldag en skooljaar was wonderlik."[57]

Audrey with her lively brown eyes and captivating smile took to school like a duck to water. In Grade 5 her inquisitiveness and love for books and learning made her the recipient of an award at the school's 1999 diploma ceremony. The following year, she was elected to the school's Prefect Council.

At the beginning of 2001, Audrey and a circle of close schoolmates at Esselen Park Primary School resolved to make the best of the year by not causing trouble or problems: *"Nie deur moeilikheid of probleme te veroorsaak nie, maar deur ons skool se naam hoog te hou."*[58]

Following from their new-year's resolution, Audrey started playing chess and joined the school's new chess club and the drama group. She even started singing soprano in the school choir. She also became involved in the anti-AIDS LoveLife campaign and in an anti-drug programme, "Geraas teen Dwelms".

"Die Monster", a poem published in the local *Worcester Standard*, earned Audrey a first prize. The last verse reads:

Al wat ek, self 'n jongeling, wil vra
Is dat God ons nasie moet kom dra
Na groener weivelde
Daar waar slegs goeie dinge geld
Ja dra ook so die bouers
Dis reg, ek praat van ons seergemaakte ouers
Bring ons net weg van hierdie skelms
Die daggapyp en die dwelms.[59]

Like most children of her age, Audrey is not particularly bothered about her family's history. She realises that most people would see them merely as individuals or an ordinary middle-class coloured family. The more informed would, of course, know that they belong to the Griqua Le Fleur family. As for herself, she sees herself as part of a Griqua family living in an ordinary coloured environment, yet with a special responsibility: *"'n Khoikhoi-gesin wat onder gewone Kleurling-omstandighede woon met ekstra Griekwa-verantwoordelikheid."*[60]

Audrey is confident that, as Griqua, she has a social role to play: *"Ek sien myself as 'n Griekwa wat 'n groot rol kan speel binne en rondom die volksaak."*

She is, however, not sure whether she will remain in South Africa when she has grown up. The future of South Africa appears somewhat bleak to her if she looks at the increasing level of crime her father has to deal with daily and as reported in the media. Unless there are other individuals like her who would endeavour to change things for the better, she may well consider moving to a country like Australia: *"As dinge nie drasties verander nie, wil ek liefs padgee. Ek hoop net daar's iemand met die-selfde droom as ek sodat ons 'n verskil kan maak. As ek wel besluit om te bly en 'n verskil te maak, sien ek myself as 'n politieke leier of andersins as 'n beroepsvrou."*[61]

Her message to young South Africans – to dream of a future that can be realised by being resolute – faintly echoes the voice of her great-great-grandfather many, many decades ago. It has a new ring to it though: *"Droom oor die huidige sowel as die toekoms. En om dit so ver as moontlik te verwesenlik laat julle deur niemand of niks afskrik nie."* (Dream about the present as well as the future. And don't be daunted by anyone or anything in your efforts to make as many as possible of these dreams come true.)[62]

Audrey, 2002. Photograph: David Goldblatt.

The **Manuel** family

Near the mountain, near the sea

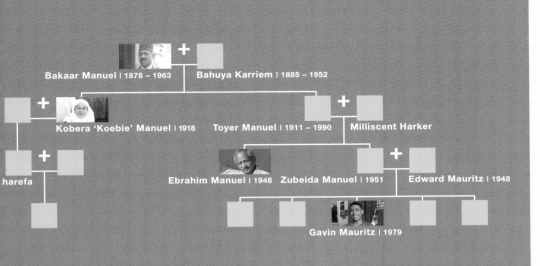

Bakaar Manuel | 1878 – 1963   Bahuya Karriem | 1885 – 1952

Kobera 'Koebie' Manuel | 1918   Toyer Manuel | 1911 – 1990   Milliscent Harker

harefa

Ebrahim Manuel | 1948   Zubeida Manuel | 1951   Edward Mauritz | 1948

Gavin Mauritz | 1979

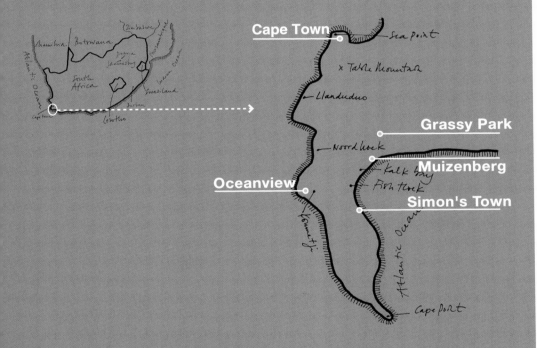

Cape Town — Sea Point
x Table Mountain
Llandudno
Grassy Park
Noordhoek
Kalk Bay
Muizenberg
Fish Hoek
Oceanview
Simon's Town

Atlantic Ocean
Cape Point

Namibia, Botswana, Zimbabwe
South Africa
Swaziland
Lesotho
Atlantic Ocean
Indian Ocean

On the slopes of the Simon's Town mountain lie two graves in wrought-iron enclosures with red and green cloth coverings. According to Ebrahim Manuel, a fisherman turned historian, these are the burial sites of father and son, Ismail Dea Malela and Jaliel, both the descendants of a sultan, Abdul Kader Dea Koasa, who – with his son Ismail – had been captured by the Dutch in the late 1700s and brought to the Cape. Ebrahim's tale is convincing, and standing high up on Dolphin Road overlooking what was once a seaside village of fishermen, laundresses, vegetable hawkers and now a thriving community of curio shops, restaurants and museums, one can almost hear the voices from the past.

It is not known for certain when the first Malays came to settle in the picturesque village of Simon's Town, but it is highly likely that they accompanied the Dutch soldiers who were sent from Cape Town by Governor-General van Imhoff in 1743 to erect a landing station for ships of the Dutch East India Company. The Malays were the real craftsmen of the Colony and, as skilled artisans, have always held their own as masons, carpenters, painters, decorators, tailors, and dressmakers. One of these early families, the Manuels, has been resident in Simon's Town since the 1700s. The first of these, according to Ebrahim, were Abdul Kader Dea Koasa and his son, Ismail, who had been captured by the Dutch and banished to the Cape of Good Hope. Ebrahim comes from a long line of men who liked to keep notes and record history, and it is these *kitaabs* (books), meticulously kept by ancestors, that have opened the door to the past. One such man, a colourful and respected Simon's Town character, is Ebrahim's grandfather, Hadji Bakaar Manuel, who recorded in his diaries all the dates, births and deaths of his family. In one of his diaries, he mentions boxes full of diaries and books dating back many years, telling the history of Simon's Town. Unfortunately, these were left behind after the Group Areas Act of 1967 saw the family moved out of Simon's Town, and the area demolished and bulldozed. One of his diaries gives a day-by-day account of his and his wife, Bahieya's travels to Mecca by ship, a journey totalling seven months and twenty-two days: *"I was born in Simonstown [sic] on 2nd January 1878. I have always lived there except for an absence of eight months in 1903 when, with my wife, I performed the pilgrimage to the Holy City, Mecca, via England and Suez."* Dr I.D. du Plessis, in his book on the Cape

Malays, states: *"The Cape Malay group consists of many racial elements: Javanese, Arabs, Indians, Ceylonese, Chinese and Europeans have mixed with Negro and Coloured (and to a lesser extent Bantu) to produce the community they form today. A mixed community, constantly reinforced by various elements, linked by one bond – religion. Of all the factors contributing to the homogeneity of this group as a distinct section of the population, the Religion of Islam has been the dominant force in spirit."*

Hadji Bakaar had been employed in the Simon's Town Dockyard. His Certificate of Service under the Admiralty records that his trade was 1st Class Storehouseman, his conduct excellent. He also performed many other public services and, between 1892 and 1961, held many positions, including that of rent collector for the Mosque, a Trustee, Convenor, First Delegate, Secretary, and Auditor.

He was also written about in an article in the *Cape Times* in 1957: *"In Simonstown, the Hadji Bakaar Manuel, my guest columnist for the day, keeps a drawerful of snapshots, mementos of all kinds of the Simonstown he has known since his father washed for Prince George of Wales in 1881, Prince Albert Victor of Wales and Prince Louis of Battenberg. The Hadji was first taken aboard a ship of the British Navy in 1881 when his father took the washing to the Admiral aboard the flagship Raleigh ... The Manuel family has served the Royal Navy from about 1859 to the present time. Malays have always been an important part of Simonstown's population. I have been looking at the Hadji's souvenir tickets to the War Fund Cricket played in 1915 between the Military XI versus Moslems XI on the Naval Recreation Ground in aid of the Governor-General's Fund. These matches at weekends were frequent, with Moslems versus Navy and so forth. All were Dockyard employees. The Hadji has among his most precious souvenirs, his 'On War Service' badge of 1914. He has faded photographs of Simon's Bay in 1897 with the naval ships Terrible, Doris, Monarch, Penelope [and] Powerful, at anchor. Another of his treasured relics is a photograph in which he is shaking hands with the Duke of Kent in 1934."*

Lady Packer's article, "Apes and Ivory", in the *Cape Times* speaks of Simon's Town's Malay Quarter, which *"clusters round the little mosque, which is also the school for the long-*

Zubeida Mauritz, Gavin Mauritz, Kobera Manuel, Sharefa Adams and Ebrahim Manuel, in front of Kobera's house in Oceanview, 2002. Photograph: David Goldblatt.

eyed Moslem children of tailors and laundresses". She speaks of another of Hadji
Bakaar Manuel's reminiscences: the little Malay
boy who was holding a captain's horse outside
the Royal Naval Officers' Club while its rider
was upstairs having a drink. *"The little boy's
mother was passing on her way to the bakery.
'Memmer, memmer, die kaptein se perd,' he
piped. 'Hou maar so, my kind,' she reassured
him. It was the regular thing in Simonstown for
small boys to hold the horses while their riders,
who had come from Wynberg Camp, took their
refreshment. Opposite the gates of the West
Dockyard can still be seen the rings and hooks
in the wall to which riders could tether their
mounts."*

Hadji Bakaar had an interesting handkerchief,
given to him in 1893 by Midshipman J.W.
Rainier. It was a handkerchief of a type
apparently widely used by junior officers in the
British Navy at the end of the nineteenth
century thickly printed with naval maxims of the
period. *"Armed with this handkerchief, the
ambitious midshipman of the 1880s need never
have been at a loss. Did a ship appear
unexpectedly ahead? A glance at his handkerchief would tell him of the rules of the road
at sea. Had a sailor fallen overboard?
The handkerchief would tell him the best
method of rescue.*

*Had he forgotten his cutlass drill? A fearsome
series of drawings would refresh his memory.
Was the bos'n piping an unfamiliar call? The
musical motif round the border of his handker-
chief would show him some 40 nautical calls."*
The handkerchief was displayed at the Moslem
Exhibition held at the Old Drill Hall in Cape
Town in 1954, and was reported on by The
Wanderer a few months later in *The Cape
Argus* of 14 December.

Hadji Bakaar was a frequent writer of letters to
the Simon's Town Historical Society. In one of
its Editorial Notes, the Historical Society
reports as follows:

*"The following letter from one of our oldest
residents, Mr H.B. Manuel of 2 Upper Sayers
Lane, Simon's Town, is a good example of the
type of reminiscence for which Mr Immelman
pleads.*

*'I beg to inform you that I have much pleasure
in the knowledge that I, perhaps the only one in
Simon's Town, still remember the first opening
of the Railway Line, which took place on the 1st
December, 1890, 70 years ago. I was then a
boy of 12 years of age.*

Zubeida and Ebrahim Manuel next to the
kramat in Simon's Town. One of their ancestors
is buried here. Photograph: George Hallett.

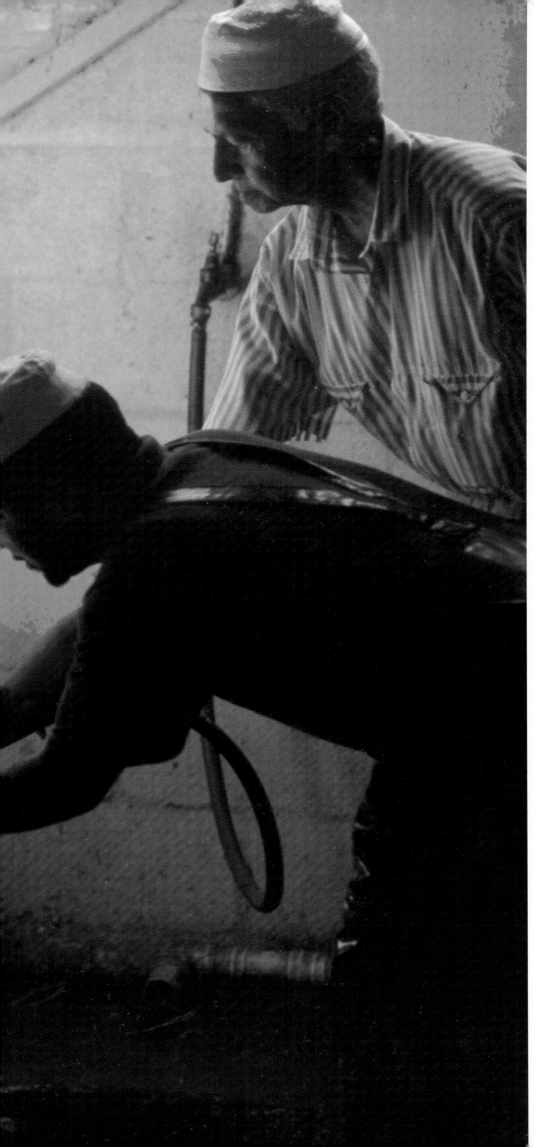

lation of the Kaaba]. *When I entered the Garam & came before the Baitollah, I was like a dumb person – oh, the Garam with the Caaba in the Centre is indeed very beautiful, the black cover over the Caaba is worked out with the words:* ya Allah la illaho allala ho mogamadara Rasoulolah – *near the top of the Caaba is a broad gold band ... Around the Caaba where you* tawarf *is all marble. The Garam is splendid, very big, soebog time is very nice to see, the thousands of people make salat [sic] [pray] &* tawarf. *After tawarf we went & drink of the Jum Jum, oh it tastes like milk. We then went & saei [walking back and forth a few hundred feet] between Safa & Marwa. After saei, we went & shaved off our head hair & then we dressed in Arabian garb & in the night you could hardly tawaaf because there is thousands of people around the Caaba & with all the lamps burning it looks just lovely.*

Ebrahim's *kitaab* was shown to the seniors of the village, who cried as they read the ancient dialect and translated it. The *kitaab* provided the missing information the villagers had sought, telling what had become of their ancestors. It was discovered that the text no one could translate had been written in the Strazontal Method. A letter from Private Museum Sultan Sumbawa (Bala Kuning) states: *"The Authentic Kitaab and other relevant material, photos, etc. that he [Ebrahim Manuel] brought with him confirms that the 'Missing' – 'Dea Koasa' and his son 'Dea Malela' – are the 'Family Members' who disappeared during the late 1700s. Our 'Original Data' states the names of the 'Missing Family Members'. The 'Strongest Proof' is the way their Grandson 'Imam Abdul Karriem Jalil' wrote in the Kitaab. It is handwritten in the 'Strazontal Method'. We are familiar with this 'Ancient Sumbawanese' writing. It is written from 'Right to Left' – 'Left to Right', 'Back to Front' – and 'Mirror Writing'."* There are no records of Abdul Kader Dea Koasa in South Africa. Ebrahim makes the connection between father and son – Abdul Kader Dea Koasa and Ismail – based on documentation and information gleaned from the villagers in Pemangong and from the oral history from the Anthony family who claim to be direct descendants of Jaliel, who was the first slave to be granted a piece of land by the government in September 1823: Erf 1240, Runciman's Drive, Seaforth, Simon's Town. A letter signed by C. Bird, Colonial Office,

Ritual slaughtering of a sheep to celebrate the end of Ramadan, 2001. Photograph: George Hallett.

19 September 1823, states: *"Whereas Abdol-gaviel Priest/Slave and Thomas & Manilla from Batavia, Manuel Joseph, January Carolus, & Rejap of the Cape and Lendor from Bengal/Free Blacks have addressed a memorial to His Excellency The Governor on the 30th Nov 1822 praying for the reasons therein stated that a certain extent of land might be allowed to them at Simonstown for the purpose of being enclosed as a burial place for the Black of the Mohametan Faith and whereas His Excellency has been pleased to accede thereto – I do therefore certify by His Excellency's desire, to those whom it may concern, that the occupancy of the ground contained in the annex diagram is hereby permitted to the abovementioned individuals as a Burial place accordingly."*

Before Ebrahim left Indonesia, he was welcomed at the palace as a long-lost son. The sultan confirmed his lineage and gave him documents relating to his family tree. He was also presented with traditional dress and family swords, and given a royal send-off. He has in his possession a Recommendation translated from the original by the Indonesian Consulate General in Cape Town, dated 9 December 1999, that he is the seventh generation of Imam Ismail Dea Malela of *dusun* Pemangong, Sumbawa. *"I stayed in Indonesia for four months, getting to know the people. I felt really at home there because the village is so similar to Simon's Town and many of the villagers looked so much like my family at home."*

Sunday 8th [November]. *Very fine weather after last night's rain. We went to Jabul Kobais ... then we went to Moshakal Kamarr, here is the place where the moon went in two to make Salaam for Rasoulolah [the Holy Prophet Muhammad] ... then to the house where Rasoulolah stayed with his wife Gadeja tal Kobera in the middle room & the room on the right where Fatima was born & the room on the left where Rasoulolah made* abdas *[ablution]* and salaat *[prayed].*

1904 January. Friday 1st. *Mogamat Armien [Son of Emam Harsiem of Cape Town] died at 6 o'clock [12 o'clock Simonstown time]. He was taken from the house to the Garam at 9 o'clock & taken from the Garam to the Mo'arla at 10 o'clock; he was buried close to Sayedna Gadeja to Cobera there was plenty people following the* kefaryat *[funeral procession].*
Monday 4th. *After* soebog *we went to Jabal Noor, the first* jeyarat *[visit] we went to was the*

Toyer Manuel, Ebrahim's father, made a pilgrimage to Mecca in 1972. His sister Kobera accompanied him.

The waistcoat which Hadji Bakaar Manuel
bought during his pilgrimage to Mecca in 1903.
He wore it during the celebrations that followed
his return to Simon's Town and afterwards
always wore it for special religious occasions.

place where Jibriel [the Angel Gabriel] took out the heart of Nabie Mogamat [the Holy Prophet Muhammad], then we went through the Rock where the Angel Gabriel appeared before the Prophet & taught him the first words of the Qur'an ... to the place where the aryat IQRAA [first revelation instructing the Prophet to read] came down, the place where Rasoulolah learned the Qur'an and made salat.

Gavin Mauritz, Ebrahim's nephew, is of the new generation. What is unique in Gavin's situation is that Gavin's mother, Zubeida – Ebrahim's sister – is married to Edward, who is a member of the Dutch Reformed Church. Gavin's father did not convert to Islam when he married Zubeida, and Gavin – and all four of his brothers – have been raised as Christians. He goes to church, but is confused about his identity, and has difficulty talking about it. Gavin is 23 years old, and will not follow in the seafaring footsteps of his uncle, Ebrahim, and other members of the family who have earned a living at sea. He is not a lover of the sea. *"There is no land. On land, I feel safe and secure. I know it's adventurous going out to sea, and you can travel and see many places, but I'm not interested in it."*
Gavin is a shelf packer at a Pick 'n Pay super-market, and is saving money to study computers. He has his own computer; he even has Internet, and has already completed a basic computer course. *"Computer science and technology is a growing industry,"* he says, *"and the market's not saturated yet."* He has an avid interest in sports, and has always been athletic, having been the leader in sports events at school. He loves soccer, cricket, and rugby. He has no girlfriend at present, but likes to go to clubs, mix with people, and enjoys discus-sion and debates. He would like to raise a family one

This small wooden board, which used to belong to Kobera's sister Murida Manuel (1904-37), was used for "riempies sny". Murida received it from a family member who made it himself. Opposite: A young girl at the annual "riempies sny", 2001. The ritual, during which the leaves of an orange tree is cut, originated in South Africa and takes place in the mosque on the Prophet Mohammed's birthday. Photograph: George Hallett.

Ebrahim Manuel during his visit to
Indonesia in 1999.

day, go overseas, and have a better environment for his children.

About his mother, he says she is a gentle woman, who works in the stock room at a Woolworths department store. They do not eat pork in the house – meaning that they follow the Muslim way in this regard, and his mother occasionally goes to *moulood*, the annual *riempie-sny* in the mosque for the traditional cutting of orange leaves on the Holy Prophet Mohammed's birthday. Gavin's father is stern, and is a regular churchgoer.

Thursday 14th [April]. *27th Moharam. About 10 a.m. Hadji Musout [brother of Hadji Saadien Dollie] fell from the Steamer & was drowned. The Steamer's Tug went round the Bay to look for him but could not find him. Musout was fishing on the port side of the Steamer. Somehow or other he fell from the Steamer on to a lighter [which was loading cargo] & from the lighter into the water. He came to the surface twice with his head bleeding. It was*

Gavin Mauritz in the Golden Cue Pool Room in Victoria Road, Grassy Park, 2002. Photograph: George Hallett.
Left: **Gavin Manuel talking with his brothers in his room.** Photograph: George Hallett.
Opposite: **Gavin Mauritz.** Photograph: David Goldblatt.

at 10 a.m. We left Cape Town for Simonstown at 2 p.m. & arrived there at 1/2 past 3. Today we are 1 month & 18 days from Mecca & today we are 7 months & 22 days gone & back. We had a Splendid travel going & coming back. Alhamdolilah [Praise be to God]. The End. Sunday 1st of May 1904.

News item, the *Cape Times*, Monday, 2 September 1963: *"One of Simon's Town's most colourful and respected characters, Hadji Bakaar Manuel, 85, who was knocked down by a car about 1 p.m. on Saturday outside the local post office, died three hours later. He and his family before him had close associations with the Royal Navy Ward Room and the ships of the dockyard for many years. He had a store of Africana of the days of sail and of the social life of the naval station in the 1800s by way of letters, photographs and testimonials. He was buried at the Dido Valley Cemetery yesterday afternoon before a large and distinguished gathering of Moslems."*

very hard for us because we could not find him. I think the reason that they could not find him is because the current is very strong setting out sea wards. In the afternoon, I & a few others went ashore. Beira is a nice place but very sandy. Everything is dear.

Kobera Manuel did not cry when the news came that fateful day in 1967 that she would be moved out of her house. Thirty years later, in her Ocean View living room, listening to birthday dedications on a Muslim radio station, the announcer played a song for the "orphans of Simon's Town". Kobera burst into tears for the first time.

Ebrahim moved to Parkwood and later to Grassy Park, where he still lives. Once he has finished researching his own story, he will help other families trace their roots. But there is still one thing left for him to do when all is done: he'll return to the sea. Gavin Mauritz will be the richer for his uncle's efforts. He smiles at the thought that he might be of royalty.

Sunday 1st [May] *At daybreak we sighted Cape Point lighthouse & arrived at Cape Town*

The **Galada** family

So many rivers to cross

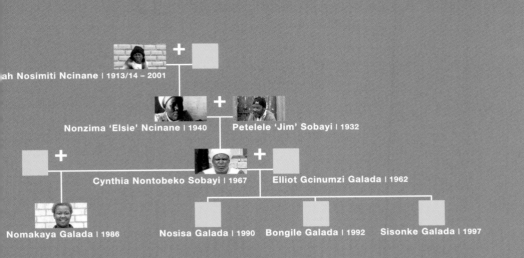

ah Nosimiti Ncinane | 1913/14 – 2001

Nonzima 'Elsie' Ncinane | 1940   Petelele 'Jim' Sobayi | 1932

Cynthia Nontobeko Sobayi | 1967   Elliot Gcinumzi Galada | 1962

Nomakaya Galada | 1986   Nosisa Galada | 1990   Bongile Galada | 1992   Sisonke Galada | 1997

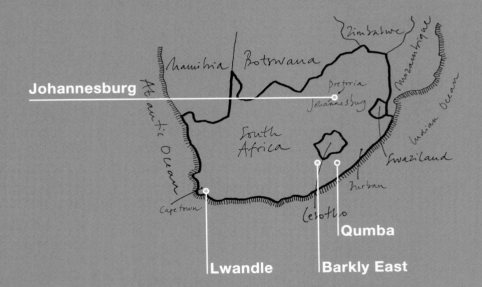

Johannesburg

Lwandle   Barkly East   Qumba

Cynthia Nontobeko Galada was born on a white-owned farm in the Barkly East district of the Eastern Cape in 1967, and spent her entire childhood on similar farms in the district. Barkly East is an extremely cold place, and many Xhosa-speaking people introduce themselves by saying, "Sazalelwa kulo makhephu ase Barkly East" (We were born in the snows of Barkly East). Today, Cynthia lives in Lwandle – a black township 40 kilometres from Cape Town – with her husband, Elliot Galada, and their four children. Every Christmas, she takes her family to visit her parents and extended family in Barkly East.

This is the story of five generations of the Galada family. It starts with Cynthia's grandparents in the Eastern Cape and ends with her daughter Nomakaya, who was born in Barkly East, but was raised in Lwandle and nearby Somerset West.

IDAH'S STORY

Cynthia's maternal grandmother, Idah Nosimiti Ncinane, the oldest surviving member of the family,[1] is a dignified old lady with a lively sense of humour. Her memory is clear: *"I was born in Shukunxa location at Qumbu in Transkei in the year of iqhuthe [the hurricane] – before 1920. I remember my childhood very well. For young girls growing up in Qumbu, it was the fashion to wear beaded skirts made by our mothers, and we braided our hair in different styles to show the different stages of growing up. When I was a child, my family were farmers with their own land in the Qumbu district. It was a painful time for us when the family had to move to white farms."*

Black farmers have lived in the Qumbu district for many generations. Qumbu is situated in what is today known as the Eastern Cape province, far from the nineteenth-century colonial frontier. It was not directly affected by the Cattle Killing of 1856-57, when many Xhosa people slaughtered their cattle and destroyed their crops, believing that a new age, free of the invading whites, was about to dawn. Nor was Qumbu directly affected by the war of resistance against the colonial authorities in 1877-78, the so-called Last Frontier War.

The area was, however, completely devastated in 1880-81, when the people of Qumbu rebelled against the extension of British colonial authority. As a result of the Mpondomise Rebellion – as the British called it – many lost their land to white farmers and black peasant farmers who helped the British. The people of Qumbu were thus reduced to living on white-

owned farms or were confined to remote mountainous areas such as Shukunxa, bordering on the white commercial farming district of Maclear.

The period 1912-13 saw the outbreak of the terrible East Coast fever, a cattle disease that brought starvation to parts of the Eastern Cape, and many people had no option but to become farm labourers. The situation was made worse after 1936, when the Native Land Act of 1913 was extended to the Eastern Cape. The Land Act meant that black people – who comprised 85 per cent of the South African population – could no longer own or occupy land outside the "native reserves", which finally covered less than 15 per cent of the land. On the other hand, some 85 per cent of the land was set aside for white people, who comprised less than 10 per cent of the population. In effect, blacks were no longer allowed on "white" land except as servants or labourers, and could no longer be share-croppers or tenants on "white" land.

This meant that black farmers outside the reserves were forced to move, even if they had owned the land for generations. One aim of the Land Act was to force black South Africans to work as cheap labour on the farms or mines, and it was in the wake of the Land Act that Cynthia's grandmother and great-grandparents were forced off their land – and into life as labourers.

Cynthia's grandmother remembers when she was *makoti* (a young bride). *"I moved from Qumbu with my husband to live and work on a plaas [farm]. That was before the war [the Second World War.] We had eight children ... four passed away soon after birth. My husband worked on white farms until he passed away many years ago. Life was hard on the farms. But now I have my own house here in Fairview, next to Barkly East, where the government built us houses. Some young family members stay with me and my daughter Nonzima, the mother of Nontobeko [Cynthia], lives nearby. Her husband also comes from Qumbu."*

The old lady recalls how she began her training as *igqirha* (a traditional healer) while she was still *makoti*. For many years, she was consulted by people *"if they were bewitched or if they were looking for lost cattle ... for sick-ness and love problems ... and the ancestors communicated through me."* When she retired, she was close to being *igqirha eliphumileyo* –

Elliot Galada, Cynthia Galada, Nonzima Sobayi, Sisonke, Nomakaya, Bongile and Nosisa Galada in front of their house in Lwandle, 2001.
Photograph: David Goldblatt.

a full-fledged traditional healer, able to train others to become *amagqirha*.

PETELELE SOBAYI – ON THE MOVE

Cynthia's father, Petelele Jim Sobayi, was born in Mpunge location at Qumbu in 1932. At an early age, his parents left him in the care of his father's mother,[2] and he has painful memories of his childhood on white farms.

"As a young boy, I had to fetch the calves from the veld and look after livestock. I was always beaten, and every night I went to sleep with a broken heart. I left that plaas with my grand-mother's brother. We went to another plaas, taking only a water can, a cooking pot and a few blankets. We stayed there until I was old enough to work. In 1940, I was already working – looking after cattle for a shilling a month. It was hard work. In our spare time, some of the workers went to church on Sundays, while others – like myself – went to imitshotsho (traditional dances) and the girls on the plaas sang for us at emtshotshweni, the place of traditional dancing.

There were many squabbles among the workers. If you were on good terms with the plaas-owner – umnini weplasi, the other workers were jealous and, if he treated you like a foreman, they refused to listen to you."

Sometimes, squabbles led to evictions. On one occasion, his grandmother fought with another woman and the farmer accused her of making trouble and ordered her to leave the farm.

"We had to carry our things because we had no wagon, but we left at once to go to another plaas. I worked there for two months before I got fired and I moved to Danie Marais' plaas where I worked for two years before I left for Mkabhayi. The next plaas I left because I was made to look after goats. When it rains, goats hide away in the forest. One goat went missing and I could not find it. When the time came to go home, the goat was still missing. Somebody told me: 'If you don't find that goat the plaas-owner will beat you to death.' That night I slept on my knees like a hare. I woke up early in the morning. My grandmother was away working on another plaas of the same owner. Without telling anyone, I ran away to other family members."

"THE ONE WHO HAS NEVER BEEN TO THE MINES KNOWS NOTHING ..."

"When I noticed that other young men were going to Johannesburg and coming back matured and wearing smart clothes, I escaped to Johannesburg. That was in September 1952 and I was 20 years old. With other youngsters, I registered in Maclear and went by train to

Xhosa costume, consisting of a skirt, a cloak and a head dress.
The costume used to belong to Idah Nosimiti Ncinane.

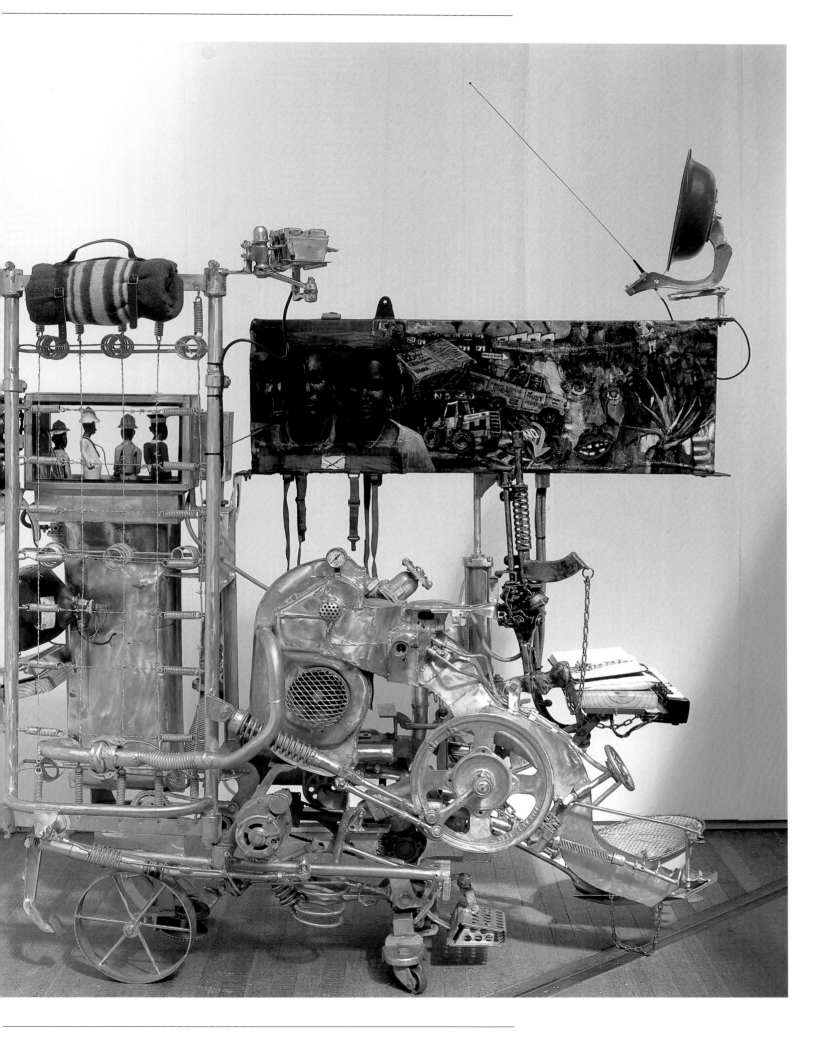

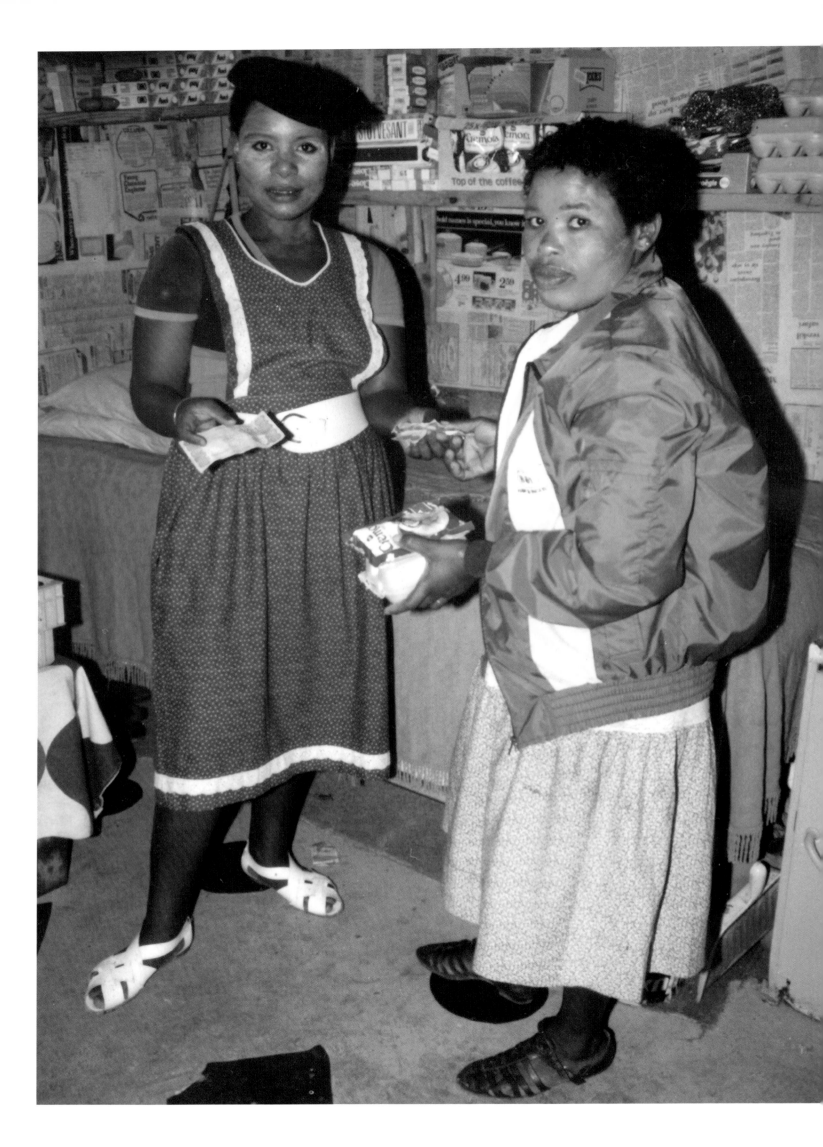

NOMAKAYA

Nomakaya Galada, Cynthia's eldest daughter, is a mature young woman with serious plans for the future, but she also has ordinary teenage interests. Asked about her stylish braids, she explains: *"I like to go to the Lwandle hair salon to braid my hair in the school holidays. If there is a certain style here in Cape Town, they will also follow it in Barkly*

persevere and after the first year I was not battling any more."

In 2001, Nomakaya entered the first year at Hottentots-Holland High School in Somerset West. Under apartheid, this was a "whites-only" school. Now, according to the principal, the

Nomakaya says: *"Of course I want to get married at some stage, but at the moment such things are out of the agenda. I'm focusing on my education right now. My aim is to become a social worker to help abused children and street children. Wherever I go, especially in*

East. There's not much difference between Barkly and Lwandle in hairstyles – we're all influenced by TV and sometimes our favourite stars."

Nomakaya now lives with her family in Lwandle after spending the first few years of her life at her grandparents' home in Barkly East. She started primary school in Barkly East and continued in Lwandle. From Xhosa-medium schooling in Lwandle, she went to the Methodist Primary School in nearby Somerset West, an English-medium school. Under apartheid, this had been a "coloureds-only" school, closed to black children.[6]

"At first I wanted to go back to my old school in Lwandle because I could not understand English at my new school. I was always quiet in class, saying 'yes' to everything, even if I didn't understand. If others were laughing, I would laugh too – sometimes even if they were laughing at me. My mother encouraged me to

school is part of the new South Africa, and is proud to have "coloured" learners as head boy and head girl.

Nomakaya likes her new school, although without her old school friends, she felt lost initially. She feels that it is like any other school – *"some are naughty, while others are nice"* – but comments on what she sees as a lack of respect: *"In this school, you don't stand up to greet teachers, you remain seated and just look at the teacher or take your book out."*

Like her parents, Nomakaya is active in the Church. She belongs to the youth guild and the choral group, and every Friday they meet to sing together and study the Bible. She enjoys gospel music and her role model is Rebecca Malope, a popular gospel singer based in Johannesburg. Asked about her plans for the future,

The Lwandle choir during a performance in November 2001. Both Cynthia and Nomakaya (center) in the choir. Photograph: Roger van Wyk. Opposite: **Nomakaya, 2001.** Photograph: David Goldblatt.

town, it worries me to see kids out of school. I think they should be in school, but some come from very poor families. After ten years, my dream is to move to Johannesburg to stay in a flat and enjoy life. That's because, after ten years, Cape Town will be boring to me. Barkly East is even worse. I only visit there in December vacations."

Cynthia says: *"I'm happy to see my daughter grow day by day. At the moment, she is following in my footsteps. She will make her own decisions in life."*

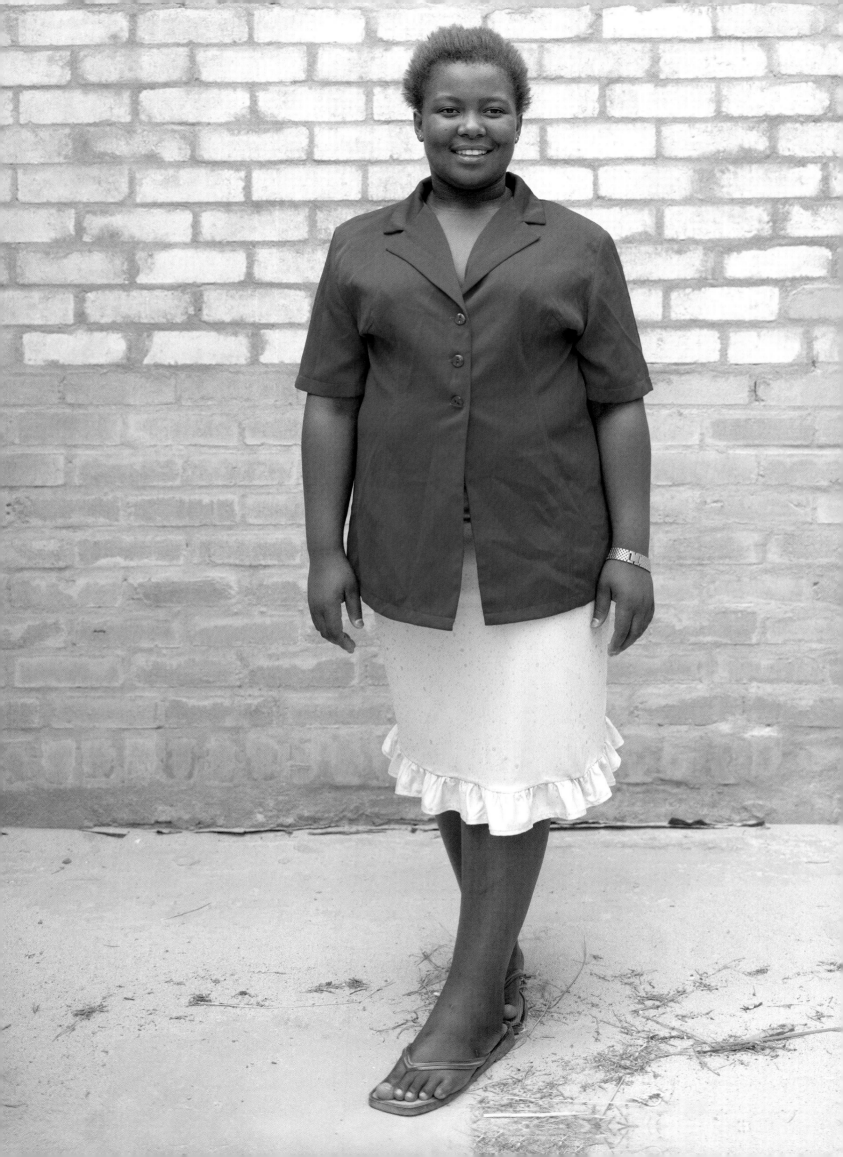

The **Juggernath** family

Coming home

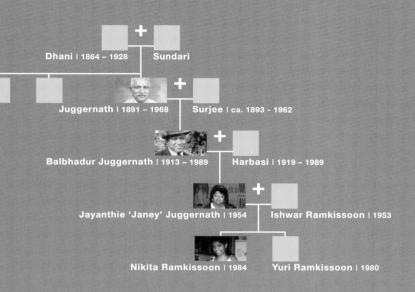

Dhani | 1864 – 1928   Sundari

Juggernath | 1891 – 1968   Surjee | ca. 1893 - 1962

Balbhadur Juggernath | 1913 – 1989   Harbasi | 1919 – 1989

Jayanthie 'Janey' Juggernath | 1954   Ishwar Ramkissoon | 1953

Nikita Ramkissoon | 1984   Yuri Ramkissoon | 1980

Durban

One day, early in March 1889, Dhani, the youngest son of Jiawon, made a decision that was to shape his life, that of his children, their children and theirs. He had had one quarrel too many with his sister-in-law. The drought that pushed so many to leave the village was causing havoc in his home. His mind drifted to the idea that had been taking root over the previous few months. He imagined himself away from this hardship, in a distant land of gold and riches. There was nothing to keep him in the village. Nothing but hardship.

DHANI (1864-1928)

And so it was, on 5 March 1889, that 25-year-old Dhani set off from the home he shared with his parents, his two brothers, their wives and children in Fyzabad, the Province of Oudh in North India.

Dhani travelled by bullock cart in the custody of labour recruiting agents to the train station, together with other young recruits from neighbouring villages. They arrived in the bustling city of Calcutta where they were held for days, prison-like in crowded, unsanitary barracks, waiting to make the sea journey. Meanwhile, the recruiting agents scoured the city and villages to secure a full shipload, including the required – but more difficult to find – 29 per cent of women. Not entirely aware of the vast distance he was to travel, the perilous sea journey that was to cut him off from his family, and the harsh treatment that awaited him on a sugar farm in Natal, Dhani was filled with thoughts of the better life that lay ahead.

After a journey of about two months across the Indian Ocean, Dhani arrived in Durban in British-ruled Natal on the *SS Congella* on 26 May 1889. After a few days at yet another barracks, he was claimed by William Campbell, a British settler and owner of sugar plantations on the Natal North Coast.

For the next five years, Dhani was indentured to Campbell, working as field hand and later in the distilling plant. The unbearably long days of hard labour in this strange land was tempered by bonds cemented with other indentured workers, and even under the restrictions of indenture, some semblance of family and community were created. A year after arriving in Natal and while still working for Campbell, Dhani married Sundari, a widow from the Barayalee district near the city of Poona. Indenture had offered Sundari escape from the suffering of widowhood. On her husband's death, she had been forced out of her home with her three children and, struggling to make ends meet in the crowded city of Calcutta, she was approached by a recruiting agent looking to fill his ship with the required quota of women. Sundari signed up for indenture with her daughter Bhagirathie, leaving her two sons to fend for themselves in the streets of Calcutta, never to hear of them again. In 1891, a year after Dhani and Sundari's marriage, a son – whom they named Juggernath – was born.

Eighty-seven years later, in 1978, Juggernath's son Balbhadur was to record his family history in a valuable diary. He tells of his grand-father's, father's and his own life. Balbhadur writes of Dhani and Sundari's time under indenture: *"During the five-year period of indenture, Dhani and Sundari encountered many difficulties. They were not at all happy of this new life in a foreign country. Hard manual work was enforced upon them for long hours in all weather and under strict supervision. They had been promised a civilised way of life. They did not anticipate that within five years of compulsory labour their youthful energy, morality, and self-respect will be seeped out for only 10 shillings, some rice, dal and salt a month."*

This *"new system of slavery"* into which Dhani and Sundari were recruited had been designed by British and European imperialists to meet colonial labour needs in the 1830s once slavery had been abolished and, from 1860 onward, indentured labour had been taken from British India to British Natal.

In the 1850s, Natal's sugar farmers, expecting their labour needs to be met by the Zulu people, had planted large expanses of cane. But the British had not yet defeated the Zulus in war: the Zulu kingdom and its economy were still intact, and Zulu people could well manage without enslaving themselves on white-owned farms. Large expanses of cane thus stood untended, ready to rot, and the farmers – desperate but with mixed feelings, since they saw Indians as the *"refuse of the Mohammedan world"* – brought in Indian indentured labour to save their crops.

By the time Dhani reached the shores of Natal, the colony had already known Indian labour for 29 years, and many ex-indentured workers – "free Indians" – were making a success of market gardening and other occupations. In addition, a second wave of Indian immigrants, referred to as "passenger Indians" as they had paid their own passage, had set up small trading stores in Durban and in Natal's rural

Ishwar, Janey, Yuri and Niki Ramkissoon, 2002.
Photograph: David Goldblatt.

Durban.

towns. By 1895, six years after Dhani's arrival, 66 shops were owned by Indians in Durban alone.

The colony offered some hope of a better life after indenture, despite the anti-Indian campaigns mounted by white settlers from time to time against Indians "encroaching" into white residential areas and competing in small trade and as artisans. These campaigns organised by the voting citizenry of Natal led to the passing of laws to restrict the advancement of Indians, who were without the vote.

In 1894, their period of indenture completed, Dhani and Sundari left Campbell's farm with three-year-old Juggernath. For the next 17 years, until 1911, they remained settled on land leased in Verulam – about 40 kilometres from Durban – from a sugar farmer, a Mr Johnson, in close proximity to other Hindi speakers who gravitated to this area and each other. The couple's children, Janki, Manki, Baijnath, Dooknee and Ramchurran, were all born on the Johnson farm and, away from the restrictions of indenture, they recreated family and community in an approximate image of village life in India, building strong relationships that last to this day. Individuals who had met under the harsh conditions of indenture now drew support, security and counsel from each other. They grew vegetables for home use and sale; built temples and prayed; celebrated marriages and festivals, where according to Balbhadur, *"specially trained young men dressed in women's clothing danced to music and sang the songs of the Hindu epics of Ramayana, Mahabaratha and Purans."* Like in village India, disputes were settled among these "villagers" through a *panchayat*, or people's court, in which Dhani's counsel was respected.

As custom dictated, the spiritual needs of family and community fell on the women. When a family member was sick or met with accident, Sundari went into a trance. Deities would reveal to her whether an evil spirit was at work and how to cure the victim. Every three years, or when a son was born, Dhani and Sundari sacrificed a goat to appease the goddess Kali.

Sundari's spiritual power gave her a certain authority in the community, so following any disagreement with Dhani, she would leave their home and spend days at a time with her cousin's family. Her grandson Balbhadur remembers in his diary: *"She enjoyed a sort of independence over everything and her finer*

Indian indentured workers arriving at Durban harbour at the end of the nineteenth century. MuseumAfricA, Johannesburg.

PH2001/3684

COPY OF SHIP'S LIST OF INDIAN IMMIGRANT.

SERIAL NUMBER   : 33

COLONIAL NUMBER   : 37750

DATE OF ARRIVAL   : 26-5-1889

NAME OF SHIP   : S.S. CONGELLA

PARTICULARS OF REGISTRATION.

PLACE   : FYZABAD

DATE   : 5-3-1889

NUMBER IN REGISTER   : 356

NAME   : DHANI

FATHER'S NAME   : JIAWON

AGE   : 25 YEARS

SEX   : MALE

CASTE   : KURMI

RESIDENCE

DISTRICT   : FYZABAD

THANNA   : SANDA

VILLAGE   : RAJAM

HEIGHT   : 5'3"

BODILY MARKS   : FACE BIRTH MARKED

NAME OF NEXT-OF-KIN   : NIL

RELATIONS ACCOMPANIED   : NIL

REMARKS   : NIL

CERTIFIED A TRUE COPY:

....

REGIONAL REPRESENTATIVE,
DEPARTMENT OF INDIAN AFFAIRS.

DEPARTMENT OF INDIAN AFFAIRS
REGIONAL REPRESENTATIVE
PRIVATE BAG X5310
18 -4- 1976
STREEKVERTEENWOORDIGER
DEPARTEMENT VAN INDIËRSAKE

qualities were noticeable. She was helpful and friendly to everyone around us. Visitors were well treated and often stayed for days."

JUGGERNATH (1891-1968)

To supplement the family income from farming, Juggernath – still in his early teens – was sent to work for William Campbell, Dhani's former employer, and the Campbells put him to work as a domestic servant for their family in Johannesburg. Balbhadur remembers: *"He worked there for two years before returning to Natal. He gained a lot of experience there as a young boy constantly amongst the whites. He could speak the English language reasonably well."* This stood the young Juggernath in good stead.

In 1910, 19-year-old Juggernath married Surjee, the daughter of Saran and Soobhagia. Unlike the marriages of their parents, contracted between indentured individuals in the absence of elders and considerations of caste, this marriage was arranged between families of the same caste and, unlike indenture where the marrying parties did not even get the day off, this marriage was celebrated with festivities that spanned over many days.

Saran, the bride's father, had settled near Dhani in Avoca after his indenture. *"He probably acquired a wife in the same way as Dhani,"* Balbhadur speculates in his diary, *"that is, from the limited lot of women from India, also indentured. Her name was Soobhagia, a very kind and obliging lady, very fair in complexion and very witty. She also believed in various deities and went into trance. I believe it was the fashion of the time that spiritual matters fell to the women. She was noted for her treatment of guests and there were many."*

But, in 1911, the growing Indian settlement on Johnson's farm was forced to break up when Johnson decided to expand his plantation. Dhani and Sundari, with their six children and daughter-in-law, leased land for the next three years on nearby Acutt's estate, adjacent to Mahatma Gandhi's Phoenix Settlement. Gandhi had established the Natal Indian Congress to resist anti-Indian legislation passed by Natal's colonial government and had set up the Phoenix Settlement on 80 acres of land. Here his followers, inspired by visions of a new society, ran a school, a newspaper, and lived off the land. Gandhi divided his time

Andrew Verster: Untitled, 2002. Oil on canvas, 204 x 85,5 cm.

Opposite: **Copy of Dhani's registration document, 1889.**

between Johannesburg and Natal over this period and it was from the Phoenix Settlement in 1913 that the passive-resistance campaign and strike against laws restricting the movement of Indians and demanding that each Indian pay a poll tax were launched. Balbhadur notes in his diary that his father and grandfather saw Gandhi at the Phoenix Settlement during their stay at Acutt's farm. And it was here, at their home on Acutt's estate, where their first child, Balbhadur, was born to Juggernath and Surjee on 23 August 1913, Lord Krishna's birthday.

Merebank

In 1914, when Balbhadur was a year old, Dhani and his family left Acutt's estate for Winn's farm in Merebank. Here they leased land until 1923 when they became landowners themselves, alongside a growing Indian farming community, many of whom had been part of Dhani's community from his days in indenture and his time in Verulam and Phoenix.

Once more, the families created a settlement that resembled village India: growing vegetables and keeping cows in the fertile valley along the banks of the Umlaas River and bounded by a ridge overlooking the Indian Ocean.

Together, the founding families of Merebank built temples and schools, instilling a strong ethic of community spirit in future generations, and laying the basis of a vibrant Merebank community. Dhani, his son Juggernath and Juggernath's son Balbhadur lived in Merebank to their last days, and Balbhadur's eldest son continues to live in Merebank to this day. When the family moved to Merebank in 1914 all Dhani's children had already married, and his daughters had left to live with their in-laws. Dhani and his sons worked the farm and tended their cows. They took their produce to the Durban Indian market and sold the milk in the Merebank community at three pence a quart. The family was now made up of Dhani, Sundari, their three sons, Juggernath, Baijnath and Ramchurran, the daughters-in-law Surjee, Maknee and Sirjatha, and Juggernath's children Balbhadur and Sookrani.

Surjee's parents, Saran and Soobhagia, were among those who moved to Merebank, and leased a large piece of land on Duranta Road, building their house near to where the Merewent oil refinery stands today. Surjee's parents were members of the Sadhu clan,

Andrew Verster: Untitled, 2002. Oil on canvas, 204 x 85,5 cm.

Opposite: **Juggernath and Surjee, circa 1960.**

followers of Kabir Das, a Hindu saint. Other members of this clan followed them to settle in Merebank, and Balbhadur records: *"As time went on, quite a number of the Sadhu clan or Kabir Panthees settled along the now Tara Road. Every member of the clan cultivated a piece of land and quite a number had cows. After the day's work and supper, the elders used to assemble in turn at the home of one of the members of the clan around 7 or 8 p.m. Each one carried with him a musical instrument called kanjri – like the tambourine, but five to six inches in diameter, covered with the skin of iguana. They would sing for hours and at intervals the host supplied them with refreshments – homemade sweetmeats made of boiled and sour milk. As the songs and kanjri music went on, the ganga cheelum [dagga pipe] was continuously going round. Ganja [dagga] was not illegal then, and was grown around the house.*

Each person of this clan added the word Das to their name – such as Ram Das, Thulsi Das. The word Das means 'servant', and in their case it meant servant to humanity and God. Followers of Kabir Das date back to some 500 years ago in India. Kabir Das grew up from a humble family and preached the gospel of non-attachment. He condemned the caste system strongly, and preached for the equality of mankind. He had a great following. Grandfather Saran was very much influenced by the teachings and songs of Kabir Das."

Close to the farms of Merebank were the emerging factories of neighbouring Jacobs and the Clairwood Race Course. Income from employment, added to income from the land, enabled Dhani's family to meet their material needs. Juggernath worked at the Surprise Soap Factory and later at Clairwood Race Course, and his strong personality and ability to speak English saw to it that he was employed in supervisory positions.

Ramchurran joined his brother Juggernath at the Clairwood Race Course, while Baijnath, a third brother, leased another farm along the sea and bought a brand new spring cart to transport their farm produce to the market. With their pooled income, the family bought an acre of land adjacent to their property in Duranta Road where they built a large house. So, by 1923, the family lived on their own land for the first time.

In his twilight years, Dhani's dream of a better life was realised. By now, Dhani had retired and yet his days remained full. He would wake at 8.30 a.m., tend his fruit trees and lovingly attend his cow. Dhani died at the age of 64. Balbhadur writes: *"Grandfather died on the 10th*

July 1928. After grandfather's death, grandmother began to sink gradually and died a few years later. She was very anxious that I should marry within her lifetime, but it was impossible as I was very young then. However, she made and left a beautiful set of earrings for my wife. My wife received the earrings when we married and she is wearing them even to this day."

With the passing of Dhani and Sundari, the family's direct link to India was gone. Neither had kept in touch with their families in India, but they had handed down religious beliefs, customs and traditions, which their offspring continued to observe.

BALBHADUR (1913-89)

By 1928, Juggernath and Surjee had had 11 children – six boys and five girls. Balbhadur, the eldest, left school in Standard Four and continued working on the farm with his uncle Baijnath. There was no school nearby that offered an education beyond Standard Four, and farming seemed to offer a reasonable way of life. Balbhadur notes in his diary:

"We acquired an additional 10 acres of virgin land on lease. Part of this is now the cutting of Umlaas Canal. We employed a few more African labourers and when the farm was brought under control, Uncle remained on the farm and I started working at the Clairwood Race Course."

Like his father, Balbhadur was to spend the greater part of his working life in industry. After six months at the Clairwood Race Course, he started work in the biscuit department of Bakers Limited and remained there until 1931, when he lost this job as a result of the Depression.

"Things were pretty bad. Many well-established firms had to close down. Europeans, mostly Afrikaners, joined in as relief workers earning 2/6d a day. The plight of Africans, Coloureds and Indians was even worse. To get employment of any type during the depression period for any person without a trade was impossible ... As a result of being unemployed, I once more joined Uncle Baijnath on the farm and added a few acres of land on lease for cultivation. There was a lot of land available and quite a number of people took up growing vegetables as a means of livelihood during the depression period."

Indians were not permitted by the laws of the time to become apprenticed for a trade, but Balbhadur soon found employment once more. Between 1934 and 1937, he worked as a messenger at a printing firm – Electric Process in Grey Street, Durban's commercial centre. While he worked at Bakers, Balbhadur had attended night classes at Carlisle Street in Durban and passed Standard Five. *"But before I could write the Standard Six examination, I lost my job and it became impossible for me to continue."*

In 1935, at age 22, Balbhadur married 16-year-old Harbasi. This marriage, like that of his parents, had been arranged in true Indian tradition. The families of bride and groom had sealed the match two years previously, but the couple did not see each other until after the wedding ceremony. The wedding was celebrated in splendour over a full week, and the homes of bride and groom were filled with joyous celebration as friends and family gathered to prepare for the wedding weeks in advance. The women cleaned and cooked and sang songs, teasing the bridal couple. The men put up bamboo poles to hold up the canopy under which musicians would entertain, and priests would call on the blessings of deities. According to custom, the wedding was held at the bride's home in Cavendish to the south of Merebank. The men from the groom's family made their way to the marriage ceremony in hired cars, while the women stayed home, preparing to receive the bride. Harbasi – dressed in a pale pink sari embroidered with gold thread, bejewelled in leaf-patterned gold and garlanded with flowers, her face covered – waited for the groom's party to arrive. Balbhadur – in a new suit, turbaned, a sash across one shoulder – was welcomed in traditional style on his arrival at his bride's home with his male family and friends. The priest led the couple in their vows as they circled the flames in the centre of a garlanded canopy. Family and friends showered their blessings and feasted on the vegetable curries and *poori* prepared in the early hours of that morning. Balbhadur noted in his diary 43 years later: *"It may seem very strange that we were married without even knowing let alone seeing one another. Needless for me to say that 95 per cent, as in my own case, married under the above circumstances, has been extremely*

successful. I certainly do not advocate that the above system should have continued, considering the present-day ideological context.

We are married for the past 43 years and during this period we too lived a very affectionate life. I might add that during our marriage there were moments of anxiety and disappointment, and equally of joy, yet she had steadfastly stood by me in every respect. We had ten children – six sons and four daughters. One of our sons died at a very early age of one year. Presently, all our children are married and living reasonably well. It is my earnest submission that in my endeavours to whatever achievements are accredited to me, my wife Harbasi was equally responsible in every respect. Even now, though old, her wisdom and humble disposition is cherished, not only by me and my children, but to a great extent by my entire family."

Back in 1935, the family members continued to pool their resources and in this way continued to prosper. Added to the family's farming income was income from employment in industry. Two of Juggernath's daughters had married and left home, and his younger children were either at school or too young to attend school.

But the happy living arrangement among the three brothers gradually began to crumble and, a year after Balbhadur's marriage, tension between his father Juggernath and his brothers and their wives was evident. One day in 1936 there were heated exchanges of words and from then on the families of the three brothers cooked separately, although they continued to live in the same house.

That same year, on 12 December 1936, a son they named Sunjith was born to Harbasi and Balbhadur, and as the family of each of the brothers – Juggernath, Baijnath and Ramchurran – grew in number, additional rooms were added to the original house at 60 Duranta Road. Slowly but surely it had expanded into a huge complex. A few years later, Balbhadur's younger brothers Thirubeni and Sewrajh married and, in a departure from custom, they went to live on their own.

Janey: "My grandmother had these gold earrings made for my father's bride in 1918, when he was five years old. My mother received them on her wedding day. She wore them until she died on 2 September 1989. I received them two weeks later, because my mother had bequeathed them to me. I gave them to Yuri for her 21st birthday on 12 May 2001. I hope she passes them and the story on to her eldest daughter." Fotograph: Sean Laurenz.

By this time, Balbhadur began to be frustrated at work. As an Indian, he had little hope of progressing and he could not join the printing union. He notes: *"I was quite happy working at Electric Process, but it was clear there was no prospect for improvement. I left Electric Process in 1937 and started working for Fishwick Printing & Publishing Company, with the promise that I will be allowed to join the Typographical Union."*

Balbahadur and Harbasi Juggernath, Duranta Road, Merebank, early 1950s. Photograph: Sewraj Juggernath.

four race groups in South Africa, the Durban City Council used existing legislation to curb Indians and expropriate their land, even before the advent of the apartheid government and its Group Areas Act of 1950. The Durban City Council declared Merebank a slum under the Housing Act in 1938. *"This,"* notes Balbhadur, *"was a ploy to expropriate land from Indian landowners and it prevented any development."*

In 1942, the Minister of the Interior declared Merebank an area for the development of Indian and coloured housing, prohibiting development and allowing the state to

He found, however, that although they employed him in contravention of the printing industries by-laws in a job reserved for white people, his bosses avoided paying him union rates by preventing him from joining the union. So he left Fishwick and started work at the Provincial Printing Company instead. Within a week, he joined the printing union.

Around this time, Balbhadur bought two additional acres of land in Merebank, but his plan to subdivide this plot to build houses for his brothers had to be abandoned. Bent on restricting the advancement of Indians and on demarcating residential areas for each of the

expropriate land from the present owners in order to develop the housing scheme. By 1945 however, the state had still not started on the housing development, and Balbhadur decided to build – illegally – on his two acres since space was short at 60 Duranta Road. Balbhadur's brothers Kalichurran and Dudrajh moved to this house with their families and his parents Juggernath and Surjee. Here they farmed poultry, vegetables and bananas, with all family members assisting Dudrajh, the full-time farmer, after work and at weekends. The family prospered over this period, and Balbhadur recalls: *"We bought a second-hand lorry, which served us well for transporting produce. Father was working at the race-course, I was working at Provincial Printing Company, Kalichurran at Herbert Mayne Jopp and later at NOP, and Debipersad as a teacher. We were living comfortably well, but with one disturbing factor in mind, that of the expropriation threat of the Durban Corporation."* Instead of building the promised houses on land expropriated from the Indian residents of Merebank, the City Council proceeded to reap enormous profits by selling the land to the oil refinery, the airport and other industries.

When, in 1953, 23 landowners in Duranta Road were served with expropriation notices, the Merebank community decided to take action. They set up the Coordinating Committee on Housing and took the Council to court.

Other Indian landowners around Durban were similarly affected and the Merebank resistance was part of a broader resistance on the part of Indians who were once more faced with a racist onslaught. Balbhadur and his brothers were active in organising the community around this housing campaign but, faced with powerful resistance from local authorities, the community lost its case and in 1958 the Durban City Council finally expropriated the Juggernath family's properties together with other Indian-owned land in Merebank. The following year the Merebank housing scheme was started, and the previous owners of the expropriated land were given options to purchase land or to rent council-built houses. Balbhadur and brothers Sewrajh and Debipersad opted to purchase plots, on which they built their own homes in 1962, while brothers Kalichurran and Thirubeni and their father Juggernath opted to rent homes built by the Council.

While the families were getting ready to move into their new homes, tragedy struck and in August of 1962 Surjee passed away. She had suffered years of ill health, and her passing heralded a new era for the families. Juggernath, now retired, spent his time rearing poultry on a small scale. His health

and electric bills in addition to the upkeep of a growing family."

Balbhadur was now 49 years old and his sons Sunjith and Rundheer were employed as a teacher and clerk respectively. His other children were still at school. Within a few years, his two older sons and two older

"I enjoyed good health throughout the major part of my life. I used to play soccer, as the game every youth of my time liked to play. I enjoyed swimming, golfing at Curries Fountain, cycling, running. I seriously took up physical training and wrestling. I continued these sporting activities until the late 1940s."

Balbhadur may have retired, but he continued to spend his days engaged even more

had deteriorated in the early 1960s and, in August 1968, he too passed away while resting after lunch.

ARCOT PLACE

By 1962, the grandsons of Dhani had finally been forced to part ways and each now coped individually to make ends meet in the new housing scheme. Balbhadur notes in his diary: It was pretty hard to meet the new living conditions, which involved paying instalments

daughters married, with the two sons continuing to live with Balbhadur and Harbasi at 24 Arcot Place, their new home in the Merebank housing scheme. In 1970, the family added four rooms to this house to provide for the growing families of their two sons. Balbhadur worked at Provincial Printing until August 1962, when he left to join a printing firm, John Dickinsons, as a machinist. Due to ill health, however, he left Dickinsons in August 1977, a year before retirement age.

A Juggernath family gathering at Duranta Road, Merebank, to celebrate the double birthday of Shyam (four), and Maltie (nine), 1957.

passionately in community service, in projects to build schools, community halls and temples, and campaigning against the injustices of the Durban City Council and National Party government. He was concerned not about simple self-advancement but for the advancement of the entire community, and he gave of himself tirelessly in order to achieve this. Through Balbhadur's work, the Juggernath name became a household name in Merebank. His philosophy and example influenced his immediate family and inspired the broader community in Merebank and beyond, but none of this would have been possible without the support of his wife, Harbasi, who kept home and cared for their children.

Of his children, Balbhadur's eldest son Sunjith campaigned in the 1970s for non-racial sport and with Balbhadur's fourth born, Abhimaneu, attended the memorial service of African National Congress (ANC) president Chief Albert Luthuli, resulting in both being victimised as teachers – and never to be promoted. Together with their father's example, these older brothers and Sunjith, in particular, shaped the consciousness of their younger siblings, cousins, nieces and nephews.

When the Natal Indian Congress (NIC) was re-established in the 1970s, after years of state repression during which there had been a lull in opposition politics, Balbhadur was asked to set up a Merebank branch. The founding meeting was held at his home, but he declined an active role, leaving this to younger NIC members. Two of his children, Jayanthie and Munmohan (better known as Spider), were to play an active role in NIC activities from the 1970s to 1990s and became involved in the ANC's underground structures.

Family remained important to Balbhadur, and he spent much time with his children and grandchildren. Over weekends and on festival days like Diwali, the sounds of three generations – including the 28 grandchildren – would fill the Arcot Place house. In addition to traditional festival days on the Hindu calendar, Balbhadur instituted another festive day – 2 January – when the family would picnic on the beach and play cricket.

Highlights of Balbhadur's later years were a trip to India and the Far East with Harbasi in 1972, and the celebration of their fiftieth wedding anniversary. His daughter Jayanthie says, *"My father loved India. But he said Arcot Place was home."*

In 1989, after a period of ill health, both Balbhadur and Harbasi passed away – Harbasi on 2 September, Balbhadur on 24 October. On his deathbed, Balbhadur worried that his children might part ways after his death, but his youngest daughter Jayanthie promised that she would try to keep the family together. True to her word, Jayanthie continues to arrange, with her siblings, regular family get-togethers and 2 January has remained a special day on the family calendar.

Celebrating Diwali, the Indian Light Festival, at 23 Arcot Place, 1976.

Abhi Juggernath, one of Janey's brothers, outside the Durban City Hall with his parents Harbasi and Balbahadur Juggernath on the occasion of his graduation in 1969. "Non-white" South Africans needed a special permit to enter the City Hall during this period.

JAYANTHIE (1954-)

Education would turn out as important for the survival of Balbhadur's children as land had been for the survival of his father and grandfather. Balbhadur, realising this, ensured that his five sons were educated to tertiary level. But he did not regard further education as necessary for his daughters. Of his four daughters, only the youngest, Jayanthie – born in 1954, six years after the Nationalist government introduced apartheid – ironically had this opportunity. Jayanthie, who chose a teaching career, asked her father about this in his last years. *"He said he was schooled in that old ideology where women marry and stay at home. He accepted equality of the sexes very late in life,"* she now recalls. *"When I completed high school, many women were in jobs outside the home so it was not an issue. Times had changed. But six years before this, he stopped my older sister from going into nursing. He later regretted that, and he told her this."*

Jayanthie remembers her father's involvement in community struggles as a strong influence in her life. Among her more vivid childhood memories is the day the security police visited her father in their Duranta Road home in 1960. *"I remember my dad burying a whole lot of books and typed material. I was about five or six. I had no idea why he was doing it. Then suddenly a whole lot of big burly white guys came up to the house and started searching every corner, even under the beds. I remember my dad telling us not to say a word. At that time, a number of people had been detained for 90 days."*

Listening to the conversations at her father's meetings at home, Jayanthie grew up with a keen sense that Indians were being treated badly by white people. *"It was so bad that at one stage I thought God was white because it rains on Diwali day and not on Christmas Day."*

It was, however, her older brother Spider who most influenced Jayanthie's politics:
"When I was in Standard Eight, Spider (then in matric) gave me a book by Huberman, called Introduction to Socialism. This was the first book I ever received as a gift, and he inscribed it with the words 'May our relationship spread.' Spider's relationship with me is very special. There is that bond – and that bond is our life in the Struggle. He was the single individual who influenced me to get involved in the Struggle."

Jayanthie accompanied Spider to meetings organised by the black consciousness South African Students Association (SASO) at the Alan Taylor Residence for black medical students –

Thaj Mahal Replica. Aumizal

Balbhadur and Harbasi Juggernath in India, 1972.

a hotbed of political activity in the 1970s – in Merewent, where in earlier times the home of Balbhadur's grandfather Saran stood. Here she made contact with African, Indian and coloured students and heard Steve Biko speak.

It was also Spider who introduced Jayanthie to the Phoenix Settlement, where in the 1970s Gandhi's teachings continued to be integrated into the struggles against apartheid. In 1972, Jayanthie attended a work camp at the Phoenix Settlement and it was around this time that Spider, with the assistance of other activists, started a newspaper, *The Sentinel*. Reading this and other "subversive" material added to Jayanthie's growing political awareness, but Spider's activities caught the attention of the

security police and in the 1980s Spider was detained and held in solitary confinement. This had a great impact on Jayanthie, and she recalls one of the visits to Spider by the security police:
"Spider had a cellar room in Arcot Place. All our activities centred there. Friends would meet there. All our books were there. One day it rained and Spider and I mopped up the floor, and lit incense. The security police then came in and began searching this room. Just before they could get to Spider's material, the incense got the better of one. He could not bear it. He left the room saying: 'I'll come back another day.' After that Spider just loves incense!"

The hippie movement, too, had a strong influence on Jayanthie: *"Oh, that was an exciting part of our lives. When the mini skirt came in, my father was absolutely shocked that we could dress like that. So we wore bell bottoms, kurtha tops, bandana and beads. We listened to the Beatles. Music influenced us a lot."*

Even though she was relegated under apartheid to a group area set apart for Indian South Africans, the influence of Black Consciousness and the ideas of leaders such as Steve Biko caused Jayanthie to see herself as black, rather than Indian.

"[During the 1970s] we always referred to ourselves as black. We shied away from an Indian identity. We were South Africans. So wearing a sari or punjabi, was an issue. You did not want to wear a sari because you are not an Indian. We did not listen to Indian music.

Prior to that, I had very firm Hindu roots. We used to watch a lot of Hindi movies and my older brothers and sisters would listen to Indian music. Although we were not taught to read and write in Hindi, I picked up a lot of spoken Hindi so I can understand Hindi. My father was very Indian – our home was very Indian. There was no English food, no alcohol in our home. As far as friends [were concerned], we socialised only among Indians. Through activist work, we made contacts with coloured and African comrades [for the first time]."

Jayanthie married Ishwar, also an activist, in 1977, but – for all her growing consciousness – Jayanthie found that women did not gain easy acceptance into the ranks of political activism.

"My dad's meetings were only men. Spider's group was also only men. Spider's group [only] started to let me in when I started going out with Ish, but then, too, I'd be seen as Spider's sister or Ish's girlfriend. I wasn't me. It was [really] only after 1979 that I became a person in the Struggle. By then, I was married and expecting Yuri. We were the only ones with our own place among the activists, so my home became the meeting place during the 1980 schools' boycott. I was at home. Merebank High was close to our flat. Pupils would come to the flat to make banners and so on. I typed, sent out pamphlets, and organised students."

Ish and Jayanthie's lives together were directed by the Struggle

and there was no time for a honeymoon. Jayanthie remarks: "We were involved in the Struggle from day one of our married life." This included involvement in Merebank's housing issues, students' and women's organisations, the Natal Indian Congress (NIC) and the United Democratic Front (UDF) – formed in 1982 to resist apartheid – and in campaigns to boycott the elections of government-imposed institutions that made the pretence of offering Indian South Africans representation at various tiers of government.

From the late 1970s, at a time when such activity was an act of treason, Jayanthie, her brother Spider and her husband Ish were also involved in underground activity of the then-banned ANC.

Opposite: **Janey in her bedroom, 2001.** Photograph: Sean Laurenz.

Bottom: **Some of Balbhadur Juggernath's personal belongings, saved by his daughter Janey.** *"My father was always cleanly shaven. In Arcot Place, there was always a queue for the bathroom when my father and his five brothers had to shave in the morning. My father always had a pocket knife with him. He did not like to lend it to others. The cuff links were a birthday present. We celebrated my father's birthday every year after his 50th birthday in 1963. He always received a lot of presents, but he considered them to be a waste of money. The wallets are more than 80 years old. My father was short-sighted and always wore glasses. My mother was illiterate. My father read the paper and patiently translated the news into Hindi for her."*

"Once we got a whole lot of ANC handbooks. We had to type out names and post them. This was early in my involvement – in 1979. It was frightening. There I was, sitting with this old typewriter, with my gloves on so as not to leave finger prints.

The dangerous part of our involvement was Operation Vula. We made two trips across the border. In 1980, Ish and I made our first trip to the ANC in Swaziland. Yuri was just a baby. We spent time in a safe house. This house was bombed a week later. I was never so scared in my life as on that night."

Their two daughters, Yuri and Nikita, were born in 1980 and 1984 respectively. Jayanthie says of the years that followed: "Between 1984 and 1994, we had no family life. There was no such thing as Ish and I packing a picnic basket and taking the children to the park. Although we tried to fit this in.

I would attend extended family events, but Ish would not attend – he would be busy with some community or political activity. There were times we would sleep at two or three in the morning and wake at six and go to work."

In 1990, the ANC was unbanned and ANC branches were set up all over South Africa. Together with other activists, Jayanthie established an ANC branch in Merebank, and she also became an active member of the newly launched South African Democratic Teachers Union (SADTU) and was elected secretary. In 2000, Jayanthie visited Cuba as part of a work brigade, organised by the Friends of Cuba Society, to pick oranges and work in construction. She considers this a pilgrimage and the culmination of a dream. "I have always been

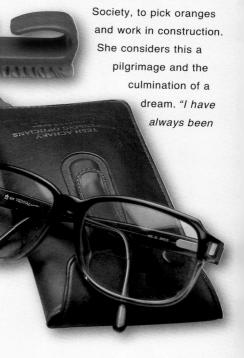

passionate about Cuba and Castro," she says. Today the ANC is no longer active in Merebank. The heady days of the political struggle are long past, and Jayanthie finds adjusting to the new context difficult: *"For me, personally, it's quite a big adjustment to give up being an activist. I had problems adjusting – mentally and psychologically. I had to work through this over the last four or five years. There was I, a full-time worker, full-time mother, full-time activist, a full-time everything and suddenly I could get a maid so I'm not a housewife any more, my children are grown and don't need me, the Struggle does not need me. Adjusting is a struggle. Some people came off okay, but I felt a total sense of worthlessness."*

Jayanthie finally became disillusioned with teaching, and resigned from her job in mid-2001. Although she is critical of the new South Africa, where the needs of many continue to go unmet and where racial inequalities remain, she has no regrets about the role the Struggle played in her life.

Janey at the wedding reception of her niece, Suvashnie Juggernath, and Marlan Chetty, Pietermaritzburg Town Hall, 1 September 200.
Photograph: Sean Laurenz.

Janey paying a visit to Settlers Primary School, where she worked from 1980 to 2001.
Photograph: Sean Laurenz.

"I'm not going to be bitter and say it was all for nothing. I'm pleased that the country has been liberated. But things are not moving as fast as they should. We are in the eighth year of our freedom and little things should change. If I had to do it again, I would be involved in the Struggle more vociferously."

In 1993, with reforms sweeping across South Africa on the eve of the country's first democratic election, Jayanthie, Ish and their daughters Yuri and Nikita moved house from Merebank to Montclair – a white group area under apartheid – to the west of Merebank, beyond the South Coast railway line. Jayanthie

says of her new neighbourhood: *"As far as relations with other races, that is fantastic. We are living among white and African families and there is no problem. People accept each other."* Jayanthie's daughter, 17-year-old Nikita, offers her view of the move from Merebank, a working-class area notorious for its high levels

of pollution, to the middle-class Montclair: *"Living here was a bit of a shock because of the clean air, and living among white people took some getting used to.*

At first, I was quite intimidated, as I had neve interacted with a white person before; now w had them next door to us. Because they were so nice and friendly, it was all forgotten in a matter of weeks and I started feeling more South African than a secluded Indian. We started making friends with white neighbours We went into each other's home, had sleep-overs, swam in each other's pools."

The difference with Merebank was stark, says Nikita. *"It was very quiet in Montclair. I was used to hearing the Merebank neighbours whistling Hindi songs in the morning, feeding the birds; on the other side, somebody screaming in Tamil, and the sounds of pots and pans. Here it was very quiet."*

YURI (1980-)

Like their grandfather Balbhadur and uncle Spider had influenced their mother, so too have Yuri and Nikita been influenced by their parent. Yuri started her political activity at the age of 1

The Ramkissoon Family

e Yuri
soon

Father Iskwar
Birthplace Umlaas Date 16·7·53

Mother Jayanthie
Birthplace Reezbank Date 26·12·54

grandfather Munmohan	grandmother Ramdhasie	grandfather Ballhadur Juggernath	grandmother Darbasie
great-grandfather Ramkissoon	great-grandmother Lapidi Kusimi	great-grandfather Juggernath	great-grandmother
great-great-grandfather	great-great-grandmother	great-great-grandfather Shani	great-great-grandmother

Yuri's baby-book with her family tree.
Left: In 2000, Janey went on the journey of her dreams: she visited Cuba with a group of South Africans. Here they are at the Propaganda Centre in Havana. She is seated in the middle.

"I was very active in the first democratic election in 1994. I got involved in house visits, put up posters, gave out pamphlets, helped with canvassing and organising motorcades. At first, I became involved because of my parents. But later it was because I wanted to. It was quite exciting and my entire family was involved, including my cousins.
I knew that apartheid was wrong – that you can't have a government that placed one race in a superior position than another."
Yuri was well aware of class and race discrimination, even at school.
"In matric, I realised how inadequate our facilities were. From Standard Nine, we did not have textbooks. We had to share a book among six students. My school was in the lower socio-economic area of Merebank. Many children came from poverty-stricken homes, so the school could not raise much money by way of school fees.
And we hardly ever mixed. There was class segregation, race segregation in the school.

We, in the A class, were mostly from upper- to middle-income families and we tended to keep to ourselves, not mixing with those from B to F class, who came from lower-income families. African students started attending Merebank schools when I was in Standard Five. In Standard Six, about 15 per cent of the kids were African kids. When I was in matric, about 40 per cent of the kids were African kids. All our teachers were Indian. The kids did not mix across race. In all my school years, I had one African friend and I have lost contact with her now."

Today, Yuri is a fourth-year Bachelor of Science student at the University of Natal, formerly a white university where Indian students now make up 60 per cent of the population, but where racial mixing does not come easily. She says, *"The Indians stick together, the whites stick together. The African and international students are a minority – you hardly notice them."* Yuri also finds that very few of her contemporaries share her strong commitment to the values of equality and justice.

NIKITA (1984-)

As politically aware as her sister and parents, Nikita was active in the ANC Youth League during the 1999 national elections.

"I went with my parents on house visits to give out pamphlets. My parents were involved in politics to achieve freedom – they were more selfless and worked hard to see the country develop. On a more personal level, they wanted out from polluted areas like Merebank; they wanted better jobs. They did the right thing. We were brought up well."

Nikita also found herself in unfamiliar situations in the two formerly white schools she attended. In contrast to the predominantly Indian school in Merebank, 50 per cent of the girls at Mowat Park Girls High were white, the rest African, Coloured and Indian. In addition to meeting schoolmates of different races, she also came into contact with Indians who were different from those she knew in Merebank.

"Indians here were extremely snobbish. They were mostly upper-class Indians whom I did not really want to connect with because they were narrow-minded and did not know what the Struggle was like. I made friends with those who understood and could accept people for their differences. In our group of friends, there were some Indians, a few Africans and lots of whites.

Andrew Verster, Untitled, 2002. Oil on canvas, 204 x 85,5 cm.

Some teachers were racist. Their racism was subtle and this kind hurts the most because you can't really do anything about it. The majority of the teachers were white."

At her present school, Crawford College, in Durban, the majority of students are Indian and the majority of teachers white, and Nikita still finds racist attitudes among her classmates: "The majority are upper-class, factory-owning, business-owning Indians and, sad to say, these upper-class Indians are racist and don't like mixing with other race groups.

My best friends include a [Indian] friend from Merebank and a white girl from this area. They are both very different. At school, my best friend is a white boy in Grade 11 – I am in Grade 12. He lives in Mariannhill and the only time we get together is in school.

Most of my friends have boyfriends or girl-friends from their own language and religious groups. But there are a few exceptions. Like we have Muslim-Hindi relationships, that kind of cross. One Indian girl who is now at UCT [University of Cape Town] is going out with a white Jewish boy. They were the talk of the town, but people have now learnt to accept that. I would, preferably, choose to be in a relationship with a Hindu. But at the moment its too early."

Initially, Nikita saw being Indian as a restriction – forced to live in an Indian group area, for example. Today, however, she is proud of her Indian origins, and is the president of her school's Hindu Association. "We organise Bhangra evenings, prayer meetings, eastern dances, mehndi day, a day when everyone – not only Indians – dresses up in traditional dress. I feel proud of my Indian culture. I try to uplift my culture as much as possible."

She, nevertheless, see herself as South African in her Indian-ness.

"South Africans don't really have a 'fixed' culture. I am South African in my Indian-ness because now Indians are a part of South Africa. We were born here and brought up

Top: Eight-year-old Niki, front, second from the right, in Grade 3 in Nizam Primary School, 1992. "This was my first class. I did not have much contact with the others. I was the one who won all the prizes. The others were quite a bit behind."

Middle: Niki, left in front, in Grade 8, with the Mowat Park Girls High choir, 1997. "It was a strict Christian school. I was the only one who wasn't a Christian. The pupils are now mostly African."

Bottom: Seventeen-year-old Niki, reclining in front, at Crawford College, 2001. "The noisiest and worst behaved class in the school."

Hindu ritual of lighting a lamp every evening in their home.

"Yuri and I got sick of politics after a while ... We said this is getting a bit much now, we might as well do what we feel is right – I was about 11 or 12 then. My dad was not religious. My mom made us aware of the Hindu culture but not religion. Yuri and I light a lamp every evening; we fast, like four-day fasts. Gradually, we might become vegetarians. Yuri and I are more spiritual than our parents. My mum is a Marxist, but she sits for Havan prayers with us. Hinduism is very much alive in this house."

Nikita bubbles with enthusiasm as she talks about her family origins.

"I did not really understand my grandparents' lives or great-grandparents' lives until I read the memorial brochure prepared by my uncle on our family. I then wanted to find out more about my family history – especially the

here. Some of us don't want to go back to our roots – in fact, we have never seen India; we don't know if we will like it or not.

In history class we talk about culture a lot. We are a very unique country in that we have so many cultures. A true South African is a person who accepts all other cultures of the country, while keeping alive their own. Indian culture is very beautiful; we should keep it alive."

Nikita and others of her age group of Indian origin do not speak any Indian language, but she is learning Hindi from her aunts and there is a swing back to an appreciation of their Indian roots: "My cousins and Indian friends are very attached to our culture. We watch Hindi movies [and] are very proud of our culture, but we are also very westernised.

I listen to a range of music – a kind of R&B, which Indians listen to. When I went to Mowat Park, I listened to Brit pop, a kind of London underground music. Now I listen to a balance, like U2 and Oasis. I also listen to a lot of my parents' stuff – Beatles, Bob Dylan, Crosby Stills Nash and Young. I listen to kwaito and South African R&B.

My dream is to study art in India. I want to go to India. I wanted to go next year to study fine arts but my mum wants to keep me here. If I study in South Africa, I am thinking of studying Journalism or Drama."

Nikita, like Yuri, remains concerned about the prejudice she sees among her contempo-

raries: "We now have an African president in our country. This is a huge jump from where we were. We still need to struggle against the prejudice that you are Indian, you are African and you are White. It's like us and them. That has to be overcome. Also, the class system, because we have different classes within race groups."

Religion plays an important part in Yuri and Nikita's lives and they have instituted the

Niki in her room, 2001. Photograph: Sean Laurenz.
Opposite: Niki, 2002. Photograph: David Goldblatt.

Merebank family. And Indians in South Africa. Because we were basically taken out of our home country and plonked here, I wanted to know how we grew up from absolutely nothing to what we are today."

Family histories of the contributors

Willie Bester

Conrad Botes

Henry Bredekamp

WILLIE BESTER

I began my career as an artist when I was still very young, making cars from wire and other scrap material for my friends in Montagu in the Little Karoo, where I was born in 1956.

My mother was from the local "coloured" community, but my father, a Xhosa-speaking migrant labourer, came from Cradock in the Eastern Cape. Because he was considered a temporary resident under apartheid law, he was supposed to live in a hostel for migrant labourers, so we never had any legal access to land. Throughout my childhood we were therefore forced to occupy makeshift accommodation in the back yards of other families living in the segregated "coloured" township of Montagu. To this day, I have very vivid memories of the humiliation and abuse my parents and other people in our community suffered at the hands of the police and the local white shop owners and farmers. These memories inform many of the ideas I explore in my mixed media works and salvage sculptures.

CONRAD BOTES

My father is the son of a railway worker from Bellville and my mother is the daughter of a sheep farmer from Uitenhage in the Eastern Cape. After they got married, they moved to Ladysmith in the Little Karoo during the late sixties, where they both taught at the local primary school. Two sons were born in Lady-

Lien Botha

smith. I am the second son. A third son was born after their return to Bellville in the Cape during the early seventies.

I met my wife, Jeanne Labuschagne, at the Art Department of the University of Stellenbosch in 1997. We work and live with our dog, Yster, in Woodstock, Cape Town.

LIEN BOTHA

To live in the place where your grandfathers lived. For a long time I found solace in the thought that my maternal ancestors came from Italy. Twice I tried to find a trace of this as evidence, and twice I failed. They left music wherever they lived. Somewhere in 2001 I opened an old family album and the more I looked at the faces of youthful grandfathers

and their mothers, the more familiar they became. Eventually I started wearing some of the portraits since they fitted so well into standard identity tags.

It took me more or less forty years to realise that this family – stitched together by words such as *huis*, *kersfees*, *totsiens*, was all contained in a single word called acceptance. Eleven generations later, the descendants of a German soldier called Friedrich Both, who arrived in the Cape from Wangenheim, Germany, in 1678, are scattered all over the globe. Some are living in America, some have returned to Europe, but most of us are still here in this precarious place called home.

HENRY BREDEKAMP

In 1816 farm labourer "Gert" Bredekamp and his family were granted permission to settle on the Khoekhoe (Khoikhoi) mission station Genadendal. In 1821 he was baptised Jacobus. His grandson married Henrietta (1875-1960) who gave birth to my father, Phillipus Anton. My father married Martha van de Rheede (1918-1996). I had only one brother, Jacobus, who died at the age of two when he was hit by a car. My mother was subsequently admitted to a psychiatric institution. After her discharge she faithfully cared for my father till he died of TB in 1950. She then left for

Cape Town where she worked as domestic
servant, while my grandmother, Henrietta, raised
me. I matriculated from the local high school after
her death and then I qualified as a primary school
teacher. Later I enrolled for part-time studies at
the University of the Western Cape. Having
headed UWC's Institute for Historical Research
since 1995, in 2002 I became CEO of Iziko
Museums, Cape Town

Elsabé Brink

Nicky du Plessis

ELSABÉ BRINK

I am a historian and specialise in the history of
Johannesburg where I live. The lives of the
people of this metropolis, at heart still an
overgrown mining town, fascinate me. I have
written on the history of Newtown, one of the
oldest quarters of the city, for example, and on
events around the outbreak of the Anglo-Boer
(South African) War. I recently edited tran-
scribed interviews with people who were at
school in Soweto on 16 June 1976.
My forebears, who were of Scottish, French
and German extraction, include a long line of
teachers and ministers of religion; however,
both my parents became writers. On my
mother's side I am the sixth generation to carry
the name Elsabé Antoinette, a tradition that
has been extended to my daughter (19), the
seventh generation. I also have a son (21) and
am married to an architect. Currently I run Ilifa
Research, my own historical research and
tourism consultancy.

CAROHN CORNELL

I am an oral-history researcher and writer living
in Cape Town. From childhood we identified
ourselves as South Africans: it was an insult to
be called English. My father, born in 1917, was
a Cape Town journalist, and my mother, born
in 1923, a secretary. My father's father, born in
Devon in 1867, was a writer and prospector in
Brazil and California and, from 1901, in South
Africa. My Cornish grandmother had eloped to
marry him in Madeira. My mother's father, born
in Tasmania in 1889, worked in post offices on
the Rand from age 13. My one great-
grandmother was a Kimberley diamond sorter
whose Irish family farmed in the Eastern Cape
from the 1820s. My great-grandfathers, all born
in England, were a gamekeeper, a farmer, a
master builder, and an accountant who became
mayor of Kimberley, East Rand auctioneer and
hotelkeeper, and Anglo-Boer War scout.

Carohn Cornell

Paul Faber

NICKY DU PLESSIS

One of my great-grandmothers was interned in
an English concentration camp during the
Anglo-Boer War, where three of her daughters
died. She refused to speak English ever again.
My maternal grandmother was left an orphan in
the great flu epidemic of 1918 at the age 12 and
began her teaching career four years later. My
mother is an English-speaking South African,
while my father's mother tongue is Afrikaans –
because of this, their alliance was not easily
accepted at first. Our family story is a modest
one of middle-class professional lives and
aspirations, offset by the various social and
political changes that have taken place since
my birth in 1961. When I travelled to Europe as
a student in the 1980s, I sometimes pretended I
was Australian to avoid the shame of being a
white South African. I have a Master of Arts
degree, live in Durban and work in arts
administration and project management.

PAUL FABER

I am rooted in the north of the Netherlands.
My father's family has been living in Friesland
for centuries. My great-grandfather had a bar in
Leeuwarden. My grandfather joined the army to
serve in Dutch East India. Upon his return, he
started a butchery. However, in the course of

David Goldblatt

the First World War his business collapsed and
the family fell upon hard times. My father,
the eldest son, reversed the situation and
eventually became director of a chain of food
distribution shops. He married my mother,
the daughter of a municipal overseer and a
bargeman's daughter, in 1941, during the
Second World War. My mother also grew up in
Leeuwarden. Born in 1951, during the post-war
reconstruction period, I am their third and last
child. I studied history of art in Amsterdam and
started working in anthropology museums,
because it enabled me to travel endlessly,
either in reality or by means
of exhibitions. Currently I am Africa curator at
the Tropenmuseum in Amsterdam.

DAVID GOLDBLATT

I was born in Randfontein, South Africa, in
1930, as the third son of Eli Goldblatt and

Paul Grendon

Petros Gumbi

Catherine Henegan

George Hallett

Rayda Jacobs

Olga Light, both of who came to South Africa as children with their parents, to escape the persecution of the Lithuanian Jewish Community in the 1890s. I became interested in photography in high school, but after trying unsuccessfully to enter the profession I went to work in my father's men's outfitting store. After the death of my father in 1962 I sold the family business and have since then devoted all of my time to photography. My professional work has involved assignments for magazines, corporations and institutions. My personal work consists of a series of critical explorations of South African society, a number of which have been exhibited and published in book form.

PAUL GRENDON

Frederick Kruger, of German descent, was born in Prince Albert, a small town in the Karoo. He drove the mail coach (*poskar*) before becoming a train driver. He married Elizabeth Theron, of French descent. In 1927 their daughter Anna (1909) married Frederick Mears (1900), also a train driver. Their daughter Freda Mears, who became my mother, was born in 1930. After the family moved to Cape Town she met my father William Grendon. They married in 1953. Joseph Grendon was a guano trader who operated between Cape Town and Windhoek in Namibia. His wife came from the Isle of Wight. Their son became a shoemaker in a suburb of Cape Town. My father was born in 1923. He has worked as a fitter and turner in the engineering trade. I was born in Cape Town in 1954 and have worked as an artist and photographer since 1982. My sister Karen (1956) died in a car accident in 1975.

PETROS GUMBI

My mother died when I was a year old, and so I grew up with my grandparents in Amahlubi Township outside Estcourt in the KwaZulu-Natal midlands. I enjoyed science and football at school, but was forced to leave in Standard

Seven when my family could no longer afford to educate me. I worked at the post office for a short while and then at the NuHair factory in Johannesburg for two years. On a home visit my uncle suggested I try doing art at Ardmore. At first I added the sculptural decorations to the functional ceramic ware, but while Matthew Stitzlein worked at the Studio I was inspired to create my own work. I am saving money to pay *lobola* (bridewealth) so that I can marry my girlfriend.

GEORGE HALLETT

I grew up in the picturesque fishing village of Hout Bay during the fifties. My family and friends were of many colours and religious persuasions. Race, as a distinguishing feature, was introduced to my community and, therefore, my consciousness, by the Nationalist Party. The scale of complexions from white through the various hues of brown to black determined the social pecking order. Families of mixed ancestry would talk about their European descendants, leaving the indigenous family out. It became clear very early on that my father's father was English; that he was an officer in the British army; that he married a woman from St Helena Island called Rebecca. However, my mother's parents were never

spoken about. After my mother's death, my uncle informed me that my mother's parents were Indian and Chinese. There is a photograph of a very stern-looking Asian gentleman in my family's collection. This apparently is my mother's father. Why is there still so much secrecy surrounding my family's ancestors? One thing is for sure, I am very happy in my skin and not a *pigmentocrat*.

CATHERINE HENEGAN

I was born in Johannesburg in 1968. Since 1992 I work as a theatre-maker and multi-media artist, living and working between Johannesburg and Amsterdam. My father, born in 1930, lived in Johannesburg most of his life. His mother's father was a missionary who came out from England to South Africa in the late 1800s and married another recent immigrant from Nottingham. My paternal grandfather's parents were Irish 1820 settlers. My mother was born in Kitwe, Zambia, in 1933. Her parents worked on the copper mine for some time. My maternal grandmother was born in 1911. She was the descendent of Scottish settlers from around 1820 and early Dutch settlers in the Cape. My maternal grandfather was born in 1905. His father was scout for Lord Kitchener. He came out from

Anton Kannemeyer

Steve Lebelo

Sonja Loots

Sean Laurenz

Canada during the Anglo-Boer War and fell in love with a Boer.

RAYDA JACOBS

My parents are Muslim, with a white grandfather in the mix. I grew up in Diep River, the eldest of seven children. I started writing at a very young age, and sent my first story off to Springbok Radio at age 12. I left South Africa in 1968 – a kind of forced departure – and lived in Canada for 27 years. A first collection of short stories, *The Middle Children*, was published in Canada in 1994. Three novels followed: *Eyes of the Sky*, *The Slave Book*, and recently, *Sachs Street*. I have also written various articles and hosted two radio programmes on culture, identity, and religion, and have produced three documentaries

ANTON KANNEMEYER

My grandfather, Jan Broer, had a tobacco shop in Amsterdam for many years. I once visited him, back in 1979. He still lives in Amsterdam, but has serious health problems, as he used to be a heavy smoker. My mother was born in Amsterdam in 1943. At the age of 12, she moved to South Africa with her mother and stepfather. He was the owner of a weapons factory. My mother met my father, John

Kannemeyer (1939, Robertson, South Africa) in Cape Town, a lecturer in Afrikaans and Dutch at UCT at the time. My mother studied languages as well, specialising in Afrikaans and French. I was born in 1967 while she was writing her final Honours exams in Afrikaans. My father's father was born in Vanwyksdorp in the Klein Karoo and grew up in Ladysmith. He was a carpenter and businessman. The Kannemeyers originally came from Elsas-Lotharingen. Today most Kannemeyers are from the "Coloured" community – the most famous being a fullback for Bafana-Bafana, the national soccer team.

SEAN LAURENZ

I was born in Durban in 1970 and have one younger brother (also a photographer). My mother is of European descent. Her family left France in the mid 1800s to farm sugar in Mauritius. When she was 18, her mother and elder sister, Françoise, left Mauritius and settled in Durban (her father died when she was three years old). Her other three sisters had already married and settled in Melbourne and Sao Paolo, with the eldest remaining in Mauritius. My father was an only child, born in Cape Town. He spent his childhood and teens in Kimberley where he began working for De Beers. His father died when he was 12 and his mother raised him. I was married two years ago to my wonderful wife Liesl Coppin, who is an actor and a singer. We recently had a beautiful boy, Noah Luc.

STEVE LEBELO

I was born in Orlando East in 1958, one of the oldest townships in Johannesburg. In 1962 my family moved to a new township, Diepkloof. In 1976, when I was in Grade 11, the Soweto student uprising broke out. I was an active

member of the Soweto Students Representative Council. So I stayed in Lesotho for some time, was arrested and returned to school in 1980. I studied history at the University of the Witwatersrand and have lectured and done research in this field. Since 2000 I am Development Officer of the Wits University Foundation.

SONJA LOOTS

My family originally came from Amsterdam, where the first Jan Loots was commander of the pilot boats in the Amsterdam harbour, circa 1600, and his eldest son, "de jonge Jan Cornelisz Loots", was mayor (the name Loots is derived from the old Germanic word *Hloede*, which means leader or pathfinder). In 1719 their descendant, Jan Loots, emigrated to the Cape while in the employ of the Dutch East Indian Company (VOC). When I was a child, my father used to tell me that this ancestor of ours was a sailor – and that this was why his descendants swore so much. However, a family register tells me that on the journey to the Cape Jan Loots was the *"scheepsjoernaal schrijver"*. I like this because, like my forefather, I also earn my living as "schrijver" – not of ships' journals, but of newspaper and magazine articles, fiction and television scripts. In more recent times my Loots ancestors have been farmers, hard workers and jovial cursers.

ROBERT LUNGUPI

I was born on 15 October 1962 in Bulawayo, Zimbabwe. My father, a motor mechanic and driver, came from Tanzania in search of work. He married my mother in 1961, but already had five kids in Tanzania. My mother was Ndebele, and had four kids. I'm the last born on both sides. My father took us to Tanzania in 1968, where with my mother's support I started school in 1969. In 1970 my mom went back to Zimbabwe, leaving me with Dad, who then

Robert Lungupi

Motlhalefi Mahlabe

Shamim Meer

Langa Magwa

Bongani Mgijima

married a Tanzanian woman. After my mother separated from my father, no one cared about me. I only completed Form II. I learnt motor mechanics and welding, and later did some construction work on the Tanzanian pipeline. In 1985 I recognised art as a natural talent. In 1989 I had dreams about my mother, searched for her and finally found her in Zimbabwe. I came to Johannesburg in 1990 as freelance artist. Here I met Brett Sher who acts as my promoter and has arranged many exhibitions. We now teach apprentices and new artists.

LANGA MAGWA

My heritage is drawn from three diverse cultures: Swazi (my paternal grandfather), Zulu (his wife, and my father) and Xhosa, from my strong-willed mother. I spent most of my childhood with my Xhosa maternal grandfather, who was "good with his hands" – always constructing, fixing or carving something. He'll always be the core of my inspiration. Sadly, he passed away seven years ago. I underwent customary Zulu scarification because of my father, but this made me different from the other Xhosa children. I then also underwent the Xhosa ritual initiation ceremony of circumcision into manhood, which is not practised in Zulu culture.

The quest for my identity, the many unanswered questions, my roots in different cultures, the

implications of scarification, exposure to western art in a formal institution – all have had a profound influence on my work. My art is a tool in exploring the realities about the essence of my tribal customs.

MOTLHALEFI MAHLABE

I was born in 1965 in a small rural village called Ganyesa in the Vryburg district of the North West Province. Growing up in a highly religious family with a father belonging to the NG Kerk (Dutch Reformed Church) was never smooth. My mother, who is very creative and artistic, was employed as a domestic worker and supplemented the meagre salary of my father by sewing cloths. I am the first-born in a family of five children. After surviving a car accident and loosing a brother who shot himself, I found a well-balanced perspective on life. I matriculated in 1984, worked for book printers for three years and studied briefly at the University of South Africa. I then joined the Market Photography Workshop and *The Star* newspaper. I am slowly turning into a businessman and manage a photographic marketing and communications company. The Market Photography Workshop has become my second home.

SHAMIM MEER

I was born in Durban in 1953, the eldest of three. I had a deep sense of South African-ness. India was a place of my grandmother Khatija's childhood stories.
My grandmother Rachel was born in Kimberley of Irish, Dutch and Russian ancestry.
My grandfathers Moosa and Chota and grandmothers Khatija and Rasool came from India. Moosa ran a newspaper, *The Indian Views*, in Durban. My father, Ismail, a lawyer involved in the liberation struggle from his

youth, was active politically until his death in 2000. My mother Fatima, a professor of Sociology, fought apartheid all her life and at age 74 continues the fight for a more just society. I have worked as women's rights, media and political activist. I live in Johannesburg with my partner Bobby who I met while we were student activists in 1972. We have two children.

BONGANI MGIJIMA

My parents Sipumelele ("We have triumphed") and Ntombizandile ("Enough girls") Mtimkulu both hail from the Eastern Cape. For almost twenty years my father worked as a migrant worker for a dynamite-manufacturing factory in Somerset West. Out of the small salary he earned, he managed to send me and my sister, Nonkosi, to study at the University of Western Cape. I have two younger brothers, Mlungiseleli (1982), Yongama (1987), and one sister Nonkosi (1979). My siblings grew up and went to school in Alice. Because of the racist laws of the time we could not visit our father in Somerset West until 1990. The Mgijimas are quite a big family, based in the Sheshegu village of Alice. My grandfather Nkosinkulu Mgijima worked in a glass-manufacturing factory in Port Elizabeth. There is little known

Sibongiseni Mkhize

Sam Nhlengethwa

Cedric Nunn

Ruth Motau

Dumisane Ntshangase

about him, but according to oral tradition, his father was Kolisi, the son of Balincwadi, the son of Kapoko, the son of Mgijima.

SIBONGISENI MKHIZE

According to oral tradition my great-grand-father, Tibela Mkhize, married a woman from the Ndlela clan in the nearby Impendle during the 1910s. One of their children, Vukuza, married a woman from the Sokhela clan in Bulwer during the 1930s. One of their sons was my father, Zwelakhe. In 1971, Zwelakhe got married to Thembeni Hlela and I am their first-born. My grandmother, born in 1924, is the only surviving grandparent and she has passed down many invaluable family traditions to me.

I started school in 1978. In 1985 I went to live with my father who was a migrant worker at Pietermaritzburg. That move introduced me to an urban way of life. I'm now Director of the Voortrekker Museum in Pietermaritzburg.

RUTH MOTAU

I was born 34 years ago from Susan Phale and Adam Motau. My grandfather died when my father was five, therefore we don't know anything about him. My grandmother Ruth remarried a priest, Thomas, and had six more

children with him. They moved to Johannes-burg to look for employment in the early forties. My grandparents on my mother's side, Johanna and Solomon, were blessed with eight children. Solomon and Johanna stayed in the rural area of Pankop in what is now the North West Province. When they were old enough, their children went out to work and sent money home every month. All my grandparents died. I'm lucky to still have both my parents. My parents have nine children; I am the youngest. All my family is alive. We are not living together but are also not far from each other. I have an eight-year-old son named Bogosi who is in his second year of primary school.

SAM NHLENGETHWA

I was born in Payneville, Springs, in 1955, the fifth of eight children. I was a sickly child, so my mother took me to her mother Sophia Mokoena in Heidelberg because she thought I would then survive. I stayed with my grand-mother until I was 15. She sold second-hand clothes. Then I returned to Springs. My mother was a domestic worker and my father worked in a factory in Payneville. He died in 1975. With so many mouths to feed, it was very difficult for my mother. It is tragic

that she died of long cancer in February 2002. My elder brother Rankatang was a jazz musician.

I played his records, visited *shebeens* with him. He died in 1988. When I didn't listen to jazz, I was drawing. After 1976 I followed an art course and in 1990 I had my first one-person exhibition. Since then I have had many exhibitions and commissions.

DUMISANE NTSHANGASE

I was born in Soweto in 1965. Like all black children who grew up in Soweto in the 1970s, my life was affected by the political events unfolding in that community at the time. During my youth, I was exposed to a vibrant cultural life in Soweto, particularly through *stokvels*, shebeens and outdoor social and cultural events. Through this I was introduced to the name and fame of, among others, Dolly Rathebe. I went to school in Soweto and completed my university degrees at the University of the Witwatersrand. I am currently pursuing a PhD in forensic linguistics at the same university. I have taught at the Johannes-burg College of Education and the University of the Witwatersrand. I am the father of three lovely children.

CEDRIC NUNN

I was born in 1957 as the fifth of seven children born to Herbert and Lily Nunn. My parents lived and worked at a store in Hluhluwe, KwaZulu-Natal, where I grew up. When I was seven or eight years old, I went to primary school at Mangete, about 300 km from home. Mangete was the home place of my father's mother, Elizabeth Nunn (née Dunn), and my dad inherited land from her. Later I moved to the junior high school in iXopo in the Natal midlands, from which I was expelled a few years later. I worked in the Amatikulu Sugar Mill for eight years before embarking on a career in photography. Self-taught, I joined the

Wonderboy Thokozani Nxumalo

Claudette Schreuders

Penny Siopis

Robert Papini

Berni Searle

Afrapix Photographers Collective and was a member till its demise in the early nineties. I have been free-lancing since then, with a two-year stint as part-time director of the Market Photography Workshop, in 1999 and 2000. I am now living in Johannesburg.

WONDERBOY THOKOZANI NXUMALO

I was born in Greytown, KwaZulu-Natal, and grew up on a farm where my father was employed as a farm worker and my mother as a domestic worker. My father died when I was six years old and I could attend school only up to Grade 6. My mother's employer saw my sketchbooks and phoned Fee at the Ardmore studio to ask if I could work with her. I started there in 1994. Fee showed me the work of the Namibian artist John Muafangejo, and in 1995, I received training in graphic techniques at Caversham Mill. I strongly believe in peace and that people should not kill each other. I'm a vegetarian and do not drink or smoke.

ROBERT PAPINI

I was born in Mombasa, Kenya, in 1960. My Tuscan-born father moved here after the Second World War, during which he was a Blackshirt youth volunteer against the USSR. During the Nazi occupation of Italy, his mother was killed in crossfire while she took provisions to her husband, a socialist school-teacher, who was in hiding in the country.

My father built Lokitaung gaol in northern Kenya where Jomo Kenyatta was held during the independence struggle.
My mother's Welsh-Irish father, a Johannesburg orphan, took his young family to Southern Rhodesia in the 1930s, to pioneer two gold-mines that remained relentlessly low-yield. My English grandmother's family boasted a major who was beheaded in some cavalry charge in British India.
I have lived in Africa for 35 years and among other things have taught English in Sudan and Zimbabwe. Four of the remaining six years of my life I spent chasing a degree at Canterbury and Oxford. Currently I am attached to the KwaMuhle Museum in Durban.

CLAUDETTE SCHREUDERS

Three of my grandparents were Dutch. My one German grandmother, Marie Luise Dettmar, was adopted by a Dutch family. My father grew up in Tiel, Holland. He came to South Africa on his own when he was 16. According to him, he was the first and last person to take part in a South African government scheme of the time to bring Dutch orphans to South Africa. He was not an orphan, however, he just wanted to live in Africa. He finished school and university in South Africa and then hitchhiked back to

Holland through Africa. After a few months he returned and met my mother. Her father grew up in Boskoop, Holland. Of the 11 children, five immigrated to South Africa. My grandfather became engaged to my German grandmother and they got married in South Africa a year later. He was a *dominee* in Volksrust for many years. My mother studied graphic art and painted while we (her four children) were at school. It was from her that I got the idea to become an artist. Neither I nor any of my three siblings speak Dutch.

BERNI SEARLE

I was born in 1964, in Cape Town, where I grew up and later pursued my studies at the Michaelis School of Fine Art. I taught art at secondary school level and at Stellenbosch University for three years before becoming a full-time artist. In the "Colour Me" series, I used spices to explore ideas relating to identity, heritage and memory. On a personal level, the use of spices refers to the tentative connections between me and my maternal great-grandfathers who came from Mauritius and Saudi Arabia. I feel equally distanced from the heritage of my paternal great-grandfathers who came from Germany and England. I know very little about my great-grandmothers. Working on this project with the Manuel family has been an inspiration for me to continue trying to find out more, whatever the obstacles may be.

PENNY SIOPIS

My father, Constantinos Siopis, was born and bred in Thessaloniki, Greece. In 1942, sick and wounded after battling the Allied forces in Egypt, he was sent to South Africa to recuperate. He met my mother, Anna Frangetis, at Baragwaneth hospital in Johannesburg.

Derrick Thema

Annari van der Merwe

Bie Venter

Roger van Wijk

Andrew Verster

My father never really adjusted to South Africa and many years later returned to Greece, where he died in 1997. My mother's father was also Greek. He left his island Andros as stowaway when he was sixteen. Later he became involved with the film industry and eventually owned several bioscopes. He also had business interests in other parts of the world and owned a bioscope in Smyrna. Between 1919 and 1929 he stayed in Europe and Turkey with his wife and child (my mother). My mother's mother, Dorothy Tothill, was of English descent. She came to South Africa with her parents at a very tender age.

DERRICK THEMA

I am a Johannesburg-based journalist and writer. I have worked as a journalist for 26 years, for *The Sowetan*, *The Star* newspaper and *Tribute* magazine. I was born in Sophiatown, Johannesburg, but grew up in Meadowlands in Soweto where the former residents of Sophiatown were relocated after the forced removals of the 1950s. My father and mother came to seek greener pastures in Johannesburg from the rural area of Ga-Mamabolo, 20 kilometres north of Pietersburg, situated in the north of the old Transvaal province (today called Limpopo). My first book, *Kortboy – A Sophiatown Legend*, was published by Kwela Books in 1999.

ANNARI VAN DER MERWE

I grew up on a sheep farm in the Karoo, as the fourth child of Christoffel Philippus van der Merwe and Johanna Adriana van Heerden. I chose a career that took me away from my farming roots, unlike my two brothers and two sisters, who are all still involved with farming, like all our South African ancestors. We are eleventh generation South African.

Willem Schalk, the *stamvader* of the Van der Merwes, arrived at the Cape from Dordrecht circa 1660 and married Ann Prévot, a French Huguenot from Calais. According to an old Afrikaans family tradition I was, as second daughter, named after my father's mother. I studied literature at the universities of Port Elizabeth and Rhodes in the Eastern Cape and Utrecht in the Netherlands. After being involved with Tafelberg Publishers in Cape Town for almost twenty years, I now head a small publishing house in Cape Town.

ROGER VAN WYK

My parents met in the 1950s, flying between Salisbury and London. My mother, in a quest for independence from a wealthy Rhodesian family, unsupportive of professional education for women, took a job with Central African Airways. My father, then a commercial aviator, grew up in rural poverty in the former Transvaal through the 1930s depression and served in North Africa during the Second World War. We have ancestors on either side of the Anglo-Boer War, some fought in the same battles. My father's parents survived British concentration camps as children and later supported Smuts and Union. My brother Gary (born in 1960) and I (born in

1964) grew up in suburban Cape Town and Johannesburg in an anglicised home of modest means. Politicised and drawn to the arts, a decade of intense political and cultural activism was our reality through the turmoil of the 1980s. Gary now has a gallery of southern African arts in Manhattan and I design exhibitions.

BIE VENTER

I was born a Scorpio, second of the four children of Erla (née Louw) and De Waal Venter, in 1970, in Krugersdorp at Paardekraal Hospitaal, which is now Yusuf Dadoo Hospital in Mohale City. My parents got married in 1969, immediately after my mom qualified as occupational therapist and my dad had published two poetry anthologies.

The Venter clan came from Hameln, Germany, in the eighteenth century. There are French Du Toits on my maternal grandmother's side, and two Swedish Erlank brothers were shipwrecked on the shores of Africa. A long line of civil servants – teachers and policemen on both sides – had to explode artistically at some point. After studying fine art at Stellenbosch University, I got involved in exhibition logistics, and have since packed and exported the work of many South African artists. I live in Bertrams, one of the oldest and most run-down neighbourhoods of Johannesburg, with Toni Morkel, the funniest actress in South Africa.

Endnotes and sources

Paul Weinberg

ANDREW VERSTER

My grandfathers were soldiers on different sides in the South African (Anglo-Boer) War. A generation and three decades later my mother (English-speaking, Anglican), married my father, (Afrikaans, Dutch Reformed), and, in one family, at least, the War was over. We have farmers, journalists, broadcasters, a bookkeeper, chemist, butcher, miner, social worker, hotelier, singer and pianist in our various clans. My brother is clever with electrical things and I am a painter. He lives in a Spanish house in a new suburb of Benoni; my house is Edwardian and in Durban. I write plays for radio, design operas, work with architects and make tapestries.

PAUL WEINBERG

As a child I remember very clearly the black trunk that held the family heirlooms and other secrets. The letters, stamps, photographs and postcards were the connection to a world far beyond the borders of South Africa and the African continent.
My "roots" I understood to be deeply South African. The black trunk defied this. The Weinbergs hailed from Riga, Latvia. Like many other Jews in the world who found themselves in a state of turmoil at the turn of the nineteenth century, they became part of a massive migration from Europe. German- and Russian-speaking, they opted for Africa.
The one side of the family got into the hotel business. Grandpa Harry from Bella-Russia was a *hassin* (singer in the synagogue), a reverend and a *moll* (the one who circumcises). My parents benefited from the hard work of my grandparents, becoming part of the professional class of modern-day Jews. I am a product of this family, a photographer living on the southern tip of Africa.

Portraits by **Paul Faber** with the exception of Gumbi, Lungupi, Nxumalo and Thema

The Nunn Family

Sources

BOOKS

Ballard, C. *John Dunn: The White Chief of Zululand.* Johannesburg: AD Donker Publisher, 1985.
Bryant, A.T. *Olden Times in Zululand and Natal containing earlier political history of the Eastern Nguni clans* (facsimile reprint). Cape Town: C. Struik, (Pty.) Ltd, 1956.
Etherington, N. *The Great Treks: The Transformation of Southern Africa, 1815-1854.* Edinburgh: Pearson Education Ltd., 2001.
Gardiner, A.F. *Narrative of a journey to the Zoolu [sic] country in South Africa* (facsimile reprint). Cape Town: C. Struik, (Pty.) Ltd, 1966.
Guy, J. *The Destruction of the Zulu Kingdom.* Johannesburg: Ravan Press, 1982.
Guy, J. "The destruction and reconstruction of Zulu society". In Marks, S. & Rathbone, R. *Industrialisation and Social Change in South Africa, African Class formation, culture and consciousness, 1870-1930.* New York: Longman, 1982.
Guy, J. "Gender oppression in southern Africa's pre-capitalist societies". In Walker, C. (ed.), *Women and Gender in Southern Africa to 1945,* Cape Town: David Philip, 1990.
Krige, E.J. *The Social System of the Zulus.* London: Longmans, Green & Co., 1950.
Laband, J. *Rope of Sand: The Rise and Fall of the Zulu Kingdom in the Nineteenth Century.* Johannesburg: Jonathan Ball, 1995.
Malherbe, J. *Port Natal: A Pioneer Story.* Cape Town: Howard Timmins, 1965.
Moodie, D.C.F. *John Dunn, Cetswayo and the Three Generals – John Dunn's Notes.* Pietermaritzburg: Natal Printing and Publishing Company, 1886.

Morrell, R. "Forging a Ruling Race: Rugby and White Masculinity in Colonial Natal, c.1870-1910". In Nauright, J. & Candler, T.J.L. (eds). *Making Men: Rugby and Masculine Identity,* London: Frank Cass, 1996.
Russel, G. *The History of Old Durban, and Reminiscences of an emigrant of 1850.* Durban: P. Davis & Sons, 1899.
Van Jaarsveld, A. *Mtunzini: A History, from Earliest Times to 1995.* Mtunzini: Published by A. van Jaarsveld, 1998.
Webb, C. de B. & Wright, J.B. *The James Stuart Archive of recorded oral evidence relating to the History of the Zulu and Neighbouring Peoples,* Volumes I-IV. Pietermaritzburg: University of Natal Press, 1986.

ARTICLES

Pridmore, J. "'Pioneers' and 'natives': establishing the Natal 'meta-narrative'? 1825-1860". In *Kleio,* XXVIII, 1996, pp. 50-61.
Pridmore, J. "The wives of Henry Fynn: Unwritten but potentially transfiguring texts? The untold biographies of Vundhlazi of the Zelemu and Christina Brown". In *Alter Nation: Journal of the Centre for the Study of Southern African Literature and Languages,* Vol. 4, No. 1, 1997, pp.73-83.
Tosh, J. "What should historians do with masculinity? Reflections on Nineteenth Century Britain". In *History Workshop Journal,* Issue 38, 1994.

ORAL SOURCES

Interviews conducted by E Brink:
Clark, Gerald, Mangete 5 May 2001.
Davenhill, Sheila, Nongoma 4 May 2001.
Louw, Amy, Nongoma, 4 May 2001.
Louw, Ronny, Nongoma, 4 May 2001.
Louw, Tiny, Nongoma, 4 May 2001.
Nunn, Lily, Mangete, 5 May 2001.

terviews conducted by Cedric Nunn:
ouw, Amy, Nongoma, 10 April 1998.

would also like to thank Busi Xaba, Gandhi
alungane, Elsa Brink, Ron Viney and Louis
rundlingh for their help.

he Rathebe Family

Endnotes

Drum, January 1957, p. 39.
. It was a year after the National Party had
ome into power and its policy of apartheid was
lowly being implemented. The BMSC, a huge
omplex in the city centre, was the only venue
n Johannesburg where organised entertainment for Africans could be presented.
. Peter Davis, *In Darkest Hollywood. Exploring
he jungles of cinema's South Africa*. Athens:
Ravan Press/Ohio University Press, 1996,
. 28.
. Ibid, p. 20.
5. Ibid, p. 30.
5. *Drum*, April 1957, p. 63.
7. Ibid, p. 67.
8. *Drum*, February 1963, p. 14.
9. Ibid, p. 14.

Sources

BOOKS
Davis, Peter. *In Darkest Hollywood. Exploring
the jungles of cinema's South Africa*. Athens:
Ravan Press/Ohio University Press, 1996.
Molefe, ZB & Mzileni, M. *A Common Hunger to
Sing*. Cape Town: Kwela Books, 1997.
Musiker, N. and R. *Historical Dictionary of
Greater Johannesburg*. Lanham, Maryland &
Oxford: The Scarecrow Press, 1999.
NN. "This time it's for keeps". In: *Drum*,
February 1963.
Schadeberg, Jürgen. *Sof'town Blues – Images
from the black '50s*. Johannesburg: J Schade-
berg, 1994.
Themba, Can. "Dolly and her men". In: *Drum*,
January 1957.
Themba, Can. "Dolly". In: *Drum*, April 1957.
Themba, Can. "Dolly". In: *Drum*, January 1957.
Themba, Can. "Dolly". In: *Drum*, March 1957.
Themba, Can. "Dolly". In: *Drum*, May 1957.

ORAL SOURCES
Interviews with Dolly Rathebe by Dumisane
Ntshangase, 2001.
Interviews with Dolly Rathebe by Derrick
Thema, 2002.

The Plaatje Family

Endnotes

1. Solomon T Plaatje, *Native Life in South
Africa*, London, 1916, pp. 61-62.
2. H.T. Wangemann, *En Zweites Reisejahr in
Sud-Afrika*, Berlin, 1886, p. 63. Quoted in Brian
Willan, *Sol Plaatje – South African Nationalist,
1876—1932*. Berkeley and Los Angeles:
University of California Press, 1984, p. 19.
3. Ibid, p. 50.
4. J.L. Comaroff (ed.), *The Boer War Diary of
Sol T. Plaatje. An African at Mafeking*.
MacMillan London Ltd, London & Basingstoke,
1973, p. 7.
5. Ibid, p. 49.
6. Ibid, p. 87.
7. Willan, 1984, p. 106.
8. Plaatje, 1916, p. 15.
9. CO 537/1137, "(Secret) Minutes of Deputation
of South African Natives. Statement by
Plaatje." Quoted in Willan, 1984, p. 242.
10. Ibid, p. 374.
11. Ibid, p. 384.
12. Obituary: Johannes Plaatje.

Sources

Comaroff, J.L. (ed.). *The Boer War Diary of Sol
T. Plaatje. An African at Mafeking*. MacMillan
London Ltd, London & Basingstoke, 1973.
Plaatje, Solomon. T *Native Life in South Africa*,
London:, 1916.
Willan, Brian. *Sol Plaatje – South African
Nationalist, 1876—1932*. Berkeley and Los
Angeles: University of California Press, 1984.
Obituary Johannes Plaatje, Kimberley, 2001.

ORAL SOURCES
Interviews with Tumi Plaatje in 2001, 2002.

The Steyn Family

Endnotes

1. The tree still stands on the farm today and
has been declared a national monument.
Ruiter, Steyn's trusted *agterryer* in the Anglo-
Boer War, was buried there and the ashes of
his grandson, Judge M.T. Steyn, scattered at
the spot.
2. When Britain declared war on Germany,
South Africa's dominion status meant that it
was automatically at war, and its troops were
mobilised to invade German South West Africa.
This sparked the Rebellion of 1914-15, led by
former Anglo-Boer War generals. De Wet
headed one of these rebel commandos. When
Steyn sent his son Colin to try to persuade him,
it was too late, and De Wet was in no mood for
reconciliation (Meintjes: 234–237, Schoeman
1980:237). The government used 32 000 troops
to suppress the Rebellion, and more than 300
men lost their lives in the fighting.
3. In 1933, when Advocate Tielman Roos was
trying to undermine Herzog and Dr D.F. Malan
headed the new National Party, the Steyns
were divided. Colin supported Roos, Tibbie the
coalition government of Hertzog and Smuts and
her daughter Emmie the new National Party
(Schoeman 1982: 147). In subsequent years,
Tibbie's daughter Hannah Fichardt was a
general of the military women's movement, the
South African Women's Auxiliary Service;
Gladys represented the United Party in the
Provincial Legislature; Tibbie Jnr married Nico
van der Merwe, who was later appointed head
of the ruling party in the Free State; and
Emmie was a general in the subversive
Ossewa Brandwag organisation. In 1948, when
the National Party unexpectedly won the
elections, Colin and Gladys were disappointed,
Tibbie quietly pleased and Tibbie Jnr and her
new husband, Cornelius Visser, elated (Truter
1997: 243).
4. Colin's grandfather – also Colin, and the
grandson of President Steyn – was sent to war
as a child of 11 or 12 to fight as a so-called
penkop, and was handed a rifle that was
smaller than those used by adult soldiers.
5. South Africa's military intervention in Angola
followed Soviet-Cuban intervention in the
territory, created by the Portuguese withdrawal
and the outbreak of civil war between the rival
liberation movements UNITA (National Union for
the Total Independence of Angola), FNLA
(National Front for the Liberation of Angola)
and the MPLA (Movement for the Popular
Liberation of Angola) (Spence: 5, Edicao: 1).
The involvement of Russia and Cuba led to a

perception in South Africa that the Soviet-Cuban bridgehead in Angola was clear evidence of Russia's "total onslaught" against white rule, the objective of which (it was argued) was to gain exclusive access to South Africa's extensive mineral resources. The liberation movement – the ANC (African National Congress) in South Africa and SWAPO (South West African People's Organisation) in what is now Namibia in particular – thus acquired new and threatening significance for the Nationalist government in South Africa (Spence: 6). The South African incursions between 1981 and 1993 were "partly in retaliation for MPLA support for SWAPO's guerilla war against South Africa's occupation of Namibia" (Edicao: 1). Namibia only achieved independence after the South African Defence Force's failed attempt to take Cuito-Cuanavale in Angola resulted in a stalemate between the South Africans on one side and the Cuban and Angolan forces on the other. This laid the foundations for peace negotiations and, under an agreement reached in December 1988, Angola, Cuba and South Africa agreed to the withdrawal of all foreign forces from Angola. South Africa committed itself to begin an independence plan for Namibia (Maier: 5), and Namibia eventually achieved independence in 1990. The ANC was finally unbanned in South Africa. Forças Armadas Populares de Libertação de Angola (FAPLA) was one of the liberation movements in Angola at the time (Maier: 4).

Sources

BOOKS

Beyers, C.J. *Suid-Afrikaanse Biografiese Woordeboek*. Pretoria: Tafelberg, 1977.
Kruger, N. *Rachel Isabella Steyn: Presidents-vrou*. Cape Town: Nasionale Pers, 1949.
Meintjes, J. *President Steyn. A biography*. Cape Town: Nasionale Boekhandel, 1969.
Pretorius, F. (Ed.) *Scorched Earth*. Cape Town: Human & Rousseau, 2001.
Schoeman, K. *Bloemfontein: Die ontstaan van die stad 1846–1946*. Cape Town: Human & Rousseau, 1980.
Schoeman, K. *In liefde en trou: Die lewe van President en Mevrou M.T. Steyn*. Cape Town: Human & Rousseau, 1982.
Spies, S.B. *Methods of barbarism: Roberts and Kitchener and civilians in the Boer Republics, January 1900–May 1902*. Cape Town: Human & Rousseau, 1977.
Van der Merwe, N.J.V. *Marthinus Theunis Steyn. 'n Lewensbeskrywing. Deel II*. Cape Town: Nasionale Boekhandel, 1921.

Van Hemert, M. *Families van Ou Swellendam. Deel 1. Steyn*. Swellendam: Drostdy Museum, 1999.

ORAL SOURCES

Steyn, Mrs Yyvonne, Onze Rust, Kaalspruit, district Bloemfontein, 14 March and 27–28 July 2001.
Steyn, Mrs Jackie, Onze Rust, Kaalspruit, district Bloemfontein, 14 March and 27–28 July 2001.
Steyn, Advocate Elize, Tamboerskloof, Cape Town, 30 June 2001.
Steyn, Advocate Colin, Onze Rust, Kaalspruit, district Bloemfontein, 27–28 July 2001.
Steyn, Mr Theuns, Tamboerskloof, Cape Town, 30 June 2001.
Steyn, Ms Isabella, Durbanville, Cape Town, 2 July 2001.

ARTICLES

De Bruin, Philip. "Kanker word oudregter se grootste uitdaging". In: *Die Burger*, 16 February 1998.
Edição, S. "Angola Unravels. The Rise and Fall of the Lusaka Peace Process". In: *Human Rights Watch Report*, December 1999.
Fichardt, T. "The illness of President M.T. Steyn". In: *Suid-Afrikaanse Mediese Tydskrif*, 24 November 1973.
Maier, K. "Angola: Peace at Last". In: *Writenet Country Papers*, May 1997.
Spence, J.E. "Southern Africa in the Cold War". In: *History Today*, February 1999.
Thornycroft, P. "Tale of the Angolan War". In: *Mail & Guardian*, 27 October 1997.
Truter, E. "Verset en volharding: Die lewe van Rachel Isabella (Tibbie) Steyn gedurende die Anglo-Boereoorlog". In: *Literator*, November 1999.
Van Heerden, E. "Vyf se reis was een van heimwee". In: *Beeld* (Plus), 25 August 2001.
Venter, J. "Theunie Steyn, die groot skadu-boom weg. Met vaste tred het hy geloop op dié 'strand van 'n vreemde see'." In: *Rapport*, 19 April 1998.
Wald, K. "Mandela thanks Cuba for its solidarity". In: *Green Left Weekly* Home Page, accessed on: www.jinx.sistm.unsw.edu.au./~greenlft/1991/23/23p18.htm.

The Le Fleur Family

Endnotes

1. Wicomb, Zoë. *David's Story*. Cape Town: Kwela Books, 2000, p. 41.
2. Le Fleur, E.M.S. Document, 20-08-1964.
3. Anthony Le Fleur Private Archives, Knysna (hereafter "Knysna Archives"). Document (with pages missing), by A.A.S. Le Fleur on "History of 1884", written in Kraaifontein, dated 30 September 1938.
4. Ibid.
5. Davenport, R. and Saunders, C. *South Africa: A modern history*. London: MacMillan Press, 2000, p. 152.
6. Edgar, R. and Saunders, C. "A.A.S. Le Fleur and the Griqua Trek of 1917: Segregation, Self-help, and Ethnic identity". In: *The International Journal of African Historical Studies*, Volume 15, Number 2, 1982, p. 203.
7. Rainier, M. "Andries Abraham Stockenström Le Fleur and the Griquas of Kranshoek". In: *Quarterly Bulletin of the South African Library*, Volume 52, Number 2. Cape Town: South African Library, December 1997, p. 56.
8. Waldman, L. "The Griqua Conundrum: Political and socio-cultural identity in the Northern Cape, South Africa" (Ph.D thesis), University of the Witwatersrand, 2001, p. 60.
9. Wicomb, 2000, p. 46.
10. Edgar and Saunders, 1982, p. 204.
11. Knysna Archives. "Oorsprong en geboorte van Hervormer", p. 9.
12. Ibid.; Rainier 1997, p. 55.
13. *Verslag van die Grondwetkomitee van die Presidentsraad oor die behoeftes en eise van die Griekwas*, P.R. 2/1983. Cape Town: State Printer, 1983, p. 48.
14. *Kokstad Advertiser*, 4 May 1898.
15. Prinsloo, W.J. "'n Volk met baie 'vrolikheid': Griekwas kom kyk nog altyd of hu leier werklik dood is". In: *Die Huisgenoot*, 29 December 1950, p. 4.
16. Knysna Archives: Letter to Griquas from Plettenberg Bay, 12 September 1940.
17. Unisa Documentary Centre for African Studies (UDCA): E.M.S. Le Fleur Collection (hereafter "Le Fleur Collection"). Copy of original manuscript written in "Breakwater".

ape Town, 1898. Reproduced from Ratelgat redendal, 2 April 1935 (photocopy).

. *Kokstad Advertiser*, 2 December 1898.

3. Le Fleur Collection. Document, 20 August 984.

9. Le Fleur Collection. Document, "Breakwater", 1898.

0. Le Fleur Collection. Document, 20 August 984.

1. "The late Griqua leader: 'A Christian and a Gentleman'". In: *The Sun*, 4 July 1941.

2. Edgar and Saunders, 1982, p. 201.

3. Lewis, G. *Between the wire and the wall.* Cape Town: David Philip, 1987, p. 81.

24. Wannenburg, A. *Forgotten Frontiersmen.* United Kingdom: Timmins Publishing House (undated), p. 187.

25. Davenport and Saunders, 2000, p. 153.

26. Edgar and Saunders, 1982, p. 212.

27. Cape Archives. Document, CMT 3/874 644, Resident Magistrate (Kokstad) to Secretary for Native Affairs, Pretoria, 16 July 1920.

28. *Kokstad Advertiser*, 3 December 1920.

29. *Cape Times*. 24 September 1921, cited in Edgar and Saunders, 1982, p. 214.

30. Unisa Documentary Centre for African Studies (UDCA): Le Fleur, Thomas L. "Griekwa Independente Kerk van S.A.: 'n Korte oorsig' (undated), loose page.

31. Wannenburg, (undated), p. 187.

32. Prinsloo, W.J. *Die Huisgenoot*, 29 December 1950, p. 4.

33. Ibid.

34. Edgar and Saunders, 1982, pp. 215-16. Letter. Anthony Le Fleur to author, 22 June 2001.

35. *Die Banier*, September 1963.

36. Ibid.

37. Letter. Anthony Le Fleur to author, 23 October 2001.

38. Letter. Anthony Le Fleur to author, 22 June 2001.

39. Interview. Andrew Le Fleur, Worcester, 7 April 2001.

40. Letter. Anthony Le Fleur to author, 23 October 2001.

41. Ibid.

42. Ibid.

43. Letter. Andrew Le Fleur to author, 23 July 2001.

44. Knysna Archives. Copy of original.

45. Letter. Anthony Le Fleur to author,

Annexures A to D, 22 June 2001.

46. Interview. Andrew Le Fleur, Worcester, 7 April 2001.

47. Letter. Andrew Le Fleur to author, 19 June 2001.

48. Ibid.

49. Letter. Andrew Le Fleur to author, 23 July 2001.

50. Van der Ross, R. *The Rise and Decline of Apartheid*. Cape Town: Tafelberg, 1987, p. 268.

51. Letter. Andrew Le Fleur to author, 23 July 2001.

52. Ibid.

53. Ibid.

54. Prinsloo, W.J. *Die Huisgenoot*, 29 December 1950, p. 7.

55. Letter. Andrew Le Fleur to author, 23 July 2001.

56. Ibid.

57. *Worcester Standard & Advertiser*, 5 July 2001.

58. Letter. Andrew Le Fleur to author, 23 July 2001. Interview in Worcester, 28 July 2001

59. Ibid.

60. Ibid.

The Galada Family

Endnotes

1. Idah Nosimiti Ncinane passed away 13 December 2001.

2. In the African extended-family system, it is quite common for children to be raised by a grandmother or other relatives. For more than a century, the migrant-labour system – and, more recently, the AIDS epidemic – has made this a painful necessity.

3. Round, single-room dwellings, often thatched.

4. A farm school is a primary school located on a white farm. The farmer is responsible for building the school, but the teachers are paid by the government. The farmer is usually the school manager. White farm schools had much better facilities and the government provided free transport for white children attending farm schools.

5. Many black people have a "white" name in addition to their African names. They may use the "white" name only among whites, or they may choose to use it generally. This practice has its roots in the inability or unwillingness of many white people to learn African names.

6. Under apartheid law, people were classified as "white", "Indian", "coloured" or "African". In the Western Cape, the majority of "non-white" people were classified "coloured" – a term the government struggled to define. The Galada family are black ("African").

Acknowledgements

The publishers wish to thank the Tropenmuseum in Amsterdam for initiating his project.
Without its wonderful cooperation and support
this publication would not have been possible.

Copyright English version © 2003 Kwela Books
and Tropenmuseum.

This book is a co-publication of Kwela Books,
Cape Town, and KIT Publications, Amsterdam.

Kwela Books
PO Box 6252
Roggebaai
8012 Cape Town
e-mail: kwela@kwela.com
http://www.kwela.com

KIT Publishers
Koninklijk Instituut voor de Tropen
Postbus 95001
1090 HA Amsterdam
e-mail: publishers@kit.nl
http://zuidafrika.tropenmuseum.nl

Design by Mulder van Meurs, Amsterdam
Set in Helvetica GX and FF Scala
Printed and bound by Meester en de Jonge in
Ljubljana, Slovenia.

First edition, first printing 2003
ISBN 0-7957-0139-X

The publication of this book was made
possible with the generous support of:

HGIS-Cultuurprogramma
(Netherlands Culture Fund)

Prins Bernhard Fonds

Ministerie van
Buitenlandse Zaken

Mondriaan Stichting
(Mondriaan Foundation)

OCenW
Ministerie van Onderwijs
Cultuur en Wetenschappen

VSB FONDS